DATE DUE			

Critical Essays on
THOMAS BERGER

CRITICAL ESSAYS
ON
AMERICAN LITERATURE

James Nagel, General Editor
University of Georgia, Athens

Critical Essays on

THOMAS BERGER

edited by

DAVID W. MADDEN

G. K. Hall & Co.
An Imprint of Simon & Schuster Macmillan
New York

Prentice Hall International
London Mexico City New Delhi Singapore Sydney Toronto

G.K. Hall & Co.
An Imprint of Simon & Schuster Macmillan
866 Third Avenue
New York, N.Y. 10022

Library of Congress Cataloging-in-Publication Data

Critical essays on Thomas Berger / edited by David W. Madden.
    p.   cm.—(Critical essays on American literature)
   Includes bibliographical references and index.
   ISBN 0-7838-0029-0
   1. Berger, Thomas, 1924– —Criticism and interpretation.
I. Madden, David W., 1950– . II. Series.
PS3552.E719C62   1995
813'.54—dc20   94-41106
                                            CIP

10   9   8   7   6   5   4   3   2   1

Printed in the United States of America

Contents

◆

General Editor's Note

◆

This series seeks to anthologize the most important criticism on a wide variety of topics and writers in American literature. Our readers will find in various volumes not only a generous selection of reprinted articles and reviews but original essays, bibliographies, manuscript sections, and other materials brought to public attention for the first time. This volume, *Critical Essays on Thomas Berger*, is the most comprehensive collection of essays ever published on one of the most important modern writers in the United States. It contains both a sizable gathering of early reviews and a broad selection of more recent scholarship as well. Among the authors of reprinted articles and reviews are Brom Weber, Anne Tyler, John Carlos Rowe, and Lore Dickstein. In addition to a substantial introduction by David Madden, there is also an original essay commissioned specifically for publication in this volume by Patrick O'Donnell. Of special interest are an interview with Thomas Berger conducted by David Madden, an essay by Berger about his unpublished play *Other People*, and the entire play itself, published here for the first time. We are confident that this book will make a permanent and significant contribution to the study of American literature.

JAMES NAGEL
University of Georgia

Publisher's Note

♦

Producing a volume that contains both newly commissioned and reprinted material presents the publisher with the challenge of balancing the desire to achieve stylistic consistency with the need to preserve the integrity of works first published elsewhere. In the Critical Essays series, essays commissioned especially for a particular volume are edited to be consistent with G. K. Hall's house style; reprinted essays appear in the style in which they were first published, with only typographical errors corrected. Consequently, shifts in style from one essay to another are the result of our efforts to be faithful to each text as it was originally published.

Acknowledgments

◆

In preparing a volume like this, one incurs many debts of gratitude, and I wish to acknowledge a number of people. I first want to thank all the periodicals, journals, editors, and authors who permitted the reprinting of their work. I also thank the Research and Creative Activity Committee and the Professional Leave Committee at California State University, Sacramento, for the released time and the sabbatical that allowed me to review Berger scholarship and gather what would become the contents of this book. I appreciate all the help offered by my friend, Terry Manns, in the Office of Research and Scholarly Activities, in preparing this and other of my projects. I also want to thank my department chair, Vernon T. Hornback, for his patience and understanding, and all my colleagues in the English Department, especially Linda Palmer, Jon Price, Mark Hennelly, Bob Olmstead, and Ron Tanaka for their support and encouragement. Various friends have been particularly heartening, among them Joe Rasch-Chabot, Gerry Wentworth, Kurt Grossheider, Patrick O'Donnell, and Scott Simmon. My wife, Mary Davis, and daughters—Annie and Maggie—have all been more than reasonably patient with my many hours spent at the desk or before the computer terminal; to them I send all my love. Thomas Berger I wish to thank for agreeing to publish his first play, for answering countless pestering questions, and for always responding with great cheer and enthusiasm; what merit there is in our interview is due entirely to him. Finally, I want to acknowledge and dedicate this work to my mentor and friend, Brom Weber, who long ago encouraged me to write about Berger in my dissertation and who has been a constant source of support in my research over the years. My thanks and best wishes to you, Brom.

Introduction

◆

David W. Madden

Thomas Berger has been publishing novels since 1958, when he made an auspicious debut with *Crazy in Berlin*, and since that time he has written a quartet about Carlo Reinhart, a warmhearted loser fitfully making his way through contemporary America, two novels about graduate student/playwright cum detective Russel Wren, a modern masterpiece about the American West in *Little Big Man*, and numerous reinterpretations of established fictional genres—*Who Is Teddy Villanova?* (hard-boiled detective novel), *Regiment of Women* (science and futuristic fiction), *Killing Time* (crime fiction), *Arthur Rex* (Arthurian legends), *Orrie's Story* (Oresteian trilogy), *Nowhere* (utopian novel), and the recent *Robert Crews* (modernization of Defoe's *Robinson Crusoe*). Berger is a remarkably inventive and prolific writer totally dedicated to the art of fiction.

Scholars and critics have continually seen in Berger's writings the reflection of their own predilections. To read them is to view a novelist who has done and been it all, and at almost every turn Berger has demurred or rejected their estimations. Early in his career he was solemnly declared a black humorist, a label that persisted throughout the 1960s and well into the 1970s, but the author has disavowed his relationship with those writers, preferring instead the company of Vladimir Nabokov.[1] He has been described as a satirist, a label he also vigorously disavows: "I don't think I'm a satirist because I have absolutely no desire to correct anybody or get anybody to do differently. In fact I enjoy enormously all these horrors of which I write."[2] Frequently critics have seen his reinventions of fictional forms as parodic, to which he has responded, "Persons who naïvely mistake me for a merry-andrew with an inflated pig's bladder can never understand that I adore whichever tradition I am striving to follow, and that what results is the best I can manage by way of joyful worship—not the worst in sneering derision."[3]

Berger most often has been proclaimed a comic novelist, for which there is ample evidence in many of his novels, yet he has consistently resisted

1

such a description: "I do not think of myself as a comic writer, and it is rarely my intent to be funny. But this statement itself, which has been made by me repeatedly, is usually taken as being facetious, and if I make it in public, is received with laughter."[4] He has been described as a searing social critic: "My interest is in creation, not in commentary. Those who believe my *intent* is to criticize society, to satirize, to write spoofs and send-ups, to be that most humorless of scribblers, the so-called comic novelist, are utterly misguided."[5] Because of a number similarities between Reinhart and Berger and because *Sneaky People* and *The Feud* are set in the Midwest and during the Depression, he has gained the mantle of autobiographical writer, which he also eschews: "Fiction must never be confused with that existence through which I make my daily slog . . . what I required by way of a hero was almost anybody but myself."[6] To those who have described him as a realist, he cites the influence of Kafka, and to others who have regarded him as a postmodernist, he has insisted on an abiding affection for classic writers such as Smollett, Goethe, Tolstoy, Melville, and Dickens.

Berger's opinions of his works are certainly instructive, but they are not the only means of approaching his canon. By the same token, attempts to pin him down to a single overriding passion or approach are equally misleading. In point of fact the problem is not that Berger's works fall in none of these categories, but that different novels partake of different traditions. Thus to a certain extent each of the critical approaches mentioned above is applicable but not wholly appropriate to his divergent canon. As some critics have pointed out, Berger finally defies easy categorization, gleefully exploiting or celebrating various traditions while never being completely contained by any of them, and as a consequence the critical response to his work has often been divided.

Berger was born in Cincinnati, Ohio, 20 July 1924, and grew up in nearby Lockland, until he attended Miami University in Oxford, Ohio, in 1941. He transferred the next year to the University of Cincinnati but interrupted his studies in 1943 when he enlisted in the army and was stationed in Berlin in a medical unit with the first American occupation forces. In 1948 he graduated with honors from the University of Cincinnati, moved to New York where he worked as a librarian at the Rand School of Social Science, and married in 1950. He did graduate work at Columbia University and began, but never completed, a thesis on George Orwell. After doing various editing jobs and publishing reviews and a handful of short stories in the 1950s, his first novel appeared. Except for sporadically publishing short stories, serving briefly as cinema critic for *Esquire* in the early 1970s, and writing some plays in the early 1970s and late 1980s, Berger has devoted himself to writing novels, the importance of which he has described: "As Henry James said of himself, I am an 'inveterate proser,' and therefore it is fiction that has been the means by which I can see myself as a wizard, ebulliently making things from the void."[7]

The critical reception, although limited, to his first novel, *Crazy in Berlin*, marked a response that would continue throughout most of Berger's career—mixed and sometimes quizzical reactions. One reviewer, for instance, noted his sense of irony and saw the novel as autobiographical and only loosely controlled,[8] and Orville Prescott denounced it as "pretentious, portentous and prolix," but declared Berger "a talented new writer."[9] More kindly disposed reviewers were also uncomfortable with the density of the prose, but commended the book for being an exceptional first novel.[10] However, the most perceptive and important review came from Harvey Swados, who offered Berger as an example of America's answer to Europe's intellectual men of letters. In dealing with the horrors of the war and the Holocaust, Berger eschews traditional liberalism "to commence where liberalism ends, in the world of ideas." He praised Berger's mixed style and pronounced, "Thomas Berger is a name to remember, an important addition to the small group of important American writers, and a novelist with a great career before him."[11]

Although still limited in number, the reviews of *Reinhart in Love* were much more favorable. Critics praised the hero, Carlo Reinhart, as "a kind of Everyman, an ever-hopeful Twentieth century Candide,"[12] commented on Berger's sense of the absurd, and even compared him favorably to Samuel Beckett.[13] The novelist Zulfikar Ghose, writing anonymously, complimented the novel's comic, absurdist, and allegorical aspects, and concluded that Berger's "writing, full of images which a poet would not have observed with greater accuracy or economy, is superbly fresh throughout."[14]

Little Big Man, the novel that firmly established Berger in the minds of critics and general readers, received more attention but was not initially a great success. The critical reaction once again revealed ambivalence. Most reviewers praised Berger's faithful rendering of Native American culture and his generally unsentimental view of the westward movement. They noted the tall tale tradition, sometimes comparing Berger to Mark Twain, but they also questioned the point of the prologue.[15] Guy Davenport offered the most perceptive and enthusiastic evaluation, praising Berger as a "superb satirist" and his style and sensibility "as robust as a tornado . . . and his novels as generously unplotted as life itself."[16]

His next novel, *Killing Time*, by far provoked the most denunciatory reactions of any of his early works. Reviewers saw it as a polemical, self-indulgent exercise, although he was compared to writers as diverse as Truman Capote, Norman Mailer, Terry Southern, and Joseph Heller.[17] Enthusiasts saw it as another example of black humor and absurdist fiction.[18] Guy Davenport singled out the main character as "one of the most complex characters in modern fiction. . . . The eeriest thing about him is that he is wholly believable, which is to say, of course, that Thomas Berger is a magnificent writer."[19]

The response to *Vital Parts* was again divided and often contradictory.

For instance, a writer for the *Times Literary Supplement* declared the book a failure and proclaimed that the protagonist, Carlo Reinhart, was "*designed* to be taken as a type, a touchstone for our civilization,"[20] while Guy Davenport saw in Reinhart "a kind of heroism . . . he is a fool, but all his greatness is in his foolishness."[21] While the *New Leader* declared that "the problem with *Vital Parts* is that its hero is no Candide in this worst of all possible worlds, but merely a Charlie Brown,"[22] John Leonard praised the book for being unique in that its "central character . . . is a Candide with private opinions, better than most of us."[23] Paul Theroux criticized the novel's style, "Nothing succeeds like excess . . . [the novel is] written in undisguised anger and disgust for the present—a tone which would be fair enough if it had a measure of art";[24] however, John Hollander asserted that "it reads like some kind of masterpiece."[25] In one of the two most penetrating assessments of the book, Richard Schickel identified a central theme in not only this but all of Berger's novels: "What [Reinhart] seeks, really, is freedom from his own concept of freedom, freedom from the old American myth of omnipotent individuality so that he can join the revel of corporate corruption with the rest of us." He sadly asserted that "Thomas Berger will never achieve the recognition he deserves."[26] Brom Weber was the most unequivocal in his contention that the novel "confirms Berger's rank as a major American novelist, one whose stylistic fecundity, psychological insight, and social knowledge are seemingly inexhaustible."[27]

Where the reaction to *Vital Parts* was confusing, the response to *Regiment of Women* was simply incomprehensible, and one wonders if reviewers were reading the same novel. These responses suggest that the novel confused a good many readers, especially Berger's attitude toward sexual politics. Reviewers saw it as a spoof on radical feminists, a critique of male chauvinists, and a send-up of both feminists and chauvinists.[28] The most perceptive evaluation, however, can be found in *Ms.* magazine, whose reviewer felt it was his best novel and argued that the "book is no more antifeminist than it is antimale; Berger is not arguing one political line. His anarchic imagination exaggerates all sexual stereotypes into ludicrous postures, perhaps to show how they rob us of our freedom."[29]

Another mixed reaction greeted *Sneaky People*, with a number of reviewers complaining about its being an exercise in nostalgia and the characters unsavory.[30] Detractors could not see any point to the novel, while those favoring the book complimented its comic gusto. Favorable reviewers saw the book as either a harbinger of the state of 1970's culture or a depiction of "anarchic American individuals *in* a particular time but *for* all time."[31] D. Keith Mano managed to discern two of Berger's fundamental concerns—the moral dimensions of his fiction and the constant motif of a search for the grail.[32]

Aside from a few equivocal reactions, *Who Is Teddy Villanova?* can easily be called a critical success. Reviewers praised its parodic dimensions and were quick to note the primary sources of inspiration as the works of Raymond Chandler, Dashiell Hammett, and Ross MacDonald.[33] These reviewers lauded the novel's baroque extravagance, and Leonard Michaels, in a witty and inspired piece, carefully probed the novel's style, and identified the central theme as being "the staggering insufficiency of an educated intelligence to such modern circumstances [as a widespread decline in amenities and manners]."[34] For the most part *Arthur Rex* was another critical success. Where detractors criticized the modernization of some characters and Berger's attempts at medieval language, others praised what one called his "embellishing rather than altering Malory's work," adding that "he bestows new, often bawdy life into these timeless tales."[35]

Neighbors received an even larger number of enthusiastic reviews, although once again critics were confused about the novel's methods and implications.[36] One reviewer claimed it had no point, another found it a parody of all the rituals of neighborliness, and another contended that it dealt with the reader's apprehension of fiction.[37] Berger's champions were generous in their praise, Thomas R. Edwards calling him "one of our most intelligent, witty and independent-minded writers"[38] and Michael Malone dubbing him "the real thing: a major, Major Writer" and comparing him with the likes of Mailer, Heller, and Pynchon.[39]

Reinhart's Women, like the two novels that preceded it, was also well received. Most reviewers commented on its buoyant, comic tone and compared Berger to Updike and Roth, each of whom had created characters who have appeared in four novels.[40] Comments about Berger's sense of the absurd continued,[41] and the novel's style also drew applause.[42] *The Feud* reinforced the pattern of mixed responses, with critics objecting to the novel's manic events and skeptical spirit[43] and complaining about the range of ironic targets[44] and about its language.[45]

The laudatory reviews seemed written almost to refute the claims of the detractors. For instance, Jack Beatty addressed the issue of language and subject by tersely commenting, "Thomas Berger is an exquisitely subtle artist who can conjure character and emotion from the slightest verbal means."[46] Anne Tyler offered an incisive explanation of Berger's vision: "There is a certain sharp edge to his vision that identifies all he writes. He appears to see his subjects in a uniquely clear, hard light. . . . When Thomas Berger pokes fun at his characters here, he does it fondly, with inspired perception. When he describes an event, it seems the event is taking place of its own volition; it fairly tumbles out. As a result *The Feud* is both endearing and surprising—a comic masterpiece."[47]

Nowhere was unquestionably Berger's critical failure, with most reviewers criticizing what they regarded as his social and cultural didacticism. They were quick to note the novel's utopian antecedents but found "some vital tension . . . missing."[48] They were, however, slightly more generous with *Being Invisible*. The negative views criticized the work's structure and style and what was regarded as its unsatisfactory conclusion.[49] On the other hand, many praised the shrewdness of the author's observations and Berger's ability to reveal the evil in the banal.[50]

Reactions to *The Houseguest* were overwhelmingly enthusiastic, yet also enigmatic in some cases. For example, Paul Gray announced that "in truth *The Houseguest* harbors no hidden messages that can stand up to a reasoned analysis. The novel instead is a rare example of buoyantly irresponsible comedy, a piling up of non sequiturs for the pure pleasure of creating progressive confusion."[51] However, John Clute argued that here, as in earlier books, "appearances can only be maintained by a kind of social compact— or conspiracy—not to challenge the rituals which enable humans to make sense in the social world."[52]

As with *Nowhere*, critics again had difficulty accepting Berger at his most fabulous in *Changing the Past*,[53] and *Orrie's Story* also provoked mixed reactions, many centering around Berger's modernization of the Oresteian trilogy,[54] but Thomas Disch praised its treatment of the mores and folkways of the Midwest and its measured tone, and asserted that it "must rank among his best novels."[55] Bill Marx took the occasion to reassess Berger's career, which he explained is characterized by "restless experimentation . . . a progression of intelligent, skeptical, and voracious comedies that should be recognized as substantial achievements in contemporary American literature."[56] *Meeting Evil* elicited a host of laudatory reactions, many of which touched on the complex moral dilemma the protagonist faces, while the issue of style drew contradictory reactions.[57]

Where reviewers have expressed ambivalence, confusion, or simply distaste, scholars have been far more favorable of Berger's canon and far more probing in their examination of his art. The first of these evaluations came from Ihab Hassan, whose essay "Conscience and Incongruity: The Fiction of Thomas Berger" raises a number of issues that successive scholars have returned to and developed more fully. Hassan limited his discussion to *Crazy in Berlin* and *Reinhart in Love* and attempted to define Berger's unique point of view as a "comic-absurd vision which we feel articulates our existential situation." He isolated a crucial Berger theme—the disjunction of appearance and reality—and the tension between this and Berger's "gnarled syntax [which] constantly searches for meaning." Although he felt the two Reinhart books have weaknesses, he saw these novels as making a significant contribution to contemporary fiction, "a more subtle sense of how Fraud and Force work to undermine our identity, of how Aggression is part of the human fundament, more damaging to commit than to endure."[58]

The next scholarly treatment was a brief discussion of *Little Big Man* by Robert Edson Lee, who dismissed it as "a product of what Berger has read, not of what he has seen and experienced. No one pretends it is literature."[59] In the same year, however, an entirely different view was offered by L. L. Lee, who insisted that this is "a most American novel [for its treatment of] all the divisive and unifying themes of the American experience, or, more precisely, of the American 'myth.' "[60] Lee viewed the novel as picaresque with a comic vision and found in the protagonist, Jack Crabb, the elaboration of the work's central theme—the truly worthy person is an individual first and the best society is an anarchistic community. America's commitment to change, he insisted, produces both vitality and destruction, and the depiction of Custer clearly reveals this paradox.

In the same year another discussion of *Little Big Man* was offered by William T. Pilkington, who credited the book as being "the most significant Western comic novel," which parodies the "staples of Western literature." Berger was compared with Faulkner for his absurd, grotesque humor, and the work was described as the "first piece of comic fiction about the West that can plausibly claim status as a major novel by anyone's standards."[61]

In the next year *Crazy in Berlin* and *Little Big Man* were cited as two among many of a growing number of contemporary American fictions that exhibited an exaggerated, grotesque form of neorealism.[62] However, in 1968 Leslie Fiedler criticized *Little Big Man* in *The Return of the Vanishing American* as an example of a new Western that demonstrates that "for all its pathos and danger, the West was and remains essentially *funny* [rather than myth-ic]."[63] In the same year Gerald Green wrote an impassioned defense of realist fiction and cited Berger's first three novels as offering "the stuff of history, of actual events, to create memorable works."[64]

Four new essays on Berger were published in 1969, two of which concentrated on *Little Big Man*. The first of these, by Brian W. Dippie, presented an overview of narratives of putative sole survivors of the Little Big Horn and declared that "in *Little Big Man*, Berger is faithful to both the West of history and the West as myth." The author refuted Fiedler's view by contending that "it is only by blending the two kinds of truth [historical and mythic] that one arrives at the West of the American mind."[65] In another essay decrying the paucity of aesthetically satisfying Westerns, Jay Gurian praised Berger for treating "Western materials as part of the greater literary tradition from which they are usually separated."[66] He found the characterizations complex, the language richly diverse, and the depiction of Native Americans fresh and imaginative.

Frederick W. Turner III, presented a subtle comparison between *Little Big Man* and Melville's *Israel Potter* as "extended cultural parable[s]," with Melville examining the contrast between the agrarian West and the urban East and Berger continuing at the historical moment where Melville concluded his novel, with Jack Crabb as "Israel reborn." Turner favorably compared Berger with Henry Miller, John Dos Passos, and Faulkner for producing one of "America's finest works." He saw the novel as a microcosm of the story of the West, whereby "America is neither near-savage and vital nor civilized but rather an unhealthy amalgam of both states, an amalgam in which the virtues of each have excelled." He credited Berger with comprehending Melville's idea of the erosion of cultural vitality and contended that Berger offers "an examination of American culture and character [that] presents to us a picture both pathetic and tragic."[67]

Reinhart in Love was discussed along with James Purdy's *Cabot Wright Begin*, Joseph Heller's *Catch-22*, and John Barth's *The Floating Opera* as an example of contemporary satire that was radical in technique and not "barren, superficial, and destructive." Marjorie Ryan saw the novel as "a mock-epic of post-World War II American society" with Reinhart appearing "almost as a latter-day and younger Babbitt."[68]

In 1971 another refutation of Robert Edson Lee's assessment of *Little Big Man* appeared, with Delbert E. Wylder arguing that the character of Old Lodge Skins, for instance, begins in absurdity and ends in solemnity, elevating him to the condition of "a Cheyenne Oedipus." This was the first article to consider in any depth the technique of using two narrators—the effete dilettante, Ralph Fielding Snell, and the earthy Jack Crabb—which emphasizes Crabb's believability and increases the ambiguity of his sardonic vision. Wylder furthermore rejected the notion that the novel was a sentimental defense of Native American culture, but instead a "commentary on the foibles of mankind itself."[69]

Joyce Hancock continued the investigation into *Little Big Man* with an essay that illustrated the separate values of the Native American and white cultures, and noted as central the symbols of the circle and the square. Where time, experience, and sex are natural, spontaneous, and connected for the Native Americans, for whites all is artificial, linear, and fragmentary. She viewed Berger's language as the means of unifying the "conflicting world views within the hero. . . . By giving the imprisoned Jack Crabb the language of liberation, and . . . by placing him and his language within the context of a rather foppish intellectual and civilized man, Berger has attempted to demonstrate that although Crabb is indeed confined at last, he still embodies those rebellious, boyhood-savage values that are represented by the Indian in the tale proper."[70]

Little Big Man drew more attention with Max F. Schulz's discussion of the novel as a parody and product of the 1960s zeitgeist. Schulz identified the objects of parody as the tall tale, the idea of Native Americans as children of nature and rapacious savages, the American dream of a virgin wilderness, and the Hollywood interpretation of how the west was won. With Crabb as the book's focus, Berger creates a "new mythic synthesis of major occurrences on the Plains . . . and a reinterpretation of [major Western figures] so convincing that no one reading the novel will be able to assent easily to the previous legends."[71] Schulz rejected Wylder's idea that the novel comments on the "foibles of mankind" to present instead a decidedly 1960s version of reality, with Native Americans as projections of youth culture and whites as representing the established order.

Historian Leo E. Oliva approached the novel as a document of exactly accurate historical fiction. "The creative artist who knows of which he writes, as in this case Berger most certainly does, adds insight and understanding to the historical record." Oliva praised Berger's sense of chronology and events but singled out his treatment of Native American culture: "His picture of Cheyenne life is so authentic that one may gain as much understanding of these people from his novel as from any other single work."[72]

Arguing against a remark of Edmund Wilson's, Brom Weber wrote an essay demonstrating how ingrained black humor has been in American literature. Weber charted the origins of the term from the French surrealists and selected Berger and Walker Percy as the two most significant black humorists working in the tradition of Hawthorne, Melville, and Faulkner. Percy and Berger "have avoided the temptation inherent in black humor to imitate disorder, to parody the incoherence of reality by slipping unself-consciously into literary incoherence. . . . These writers reassure us that black humor will not disappear from American literature."[73]

The first extensive treatment of the then Reinhart trilogy came from Douglas A. Hughes who saw Berger as closest to Dickens and Twain for his satirical vision. Hughes contended that the trilogy focused on how one maintains integrity and humanity, the quest for personal freedom, and the separation between appearance and reality. Like many reviewers, Hughes saw Reinhart as a Candide-like figure and as an American Leopold Bloom, belonging in the tradition of the "schlemiel hero, a wise fool [whose short-comings] are mitigated by his essential goodness. . . . [He is] an embodi-ment of those humanist values the author wishes to celebrate." Hughes charted the character's development through the three novels from a man who initially resists the temptations of cynicism and nihilism, to one who fails at various undertakings while succeeding morally, to a voluntary outsider, disillusioned and resentful. Ultimately "Carlo Reinhart and the imperfect humanism he has metaphorically come to represent are really indestructible.[74]

In another essay on *Little Big Man* Fred M. Fetrow reviewed scholarship of the novel and concluded that little attention had been given to its specific fictional techniques. Fetrow concentrated on the use of the frame device and the role of the narrator, Snell, whom he felt "establishes a neat balance between veracity and sheer farce. . . . Berger uses Snell to establish the prerequisite mood and to set the ambivalent tone which initiates and supports the satire which follows." Snell is a paradoxical combination of naïf and expert, fool and scholar, and he signals many objects of social satire in the novel—doctors, the aged, racial arrogance. Finally, "the frame technique and the external narrator serve the purpose of moving the reader toward where Thomas Berger wants the reader during the reading and after the digestion of the novel—in between the uncertain, amused by the tall tale, but seriously pondering the moral implications."[75]

The first extended discussion of *Regiment of Women* was a confusing, poorly developed essay that dismisses the novel.[76] The success of the film of

Little Big Man occasioned a comparison between the novel and the movie. Where director Arthur Penn sought to satirize and demythologize the Western genre, Berger set out to remythologize the image of the West. Where Penn romanticized the Native Americans, Berger displayed no tendency to idealize. Where Penn's version of Jack Crabb was that of a loser overwhelmed by experience, Berger's hero assumed legendary roles and remained "self-possessed and recalcitrant . . . a character with substance and a will of his own."[77]

In the same issue of *The Nation* in 1977, two articles about Berger appeared, one offering a reassessment of *Little Big Man* and the second an overview of his career. Frederick Turner argued that *Little Big Man* had remained underappreciated because of an ingrained American disgust for Native American culture, yet "for the first time really in American letters, *both* cultures are seen from the inside out." Berger was praised for treating each culture even-handedly, and the novel stands as a "seminal event in what must now seem the most significant cultural and literary trend of the last decade."[78]

In the first of his many articles on Berger, Brooks Landon saw him as an original defying easy classification. In examining the novelist's first eight works, Landon described their protagonists as "observing Ishmaels," seeking survival more than change. He regarded the Reinhart trilogy as possibly Berger's greatest creation, and he underscores Richard Schickel's view that Berger has " 'one of the most genuinely radical sensibilities now writing novels in this country.' "[79]

A second comparison of the film and the novel of *Little Big Man* again ranked the book as the superior treatment by using a structuralist approach of binary oppositions to reveal the film's weaknesses. Although the film can dramatize the two cultures' activities, it cannot reveal adequately what those cultures believe. The film consistently sentimentalizes the Native Americans and "fails, then, despite all Penn's admirable intentions and considerable craftsmanship, because he has not achieved a structure that will sustain the weight of his materials. . . . What vitiates Penn's achievement in the film is his failure to avoid romanticizing the past."[80]

A second essay dealing with *Little Big Man* as picaresque appeared in 1978, and dealt more profoundly than any before it with Berger's manipulation of the form's conventions. Crabb, as picaro, was seen as an heir to Huck Finn, with "a sound heart in a deformed conscience." Crabb was also compared with Melville's Ishmael for his sense of invulnerability and was seen as trickster, "[who] refuses to be recruited to specific moral views. Confronted with absurd situations, he remains a western Sisyphus in permanent exile." The result of Berger's method is that "historical reality looks like a hoax because the American past appears as a sustained tall tale. Ultimately *Little Big Man*'s picaresque adventures teach that reality is at best seen as someone's make-believe."[81]

Berger has often been compared with John Barth, but Stanley Trachtenberg offered the most trenchant comparison of the two in an essay devoted to a form of comedy in which their heroes merge with the figure of the dupe. Trachtenberg argued that current literature refuses to compete with reality, and he labeled this "hunger art:" "it is an art of displacement which hesitates to reconstruct reality or even to frame it." Linear plot gives way to random situations and emphasis is placed on literary self-reflexivity. The reassurance of comedy comes not from a vision of wholeness but from fragments that do not connect.

Trachtenberg insisted that the subject of *Little Big Man* is not the West but its myth: "Despite its vernacular diction, Crabb's account is no more real than the myths it parodies. Along with Snell's pedantic frame, the totality of the novel makes a comic statement of the impossibility of taking seriously any one version of history, even its own." Trachtenberg also discussed the role of the double in this fiction: "Sometimes real, sometimes imaginary, the double engages the self with the dilemma of ambivalence or of suppressed desires."[82] Reinhart encounters numerous doubles in *Vital Parts*, with the result that identity is fragmented and personal relationships rendered difficult to sustain.

There were at least two feminist reactions to *Little Big Man*, the first of which, by Madelon Heatherington, was the more probing and original. She began by criticizing the Western form as perpetuating a "puerile fantasy" in which the dynamics of romance are aborted. The Western, she demonstrated, is a modernization of the medieval romance in which a hero's principal duty is the deliverance of endangered, vulnerable women, and female characters are uniformly depicted as "shallow demi-types of no complexity whatever."[83] *Little Big Man* was seen as one of the best Western novels, despite its treatment of women in only narrow, stereotypical roles.

The second feminist reading, by Caren J. Deming, is little more than a facile, superficial treatment. Deming denounced the ancillary role of women in *Little Big Man*, which depicts them as either a bountiful garden to be exploited (as in the case of the Native American women) or a preserver of culture, tainted by any contact with Native Americans (as with Olga, Crabb's first wife). Deming denounces the scene where Crabb is encouraged by his wife to have sex with her sisters, and on this issue readers should compare Deming's reading with that of Joyce Hancock mentioned earlier. Finally, "the complex of assumptions behind the double standard of miscegenation denigrates all women and, ultimately, plays white women and women of color off against one another."[84]

The first scholarly treatment of *Who Is Teddy Villanova?*, by David W. Madden, argued that the novel is a parody of the hard-boiled detective form and drew extensive comparisons with Raymond Chandler's *Farewell, My Lovely*. "By imitating, and at the same time inverting, many of the hard-boiled detective story's conventions, Berger manages to sustain his unique comic-absurd vision and illustrate the artistic and cultural disparity between the values of the writer of detective fiction and those of the novelist in post–World War II America." The essay concluded that "the self-reflexive and self-conscious aspects of its hero, and finally his use of the parodic mode, place Berger in that tradition of American literature established by Hawthorne: the romance tradition."[85]

Michael Cleary examined the satiric and parodic dimensions of *Little Big Man*, asserting that "on one level [the novel] is a condemnation of the weaknesses of human nature; on another level, it is a serious indictment of American institutions, culture, values, and even history itself." Cleary praised Berger's balanced treatment of both cultures, each of which is satirized for its limitations, and the result is a commentary on humanity in general. In spite of Berger's fairness, though, the novel does reveal white culture as lacking the moral foundation that underpins Native American societies. Cleary concluded that instead of being a cynical or nihilistic exercise, it offers "a serious consideration of what it means to live well."[86]

Still another consideration of *Little Big Man*'s picaresque dimensions was offered by Richard A. Betts, who emphasized the novel's episodic plot and the antihero status of Jack Crabb. The hero's pragmatism, lack of principles, resiliency, and solitude are noted as primary attributes of a traditional picaro, and Crabb is "supremely adept at the trickery that is necessary to survival and that sometimes even results in momentary triumphs." The unresolved plot, the panoramic sense of space, and the subjective narrator are other picaresque conventions employed by Berger, and as a result, "his novel undoubtedly belongs to the mainstream of the picaresque tradition."[87]

The high water-mark in Berger scholarship was 1983, when sixteen articles appeared, and *Studies in American Humor* published two issues devoted exclusively to his work. A penetrating biographical glimpse into the author was provided by excerpts from his correspondence with longtime friend Zulfikar Ghose, letters that extend over a thirteen-year period. The topics are numerous: his newfound fascination with writing plays, difficulties in completing a new novel, love of music, disgust over an age of cultural decline, and enthusiastic appreciation of Friedrich Nietzsche. He also comments liberally on a host of writers—Petronius, Henry James, George Bernard Shaw, Thomas De Quincey, Tobias Smollett, Henry de Montherlant, Charles Baudelaire, Jane Austen, and Leo Tolstoy.

Michael Malone wrote an excellent essay in which he argued against the idea that Berger is a parodist or social critic and insisted that "it is language, not self-expression, that absorbs him; voices, not Voice." He found in Berger's fiction an "emotional yearning for human love, harmony and nobility that is persistently drawing Berger towards those romance elements of his tradition that help make his novels true comedies, always a much more serious (and moral) business than burlesque." Malone argued against other interpretations of Berger's work—sentimental, nostalgically adrift, or "romantic primitivist"—and contended that his depiction of women illustrates men's view of them as baffling and alarming. Ultimately, "the achievement of the best fiction-makers, like Thomas Berger, is to triumph over Time, not by the mocking murders of their predecessors, but by continual recreation."[88]

Myron Simon provided the first assessment of Berger's German-American background and Reinhart's confused sense of ethnicity. Much of Reinhart's craziness in the first novel results from his realizing that German history has not been entirely heroic, and his experience of being hated for his ethnicity provides him with a greater sensitivity toward others so despised (especially Jews and blacks). Reinhart eschews ideology and politics in human affairs, preferring fundamental values such as respect and decency; thus Berger "proposes a vocabulary of moral actions as profound as they are simple and communicable by gentle ways." Reinhart achieves an almost Olympian view of humans as flawed but not contemptible creatures, and *Crazy in Berlin* emerges as "one of the few truly indispensable ethnic novels in American literature."[89]

In another excellent essay, John Carlos Rowe examined Berger's existential humanism, insisting that in the novels, acts of creation are a defense against existential contingency. Rowe focused most of his discussion on *Neighbors*, and noted that while the characters of Harry and Ramona represent a popularizing of existential concepts of the antihero, they are not exemplars of authenticity. The protagonist, Earl Keese, gets the worst of what he expects from these new acquaintances, and the novel is constructed around a series of choices which are really judgments of the reader's values. Melville was invoked once more, in this case *The Confidence Man*, and Rowe concluded that in *Neighbors* Berger "uses Earl and Harry to parody the idea of art as a defense against a threatening world and to relate that aesthetic to a glib existentialist jargon. . . . [which amounts to a] transformation of Berger's aesthetic values."[90]

Brooks Landon, in the first in a series of essays devoted to Berger's stylistic experiments, examined Berger's unswervingly ironic method in *Sneaky People* and *Neighbors*. The first of these deals with the ways male-female relationships are skewed by verbal misunderstandings, while *Neighbors* is a novel "whose action consists primarily of function. . . . [It is] a book in which language becomes the only operating reality." The tenuous nature of human behavior and ethics is connected with the arbitrary nature of language among the characters. Landon showed the dialectic in the novel between freedom and victimization and was the first to acknowledge Nietzsche's profound influence on Berger. "Berger's narrative continually foregrounds the ironic ways in which the worlds of his characters' language are exposed as being at odds with the worlds of their experience."[91]

Another discussion of Berger's parodic practices can be found in an essay by Jean P. Moore. Under consideration were *Little Big Man*, *Regiment of Women*, and *Who Is Teddy Villanova?*. The discussion emphasized Berger's foregrounding of language and form, to the point that fact and fiction blend. "Because Berger does not perceive art to be a conveyer of truth, a corrective or the means through which right or wrong may be revealed, story-telling is not seen as a means to an end other than itself."[92]

Sherrill E. Grace provided an excellent comparison of *Little Big Man* and Rudy Wiebe's *The Temptations of Big Bear* that revealed the differences between the American Western and the Canadian Northern as responses to the frontier. Grace regarded *Little Big Man* as a combination captivity narrative and tall tale and noted that the two novels are structured around journey quests. "*Little Big Man* is a bawdy, secular text, truly representative of the Western paradigm . . . [it] adds to and continues the Western mythology."[93]

In another examination of the author's style, Max F. Schulz argued that in Berger's novels words are the medium of reality, and style is the underpinning of that verbal world. Berger's language performs a paradoxical function; it can be "a mimetic mirroring of existence, and an expressive distortion of its appearances." In *Neighbors* words are duplicitous and "gambits of social power," whereas in the Reinhart novels language is used and abused by a host of manipulators; in *Killing Time* words become unhinged from the reality they describe, and in *Regiment of Women* "doppelgänger diction" mixes and confuses gender referents. "Berger's many styles represent a continuing celebration of the self-regenerative powers of language. He is the closest we have today to that rare literary fauna, the writer's writer, the literate dweller among the fictional forms and styles of his tools of trade."[94]

In another discussion of the Reinhart trilogy, Sanford Pinsker placed Berger in the company of other postwar writers of serial fictions like Roth and Updike, and claimed that these three writers' works rank among the period's finest achievements. Once again Reinhart was discussed as a schlemiel hero whose life is built on comic defeats.[95] Ronald R. Janssen limited his discussion to *Reinhart in Love* to reveal the ways in which the novel fits within a tradition of fictions critical of American culture over the last one hundred years. The character of Claude Humbold was cited as the embodiment of a commercial culture that demands conformity and represses individuality.[96] In a second essay devoted to *Who Is Teddy Villanova?*, Philip Kuberski rather ponderously examined the various meanings and implications of the German word *Kraft* (power) to reveal the ways in which the novel "pursues its satisfactions (regardless of whoever would try to civilize or police or arrest them) through the constant demonstration and subversion of craft."[97]

David W. Madden examined the pervasive role of crime and the criminal in Berger's fiction, concentrating on five novels in particular. Berger's criminals are not necessarily professional miscreants, but almost anyone, and their crimes emerge most often from accident. In most of Berger's novels the line between the police and the criminal is blurred, with some police being their society's greatest malefactors. Berger's use of the ubiquitous third-person narrator promotes the sense of pervasive crime, and the often ambiguous quality of his books underscores the ambiguity of values in his fictional worlds.[98]

Little Big Man was once again compared with another Western, in this case Ken Kesey's *One Flew Over the Cuckoo's Nest*, in an essay by Patrick W. Shaw in which Western heroes were described as "a tawdry assortment of crazies, each individually pathetic."[99] Berger was credited with achieving a greater detachment from his characters than Kesey and with viewing reason as the means of individual freedom.

With his essay "Reinhart as Hero and Clown," Gerald Weales provided one of the best overviews of the complete Reinhart saga. Although noting the differences between the books, Weales defined important areas of similarity: the uncertainty about human relationships, the problem of identity, the elusiveness of truth, the inefficacy of language, the "authoritarianism of self-righteous idealism," and mortality itself. In recognizing the comic extravagances of the books, he suggests that "either his grotesques are real or his themes are too serious to be treated except in fantasy."[100] There is a typical pattern to these plots as Reinhart passes through confusion and despair to minor triumphs that leave him by the fourth novel in a condition of relative contentment.

The best essay on *Regiment of Women* was Brooks Landon's "Language and Subversion of Good Order in Thomas Berger's *Regiment of Women*," which examined the theme of individuality and freedom and the ways in which language can promote or frustrate that freedom. He developed the idea of victimization introduced in his earlier essays to show that in all of Berger's fictions victimization is primarily a linguistic phenomenon. The task of the novel's protagonist, Georgie Cornell, is to free himself of the verbal versions of reality foisted on him by others. Berger's primary concern, he explained, "is not with sex, but with power . . . [which] is almost always a function of language."[101] Landon wrote a second, much shorter, consideration of the novel by comparing it with Joanna Russ's *We Who Are About To* and Angela Carter's *Heroes and Villains*; he argues that by "using essentially patriarchal literary formulas, each questions patriarchal assumptions, a reversal that gives rise to fantastic elements in these three novels."[102]

A third reading of *Who Is Teddy Villanova?* came in an essay by Larry E. Grimes in which he compared the novel with Jules Feiffer's *Ackroyd* and Richard Brautigan's *Dreaming of Babylon*. All three are "re-visions" of the classic detective model, with Berger's being the best for its "full-adherence to the formula." As he explained, "True mystery and not the moral self, ontology and not ethics, most concern Berger and Wren."[103] Berger's revisions include an absurdist view of the city as a typical setting, a plot with infinitely incomplete actions, detectives who become writers and dreamers instead of moral arbiters, and style as a substitute for morality.

With "Acts of Definition, or Who Is Thomas Berger?" Alan Wilde offered the most challenging, far-reaching, and presumptuous piece of Berger scholarship. As the title suggests, Wilde sought to locate the author in the fiction and placed Berger in the camp of the "mid-fictionists" who "attempt to demystify the imperial ego—the self as preexistent 'psychic entity' coercing a yielding world into a transparent text." Wilde bases his ideas on the phenomenological notion of the author found *in* the text as a figure who "creates himself in and through language—or, more accurately, creates that phenomenological ego to which we as readers respond and which *does not exist* anywhere—not in things, which as yet have no meaning, nor in the artist himself, in his unformulated life."

Wilde cautioned that while Berger says his aim is to make language a theme, "his practice, the primary evidence of his *intentionality*, suggests nothing so much as an edgy discomfort with a world too effortlessly dismissed from consideration . . . [Berger acknowledges] that art can do no more than supply *a* view of what we choose to call reality." Wilde argued that Berger consistently creates "coercers of reality," monomaniacs who resist their worlds and seek to impose their wills on the world. In Wilde's view the portrait of the artist that emerges in his fiction "is in general one of uneasiness, discomfort, tension. The novels manifest, along with a determined effort to accept the contingency of reality, a more fundamentally intentional sense of the world as hostile, threatening, disequilibrating, alien, *other*."[104] The encounter with the Other—time, women, language, mortality, anarchy, evil—is at the center of his books. The determining of the self Wilde regarded as Berger's dominant theme. Wilde extended his thinking to later novels in a long footnote at the end of a reprint of this article in *Middle Grounds*.[105]

Berger's parodic practices in *Little Big Man* and *Arthur Rex* are considered in an essay by Joan F. Dean. She argued that Berger seeks to renew these myths' vitality by "demystif[ying] his material while preserving its mythic power to inspire belief and action."[106] Berger achieves these ends by emphasizing the human as well as the heroic aspects of his characters, thus emphasizing their complexity and contradictions. Berger presents a view of the world where people struggle amid good and evil, and consequently his books amount to a secular version of hagiography.

Three essays devoted exclusively to *Arthur Rex* appeared next, the first of which, by Raymond H. Thompson, was the weakest, lacking a clear thesis or approach. Nevertheless, Thompson contended that of the three typical responses to the Arthurian legend—heroic fantasy, ironic fantasy, and mythopoeic fantasy—*Arthur Rex* is an example of the second because of Berger's eye for the ridiculous.[107] Jay Ruud, on the other hand, saw the novel as pondering universal questions—what is truth, what is love, what is goodness?—and these meet in the figure of Galahad. Truth, he argued, is often only a matter of appearance, and what matters to Berger is what people *think* they are doing. Love relationships in the novel are exercises in power, and selfishness is the root of that power. Goodness is revealed to be ambiguous but "equated with truth, which is beyond the shaping power of human perceptions. It exists in the natural order of things. To see truth, to achieve true goodness, one must overcome the self. Berger has shown one path to total selflessness: true love.[108] Ruud concluded that Berger endorses a truth beyond the mundane that affirms goodness and love through self-denial, an experience Galahad undergoes.

Klaus P. Jankofsky organized much of his discussion around the figure of Gawaine and his adventures at Liberty Castle. Jankofsky argued that the novel can be read as Berger's answer to the condition of modern depravity he reveals in so many of his novels. For Jankofsky, Gawaine is the touchstone for revealing the moral issue Berger investigates. The "central issue for the modern reader [is] how to be human and live to tell; how to be a Christian knight and reconcile one's nature with the self, the world, and God."[109] From his encounter with the Green Knight at Liberty Castle, Gawaine emerges as the most likely successor to Arthur as king and an exemplum of the values Berger is promoting in the novel.

In "Language as Self-Defense in *Who Is Teddy Villanova?*," Jon Wallace analyzed Berger's style to demonstrate that the true mystery in the novel lies not with who has committed a crime but with the uses and abuses of language. Where language loses its traditional frames of reference, the novel questions "how [we are] to survive as individuals in a violent and apparently meaningless world in which language has become less an expressive and ordering medium than a dis-ordering force that helps the powerful maintain control of the powerless." Against such "nomenclatural vandalism," the hero, Russel Wren, finds first refuge and then conquest in his linguistic precision.[110]

A number of scholars have remarked that in *Little Big Man* the soliloquy Custer delivers before his death is taken directly from a portion of his autobiography. In a brief essay Jon Wallace took a semiotic approach to this passage to argue that there are two kinds of language in the novel—exploratory and defensive. Custer, he argued, is "at bottom a defender of a restricted sense of self . . . [who] for all moral purposes [is] blind and deaf to the existence of others." In his last words he denies the world, distancing himself verbally from what will soon kill him. This scene reveals in miniature a fundamental view of language elaborated in the novel as a whole: the "nature of human discourse, what it can and cannot do, how it shapes our world and vision, and ultimately limits us."[111]

In another essay on *Little Big Man*, Wallace turned his attention to the implied author, what he believed is the actual protagonist of the novel. Because Snell is presenting Crabb's words, one can never know how much of that presentation is a result of Snell's imposition on the text. "The central theme of *Little Big Man* is the restrictive power of language—the ways in which it limits our perception and understanding. . . . Crabb seeks to expose and transcend the language codes through which we have come to see the Old West—and to do so by means of an undeniably idiosyncratic style." Berger, in foregrounding language, shows how Crabb "plays the game of self-creation. . . . [By] forcing us to read [Crabb and Snell] as his own creations, Berger's implied author deepens and extends the theme of the search for selfhood by dramatizing it in linguistic as well as mimetic terms."[112]

In a second article concerning *Arthur Rex*, Klaus Jankofsky saw Berger's treatments of food and sex as elements that tellingly reveal his seriocomic approach to legendary material. In spite of humor that some critics found deflating, Jankofsky argues that Berger preserves "the essential idealism, depth, and pathos of the Arthurian story" and thus illustrates "again the perennial appeal of the Arthurian material."[113]

Brooks Landon also examined *Little Big Man*, which he called "Berger's greatest novel—not necessarily his best," and chose to look at the work in terms of its vision and style rather than its relationship to other narrative subgenres. Analyzing Crabb's amalgamation of verbal styles, Landon argued, "Just as surely as Jack's account of his life explores the nature and importance of western myths—both white and Indian—it also explores the linguistic and literary mechanics of myth-making, whether in history, anthropology, journalism, or the novel itself."[114] Landon endorsed the idea of the novel as a captivity narrative, but captivity imposed by language and standards impossible to achieve for the protagonist.

The best discussion of *Killing Time* was offered by Jon Wallace, who explored the ways that language is used to dismiss protagonist Joe Detweiler's experience and person. Wallace compared Detweiler with the actual killer upon whom he is based, Robert Irwin, and two accounts of his trial and prison statements. In *Killing Time* "Berger is specifically interested in how language serves to protect an established metaphysical frame of reference against a character whom it cannot explain." Wallace demonstrated the ways in which most of the novel's principal characters grapple with language and lead the reader to the essence of the author's method: "Berger not only reveals the limitations of labels, he also calls our attention to the limitations of language itself as a means of knowing, or revealing, the world—and persons. . . . As human beings, [Berger] seems to suggest, we will always remain in some shadowy, non-verbal other place—beyond the reach of language and the value assumptions that inform it."[115]

The one book devoted to Berger was written by Brooks Landon, in which he reprinted each of his four previous essays with revisions. The study was a general introduction that discussed all the novels up to *The Houseguest* and took for its thesis the idea that Berger's vision and method are paratactic, emphasizing a thoroughgoing dialectic. "A vital corollary to Berger's view of the way reality operates is his apparent conviction that only through a better understanding of the conflicts structuring the operation of reality—a search for truths—can personal freedom be found."[116]

Landon devoted most of his attention to the Reinhart quartet, *Little Big Man*, and *Arthur Rex*, emphasizing Berger's manipulations of language and persistent themes such as time, appearance and reality, victimization, power, identity, and freedom. The study was particularly useful for its treatment of such overlooked novels as *Nowhere*, *Being Invisible*, and *The Houseguest*, as well as the three plays from the early 1970s, which have also not yet received scholarly consideration. The book was furthermore noteworthy for the many excerpts Landon offered from his correspondence with Berger, which provide an often privileged glimpse into the writer's practice and thinking. The conclusion presented a helpful consideration of Berger's manipulations of traditional narrative forms, the role of language in the characters' lives and personae, and the inspiration of Nietzsche.

In another examination of *Arthur Rex*, Suzanne H. MacRae acknowledged the novel's contradictory reception and argued that sections of the book represent different and evolving narrative methods. Thus it progresses from ironic satire, to pathos, then tragedy, and finally realism. MacRae argued that Berger is not a misanthrope but a writer aware of the possibility for heroism despite radical human limitations. *Arthur Rex* is a "supple, sad, wise, and witty book which reincarnates the essential thing—the old story."[117]

There are also thirteen interviews, of varying lengths, that have been conducted with Berger over the years. By far the most important and revealing were with Douglas Hughes, Charles Rydell, and Richard Schickel.[118] The topics are of course diverse, with Berger explaining his writing habits, origins for characters and novels, relationship with the literary establishment, and intellectual and artistic inspirations. Most of the discussions have involved *Little Big Man* and the Reinhart saga, although one interview was devoted exclusively to *Arthur Rex* and another to Berger's theories of language and the dominant role it plays in his novels.[119] Another pair of interviews touched upon his relationship with his Ohio origins and his knowledge of New York City, among other topics.[120]

Even the most cursory review of Berger scholarship reveals that *Little Big Man* and the Reinhart novels have garnered the most attention (there are forty articles or treatments in books of the former and fifteen considerations of the quarter). While most of the novels from the 1960s, 1970s, and early 1980s have been considered by scholars, Berger's later novels (*Nowhere*, *Being Invisible*, *The Houseguest*, *Changing the Past*, *Orrie's Story*, and *Meeting Evil*) have been ignored and deserve much more attention. While there has been a good deal of attention given to his experiments with style and language and his manipulation of narrative conventions and forms, scant recognition has been given to the moral (as opposed to didactic) emphasis in his canon.

Berger has always been concerned with issues of justice and ethics, beginning with Reinhart's moral education in *Crazy in Berlin*, and he has not received the attention he deserves as one of contemporary American fiction's truly morally serious and penetrating writers.

The biographical information on Berger remains thin. He is an extremely private man, and the few details about his life must be gleaned from interviews, the introduction to Landon's book, and the usual references sources such as *Who's Who*, *Contemporary Authors*, and the *Dictionary of Literary Biography*.[121] Certainly more work remains to be done in this area, as well as some assessment of his letters and papers, which are housed in the Boston University Library. Landon's book also provides a brief annotated bibliography of primary and secondary materials, and James Bense has published a more comprehensive bibliography of materials.[122]

Notes

1. Douglas Hughes, "Thomas Berger's Elan," *Confrontation* 12 (Spring–Summer 1976): 25.

2. Tony Lang, "Close-Up: Thomas Berger," *Cincinnati Enquirer Magazine*, 8 October 1972, 22.

3. Richard Schickel, "Interviewing Thomas Berger," *New York Times Book Review*, 6 April 1980, 21.

4. Anon., "CA Interview," *Contemporary Authors*, New Revision Series, vol. 28 (Detroit: Gale Research, 1989), 57.

5. Michael Malone, "American Literature's Little Big Man," *Nation* 230 (May 1980): 535.

6. Thomas Berger, "Who Created Whom? Characters That Talk Back," *New York Times Book Review*, 31 May 1987, 36.

7. David W. Madden, "Thomas Berger: An Interview," in this volume.

8. Robert B. Jackson, review of *Crazy in Berlin*, *Library Journal* 83 (1 October 1958): 2763.

9. Orville Prescott, "Books of the Times," *New York Times*, 14 November 1958, 25.

10. Gene Baro, "Post-war Berlin in a Powerful Novel," *New York Herald Tribune Book Review*, 26 October 1958, 12; William James Smith, "The Genuine Gallows Humor," *Commonweal*, 9 January 1959, 392–93; Martin Levin, "For Diversion Seekers the No-Nonsense Novel," *Saturday Review*, 29 November 1958, 27.

11. Harvey Swados, "An American in Berlin," *New Leader*, 15 December 1958, 24.

12. Burke Wilkinson, "Carlo Comes Home from the Wars," *New York Times Book Review*, 15 April 1962, 37.

13. Granville Hicks, "Little Man, What Absurdity Now?" *Saturday Review*, 14 April 1962, 24.

14. [Zulfikar Ghose], "Innocent at Large," *Times Literary Supplement*, 21 June 1963, 457.

15. Stanley Kauffmann, "O'Hara and Others," *New York Review of Books*, 17 December 1964, 21; Granville Hicks, "Paleface in the Cheyenne Camp," *Saturday Review*, 10 October 1964, 39–40; Gerald Walker, "Pecos Picaresque," *New York Times Book Review*, 11 October 1964, 42.

16. Guy Davenport, "Tough Characters, Solid Novels," *National Review*, 26 January 1965, 68, 70.

17. S. K. Oberbeck, "Schlock Therapy," *Newsweek*, 18 September 1967, 106; Kenneth Graham, "Varieties of Picaresque," *Listener* 79 (1968): 639–40; Jib Fowles, "Mad Though Not Madcap," *New Leader*, 6 November 1967, 26–27.

18. Barbara Bannon, "PW Forecasts," *Publishers Weekly*, 31 July 1967, 53; Granville Hicks, "Not Who Done It, But Why?" *Saturday Review*, 23 September 1967, 77, 83.

19. Guy Davenport, "Masters of Time and Place," *National Review* 19 (1967): 1283.

20. Anon., "Twice as Much to Freeze," *Times Literary Supplement*, 30 April 1971, 493.

21. Guy Davenport, "A Chaplin Among the Cannibals," *Life*, 27 March 1970, 12.

22. Phoebe Pettingell, "Perpetual Sucker," *New Leader*, 11 May 1970, 30.

23. John Leonard, "Reinhart on the Rocks," *New York Times*, 31 March 1970, 39.

24. Paul Theroux, "A Hankering for the Fifties," *Book World*, 12 April 1970, 6.

25. John Hollander, *Harper's Magazine*, April 1970, 106.

26. Richard Schickel, "Bitter Comedy," *Commentary* 50 (July 1970): 78, 76.

27. Brom Weber, review of *Vital Parts*, *Saturday Review*, 21 March 1970, 42.

28. Richard Todd, "God's First Mistakes," *Atlantic*, September 1973, 107; Anon., "Notes on Current Books," *Virginia Quarterly Review* 49 (1973): cxxxvi; Walter Clemons, "Georgie's Travels," *Newsweek*, 21 May 1973, 102; Geoffrey Wagner, "Mister Ms.," *National Review* 25 (July 1973): 800; Leo Braudy, *New York Times Book Review*, 13 May 1973, 6.

29. Lore Dickstein, review of *Regiment of Women*, *Ms.*, August 1973, 33–34, 32.

30. Rene Kuhn Bryant, "Berger's Plastic Nostalgia," *National Review*, 16 October 1975, 1127; Aram Bakshian, Jr., "The Seamy Side of Main Street," *Wall Street Journal*, 29 May 1975, 12.

31. Michael Harris, "A Garden of Devious Delights," *Book World*, 20 April 1975, 3; Anon., review of *Sneaky People*, *Choice* 12 (July/August 1975): 678.

32. D. Keith Mano, "A Good Book by a Good Writer," *New York Times Book Review*, 20 April 1975, 4–5.

33. Walter Goodman, "The Shamus as Schlemiel," *New Leader*, 23 May 1977, 12; Walter Clemons, "Dashiell Chandler," *Newsweek*, 4 April 1977, 85; Roger Sale, "Hostages," *New York Review of Books*, 19 March 1977, 39–40; Paul Gray, "Loopy Locutions," *Time*, 4 April 1977, 86.

34. Leonard Michaels, "If Hammett and Chandler Were Written by Perelman," review of *Who Is Teddy Villanova?*, *New York Times Book Review*, 20 March 1977, 1, 26.

35. Barbara Bannon, "PW Forecasts," *Publishers Weekly*, 10 July 1978, 120; Edmund Fuller, "An Enchanting Retelling of Arthurian Legend," *Wall Street Journal*, 5 February 1979, 18; John Romano, "Camelot and All That," *New York Times Book Review*, 12 November 1978, 62; Curt Suplee, "Knights to Remember," *Book World*, 17 September 1978, E8; Garrett Epps, *New Republic*, 7 October 1978, 34–36.

36. Walter Clemons, "Slippery Foothold," *Newsweek*, 14 April 1980, 96B; Thomas Lavoie, *Library Journal* 105 (15 March 1980): 741; Isa Kapp, *New Republic*, 26 April 1980, 34–36.

37. Paul Gray, "A House Is Not a Home," *Time*, 7 April 1980, 84; Christopher Lehmann-Haupt, "Books of the Times," *New York Times*, 1 April 1980, C10; Georgia A. Brown, "Recent Fiction," *Yale Review* 70 (1981): 275.

38. Thomas R. Edwards, "Domestic Guerrillas," *New York Times Book Review*, 6 April 1980, 23.

39. Michael Malone, "American Literature's Little Big Man," *Nation* 230 (1980): 536.

40. Alan Cheuse, review of *Reinhart's Women*, *Saturday Review*, 8 September 1981, 60; David Montrose, "On the Gastronomic Warpath," *TLS*, 3 September 1982, 940.

41. Karl Keller, "Berger, with Relish," *Los Angeles Times Book Review*, 1 November 1981, 1.

42. J. D. Reed, "Quixote in the Kitchen," *Time*, 12 October 1981, 109.

43. Frank Burch Brown, "Books," *Christian Century* 100 (1983): 941–42.

44. W. Riggan, "Noted," *World Literature Today* 58 (1984): 276.

45. Michael Gorra, "Comic-Book Quarrel," *Nation* 236 (1983): 742.

46. Jack Beatty, "A Comedy of Bad Manners," *New Republic*, 23 May 1983, 39.

47. Anne Tyler, "Home Folks at One Another's Throats," *New York Times Book Review*, 8 May 1983, 1, 24.

48. Christopher Porterfield, "Dicey Claims," *Time*, 17 June 1985, 76.

49. Lee Lemon, "Bookmarks," *Prairie Schooner* 62 (Fall 1988): 132; Dan Cryer, "Fred and Babe and Zirko the Artist," *Newsday*, 5 April 1987, 16.

50. Marvin J. LaHood, review of *Being Invisible*, *World Literature Today* 62 (Winter 1988): 135; Francine Prose, "Outnumbered by Jerks," *New York Times Book Review*, 12 April 1987, 9.

51. Paul Gray, "When the Outrageous Is the Norm," *Time*, 11 April 1988, 73.

52. John Clute, "Outside the Social Syntax," *Times Literary Supplement*, 4–10 August 1989, 851.

53. Steve Weingartner, *Booklist* 85 (15 June 1989): 1738; Tom McKusick, "Fiction," *Utne Reader* 37 (January–February 1990): 102; Douglas Glover, "Caspar Milquetoast, These Are Your Lives," *New York Times Book Review*, 27 August 1989, 12.

54. Sybil Steinberg, "Forecasts," *Publishers Weekly*, 31 August 1990, 48; Marvin J. LaHood, "Fiction," *World Literature Today* 65 (Summer 1991): 487; William H. Pritchard, "Fiction Chronicle," *Hudson Review* 44, 3 (Autumn 1991): 508.

55. Thomas Disch, "Agamemnon and the Guys at the Bar," *New York Times Book Review*, 7 October 1990, 12.

56. Bill Marx, "It's All Greek, Berger Perfects the Slow Burn," *Boston Phoenix*, "Literary Section," October 1990, 6.

57. Louis B. Jones, "Evil Incarnate Is a Guy Named Richie," *New York Times Book Review*, 12 July 1992, 7; Robert Long, "Thomas Berger's Latest Novel Tells of a Man and a Menace," *Philadelphia Inquirer*, 27 September 1992, M3; Michiko Kakutani, "Mayhem Envelops a Normal Life," *New York Times*, 2 June 1992, C16; Roy Olson, "Upfront: Advance Reviews," *Booklist* 88 (1 April 1992): 1411.

58. Ihab Hassan, "Conscience and Incongruity: The Fiction of Thomas Berger," *Critique* 5, 2 (1962): 4, 10, 13.

59. Robert Edson Lee, *From West to East: Studies in the Literature of the American West* (Urbana: University of Illinois Press, 1966), 156.

60. L. L. Lee, "American, Western, Picaresque: Thomas Berger's *Little Big Man*," *South Dakota Review* 4, 2 (1966): 35.

61. William T. Pilkington, "Aspects of the Western Comic Novel," *Western American Literature* 1 (1966): 215, 217.

62. Paul Levine, "The Intemperate Zone: The Climate of Contemporary American Fiction," *Massachusetts Review* 8, no. 3 (1967): 509.

63. Leslie Fiedler, *The Return of the Vanishing American* (New York: Stein & Day, 1968), 160.

64. Gerald Green, "Back to Bigger," in *Proletarian Writers of the Thirties*, ed. David Madden (Carbondale: Southern Illinois University Press, 1968), p. 43.

65. Brian W. Dippie, "Jack Crabb and the Sole Survivors of Custer's Last Stand," *Western American Literature* 4 (1969): 202.

66. Jay Gurian, "Style in the Literary Desert: *Little Big Man*," *Western American Literature* 3 (1969): 288.

67. Frederick W. Turner III, "Melville and Thomas Berger: The Novelist as Cultural Anthropologist," *Centennial Review* 13 (1969): 115, 120.

68. Marjorie Ryan, "Four Contemporary Satires and the Problem of Norms," *Satire Newsletter* 6, no. 2 (1969): 44.

69. Delbert E. Wylder, "Thomas Berger's *Little Big Man* as Literature," *Western American Literature* 3 (Winter 1969): 282, 283.

70. Joyce Hancock, "Squaring the Circle: System Conflicts in *Little Big Man*," *Amanuensis* 1 (1972): 42. See also Mike Parker's "Circles and Squares: Psychologies at War in Berger's *Little Big Man*," *Mount Olive Review* 3 (Spring 1989): 15–21.

71. Max F. Schulz, *Black Humor Fiction of the Sixties* (Athens: Ohio State University Press, 1973), 73.

72. Leo E. Oliva, "Thomas Berger's *Little Big Man* as History," *Western American Literature* 8 (1973): 34, 40.

73. Brom Weber, "The Mode of 'Black Humor,' " in *The Comic Imagination in American Literature*, ed. Louis D. Rubin (New Brunswick, N.J.: Rutgers University Press, 1973), 371.

74. Douglas A. Hughes, "The Schlemiel as Humanist: Thomas Berger's Carlo Reinhart," *Cithara* 15, no. 1 (1975): 5, 20.

75. Fred M. Fetrow, "The Function of the External Narrator in Thomas Berger's *Little Big Man*," *Journal of Narrative Technique* 5 (1975): 58, 64.

76. Anon., "Thomas Berger's *Regiment of Women*: Beyond *Lysistrata*," *Studies in Contemporary Satire* 1 (1975): 1–3.

77. Mark Bezanson, "Berger and Penn's West: Visions and Revisions," in *The Modern American Novel and the Movies*, ed. Gerald Peary and Roger Shatzkin (New York: Frederick Ungar, 1978), 277.

78. Frederick Turner, "The Second Decade of *Little Big Man*," *Nation*, 20 August, 1977, 150, 151.

79. Brooks Landon, "The Radical Americanist," *Nation*, 10 August 1977, 153.

80. John W. Turner, "*Little Big Man*, The Novel and the Film: A Study of Narrative Structure," *Literature/Film Quarterly* 5 (1977): 162.

81. Daniel Royot, "Aspects of the American Picaresque in *Little Big Man*," in *Les Américanistes: New French Criticism on Modern American Fiction*, ed. Ira D. Johnson and Christiane Johnson (Fort Washington, N.Y.: Kennikat Press, 1978), 41, 43, 51.

82. Stanley Trachtenberg, "Berger and Barth: The Comedy of Decomposition," in *Comic Relief: Humor in Contemporary American Literature*, ed. Sarah Blacher Cohn (Urbana: University of Illinois Press, 1978), 47, 50, 52.

83. Madelon Heatherington, "Romance Without Women: The Sterile Fiction of the American West," *Georgia Review* 33 (1979): 645.

84. Caren J. Deming, "Miscegenation in Popular Western History and Fiction," in *Women and Western American Literature*, ed. Helen Winter Stauff and Susan J. Rosowski (Troy, N.Y.: Whitson, 1982), 97.

85. David Madden, "Thomas Berger's Comic-Absurd Vision in *Who is Teddy Villanova?*" *Armchair Detective* 14 (1981): 37, 43.

86. Michael Cleary, "Finding the Center of the Earth: Satire, History, and Myth in *Little Big Man*," *Western American Literature* 15 (1980): 196, 211.

87. Richard A. Betts, "Thomas Berger's *Little Big Man*: Contemporary Picaresque," *Critique* 23, no. 2 (1981): 92, 95.

88. Michael Malone, "Berger, Burlesque, and the Yearning for Comedy," *Studies in American Humor* 2, no. 1 (Spring 1983): 21, 27, 31–32.

89. Myron Simon, "*Crazy in Berlin* as Ethnic Comedy," *Studies in American Humor* 2, no. 1 (Spring 1983): 41, 43.

90. John Carlos Rowe, "Alien Encounter: Thomas Berger's *Neighbors* as a Critique of Existential Humanism," *Studies in American Humor* 2, no. 1 (Spring 1983): 57.

91. Brooks Landon, "The Whole Kit and Caboodle: Language as Irony in Thomas

Berger's *Neighbors* and *Sneaky People*," *Studies in American Humor* 2, no. 1 (Spring 1983): 65, 71.

92. Jean P. Moore, "Thomas Berger's 'Joyful Worship': A Study of Form and Parody," *Studies in American Humor* 2, no. 1 (Spring 1983): 81–82.

93. Sherrill E. Grace, "Western Myth and Northern History, The Plains Indians of Berger and Wiebe," *Great Plains Quarterly* 3, no. 3 (Summer 1983): 153, 154.

94. Max F. Schulz, "Thomas Berger: His World of Words, and Stereoscopes of Style," *Studies in American Humor* 2, no. 2 (Fall 1983): 87, 97.

95. Sanford Pinsker, "The World According to Carl Reinhart: Thomas Berger's Comic Vision," *Studies in American Humor* 2, no. 2 (Fall 1983): 101–10.

96. Ronald R. Janssen, "The Voice of Our Culture: Thomas Berger's *Reinhart in Love*," *Studies in American Humor* 2, no. 2 (Fall 1983): 111–16.

97. Philip Kuberski, "The Kraft of Fiction: Nomenclatural Vandalism in *Who is Teddy Villanova?*," *Studies in American Humor* 2, no. 2 (Fall 1983): 128.

98. David W. Madden, "The Renegade Mood in Thomas Berger's Fiction," *Studies in American Humor* 2, no. 2 (Fall 1983): 130–41.

99. Patrick W. Shaw, "The American West as Satiric Territory: Kesey's *One Flew Over the Cuckoo's Nest* and Berger's *Little Big Man*," *Studies in Contemporary Satire* 10 (1983): 2.

100. Gerald Weales, "Reinhart as Hero and Clown," *The Hollins Critic* 20, no. 5 (1983): 5.

101. Brooks Landon, "Language and the Subversion of Good Order in Thomas Berger's *Regiment of Women*," *Philological Quarterly* 62 (1983): 28.

102. Brooks Landon, "Eve at the End of the World," in *Erotic Universe: Sexuality and Fantastic Literature*, ed. Donald Palumbo (New York: Greenwood Press, 1986), 73.

103. Larry E. Grimes, "Stepsons of Sam: Re-Visions of the Hard-Boiled Detective Formula in Recent American Fiction," *Modern Fiction Studies* 29, no. 3 (Autumn 1983): 543.

104. Alan Wilde, "Acts of Definition, or Who Is Thomas Berger?" *Arizona Quarterly* 39, no. 4 (Winter 1983): 316, 318, 329, 335.

105. Alan Wilde, *Middle Grounds: Studies in Contemporary American Fiction* (Philadelphia: University of Pennsylvania Press, 1987), 70–71.

106. Joan F. Dean, "Thomas Berger's Fiction: Demystification without Demythification," in *Hagiographie et Iconoclastie: Modèles Américains*, ed. Serge Ricard (Aix-en-Provence: Pubs. Univ. de Provence, 1984), 56.

107. Raymond H. Thompson, "Humor and Irony in Modern Arthurian Fantasy: Thomas Berger's *Arthur Rex*," *Kansas Quarterly* 16 (Summer 1984): 45–49.

108. Jay Ruud, "Thomas Berger's *Arthur Rex*: Galahad and Earthly Power," *Critique* 25 (1984): 97. For a brief survey of medieval sources, see Beverly Taylor and Elisabeth Brewer, *The Return of King Arthur: British and American Arthurian Literature Since 1800* (Cambridge: D. S. Brewer & Barnes & Noble, 1983), 291, 298–300; for a discussion of Berger's fidelity to and deviations from Malory, see Brooks Landon, "Thomas Berger's *Arthur Rex*," in *King Arthur Through the Ages*, ed. Valerie M. Lagorio and Mildred Leake Day (New York: Garland, 1990), pp. 240–54; and for a pedagogical approach, see Harold J. Herman, "Teaching White, Stewart, and Berger," in *Approaches to Teaching the Arthurian Tradition*, ed. Maureen Fries and Jeanie Watson (New York: Modern Language Association of America, 1992), 113–17.

109. Klaus Jankofsky, "Sir Gawaine at Liberty Castle: Thomas Berger's Comic Didacticism in *Arthur Rex: A Legendary Novel*," in *Theorie und Praxis im Erzählen des 19. und 20. Jahrhunderts*, ed. Winfried Herget, Klaus Peter Jochum, and Ingeborg Weber (Tübingen: Gunter Narr Verlag Tübingen, 1986), 392.

110. Jon Wallace, "Laughter as Self-Defense in *Who is Teddy Villanova?*," *Studies in American Humor* 5, no. 1 (Spring 1986): 40.

111. Jon Wallace, "The Meaning of Custer's Last Words in *Little Big Man*," *Notes on Contemporary Literature* 17 (May 1987): 3.

112. Jon Wallace, "The Implied Author as Protagonist: A Reading of *Little Big Man*," *Western American Literature* 22, no. 4 (1988): 293, 297.

113. Klaus Jankofsky, "Food and Sex in Berger's *Rex*," *Studies in American Humor* 6 (1988): 105, 114.

114. Brooks Landon, "The Measure of *Little Big Man*," *Studies in American Fiction* 17 (Autumn 1989): 135. Another recent evaluation of the novel can be found in Michael Parker's "Religion in Berger's *Little Big Man*," *Mount Olive Review* 5 (Spring 1991): 7–14.

115. Jon Wallace, "A Murderous Clarity: A Reading of Thomas Berger's *Killing Time*," *Philological Quarterly* 68 (1989): 107–08, 112–13.

116. Brooks Landon, *Thomas Berger* (Boston: Twayne, 1989), xi.

117. Suzanne H. MacRae, "Berger's Mythical *Arthur Rex*," in *Popular Arthurian Traditions*, ed. Sally K. Slocum (Bowling Green: Bowling Green University Press, 1992), 93.

118. Douglas Hughes, "Thomas Berger's Elan," *Confrontation* 12 (1976): 23–39; Charles Rydell, "Book-Maker-of-the-Month: Thomas Berger," *Andy Warhol's Interview*, July 1975, 38–39; Richard Schickel, "Interviewing Thomas Berger," *New York Times Book Review*, 6 April 1980, 1, 21–22.

119. Dan Nastali, "Interview on *Arthur Rex*," *Quondam et Futurus* 10, no. 3 (Spring 1990): 11–17; Mary Reefer, "The Substance of Style: An Interview with Thomas Berger," *New Letters* 55, no. 1 (Fall 1988): 85–98.

120. Tony Lang, "Close-Up: Thomas Berger," *Cincinnati Enquirer Magazine*, 8 October 1972, 21–24, 26; James Knippling, "Thomas Berger: Reclusive Writer," *Cincinnati*, December 1981, 28, 30–31.

121. In *The Education of an Editor* (Garden City: Doubleday, 1980), Burroughs Mitchell, Berger's first editor, offers a rare biographical glimpse of the writer and his work.

122. James Bense, "Works By and About Thomas Berger," *Studies in American Humor* 2, no. 2 (Fall 1983): 142–52.

REVIEWS

◆

An American in Berlin
[Review of *Crazy in Berlin*]

Harvey Swados

Perhaps the most valid of the various recent criticisms of American novels and novelists has been the complaint of the intellectual discrepancy between fiction produced by half-educated Americans and that composed by Europeans who are not just novel writers, but intellectuals and men of letters too. It is true that great works have been produced in this country by men of little learning but great sensitivity and intensity, and that these men, with all their limitations, have been fairly typical in the creation of American fiction. Nevertheless, there lies at hand the contemporary achievement of truly cultivated and thoughtful European novelists, and in consequence there have sounded the discontented voices, claiming that here in the United States the writer of fiction is seemingly incapable of dealing with any problems larger than semi-private psychological states of being.

Well, here is a first novel by a young American who is not afraid to consider seriously and thoughtfully some of the central questions of European identity: What is a German? What is a Jew? Who is guilty for what the former did to the latter? And what, finally, is a man? The questions are asked, and answers are argued over (or emerge gradually and novelistically from a series of developments in the lives of the protagonists) in their logical setting, the ruins of Berlin in the autumn of 1945. This is not however the traditional liberal American novel in which the well-intentioned writer sighs over the pity of it all and invites us as readers to sigh with him while he hates the Nazi as his enemy and loves the Jew as his brother. That we can do for ourselves.

What Berger has done instead is to commence where liberalism ends, in the world of ideas. His hero, the young American occupation soldier Carlo Reinhart, is not a man of good will eager to avenge wrongs. He is more a man who listens so hard, and discovers so many contradictory facts about people, that he is driven crazy (literally—but only temporarily— which is just one of the meanings of the title) by the effort of learning so much and sorting out so much about his own German roots and his profound connections with the Jewish people.

Reprinted with permission from *The New Leader*, 15 December 1958.

No one is what he seems in this mordant and impious book. . . . It is their interacting one upon the other, in a complexly plotted story, that slowly reveals to us a picture of a city, a portrait of a culture, and an attitude toward mankind.

There are many things to praise about this brilliantly-lit narrative. Not least is Berger's audacious use of the English language. He writes in American, in an engaging mixture of the colloquial, the obscene, the slangy and the poetic; it is a style that could hardly have emerged without the new developments in American prose writing by the innovators of recent years; but it is the author's own. The result, when imposed on a steadfastly ironic point of view, is both stimulating and original. What is more, it reveals an author thoroughly faithful to the demands of the novel as a medium of communication—he is hilariously entertaining, but he is above all a man who thinks and feels, and who makes us think and feel too.

Of course this reviewer has reservations about *Crazy In Berlin*. The exuberance of language occasionally results in forcing. Similarly, the unrelentingly ironic point of view demands—and finally obtains—a kind of detachment that prevents readers from identifying whole-heartedly with characters. This is particularly true of Schild, whose background is detailed with absolute fidelity, but whose tragic fate leaves one quite cold and unmoved.

The important news, however, is not that *Crazy In Berlin* is flawed by its weaknesses; naturally it is. What matters is that it exists, that it promises a real emotional charge to those adventurous enough to plunge on past the early murky pages, and that Thomas Berger is a name to remember, an important addition to the small group of important American writers, and a novelist with a great career before him.

[Review of *Vital Parts*]

Brom Weber

The tragicomic saga of Ohio's Carlo Reinhart, World War II corporal in *Crazy in Berlin* (1958) and maladjusted veteran in *Reinhart in Love* (1962), is carried forward brilliantly into the late Sixties in *Vital Parts*, the third of Thomas Berger's novels devoted to his likable Midwestern slob. *Vital Parts* confirms Berger's rank as a major American novelist, one whose stylistic fecundity, psychological insight, and social knowledge are seemingly inexhaustible. Reinhart continues to move, clownlike, through his familiar world of "asymmetrical impulses, like a laughter hopelessly mad, hopelessly free," large in physique, generosity, honesty, gullibility, optimism, and capacity for enduring psychosocial wounds.

In *Vital Parts* Reinhart comes closer than ever before to being a total mess of nonheroism. Forty-four years old, he thinks of himself as virtually senile. His taut muscles have turned to helpless fat; he has failed miserably at real estate, film exhibiting, and sundry other forms of money-making; his twenty-one-year-old son berates him for being "far worse" than a "fascist"—namely, "a liberal, Northern style"; his wife forbids him to sleep in their bed any more; the local Italian restaurateur expels Reinhart from the "in" eatery; the whore he infrequently visits rejects his desperate offer of a post-dated check in place of the usual cash.

Similar rebuffs in earlier decades had not dented Reinhart's apparently resilient innocence. In *Vital Parts*, however, the dark undercurrents of Thomas Berger's art emerge more strongly. Reinhart's continued openness is shown to have been deliberate and desirable rather than accidental and trivial—"younger, he had sought control over experience, basic to which was an escape from imposed rituals, like church, rigid political credos, and social biases. The object was not to repeat anything compulsively." Giddy, amusing passages depict Reinhart's adventures with contemporary forms of socio-personal liberation and the startlingly foul and funny characters he encounters en route. The experience proves de-individualizing rather than liberating. Reinhart's generally laissez-faire philosophy is transformed into bitterness:

Reprinted with the permission of SR Publications Limited.

> Human beings are vile. . . . Like any other general rule it has as many exceptions as applications, but it is a useful position from which to start. Then you won't be disillusioned by swinishness on the one hand, while on the other you will be pleasantly surprised occasionally when decency appears unexpectedly.

Little wonder, then, that in exchange for $10,000 with two final weeks of life in which to spend it, Reinhart promises two ridiculously sinister charlatans—an American go-getting businessman and an alleged Swiss scientist who may well be the ex-Nazi "Schatzi" of *Crazy in Berlin*—that they may deep-freeze him into suspended animation. Their ostensible purpose is to initiate a nonprofit effort to circumvent death, though they are obviously irresponsible and self-seeking. The chicanery and slapstick that enliven this fraudulent philanthropy are enveloped in the extravagant humor which surrounded the espionage of *Crazy in Berlin* and the political skulduggery of *Reinhart in Love*.

As in earlier Reinhart novels, the pace of events in *Vital Parts* is as phenomenally rapid as the tempo of the prose, the outcome is unexpected, explanations emerge late, and one is bombarded with continual novelty. *Vital Parts* demands an attentive reader who can accept frenetic change with the aplomb of Eunice, the girl in whose company Reinhart explores youthful sex, rock, and drugs. "Jews are out, I think," she says. "Blacks may not last much longer, either. I am beginning to turn off from the ethnic bag. Do you dig soul food? It's all fried." Not surprisingly, Reinhart, whose natural optimism has been weakened by his acquired pessimism, is lured back into continued life only by a profoundly felt need to sustain his physically injured sixteen-year-old daughter, who is as fat, gluttonous, insecure, foolish, innocent, and loving as Reinhart, and as much detested and repudiated by her mother and brother.

The laughter threading *Vital Parts* brightens rather than obscures the depth of thought and emotion evoked by Thomas Berger's fiction. In *Crazy in Berlin* Reinhart had expressed in action more than in words the moral distinction between Jew and Nazi. In *Reinhart in Love* he again depicted ideas, in this case the essential humanity of the Negro and the fragility of love. Berger's newest novel dramatizes the tenuous contemporary existence of old-fashioned qualities anathema to Reinhart's son: "Our enemy is liberal, agnostic, rationalistic, moral relativists, 'men of goodwill,' 'common decency,' 'humanitarianism,' and all those frauds."

Will Reinhart, fat, anachronistic fool, survive the 1970s? One hopes so, for he has a basic humanism that should not be lost. Tricked into marriage by a false alarm of pregnancy, encouraged to scrounge for money and social prestige instead of wasting his hours studying under the GI Bill of Rights, he is the kind of decent bungler about whose existence we might well begin to care a little more. Nobody really spectacular, but at least no hot prospect for authoritarianism of any kind.

A comic allegorist of the worthwhile Middle American, skillfully wielding a colloquial diction and rhythm of extraordinary expressiveness, Thomas Berger is one of the most successful satiric observers of the ebb and flow of American life after World War II. His prolificacy promises a continued development of the tragicomic mode of vision, something American literature badly needs to compensate for the over-extended silence of such formerly active writers as Ralph Ellison, Joseph Heller, and Thomas Pynchon.

[Review of *Regiment of Women*]

Lore Dickstein

Thomas Berger is an extremely talented comic novelist. Although he is best known for *Little Big Man* (1964), a parody of the Wild West adventure novel, Berger's greatest achievement is the Reinhart trilogy (*Crazy in Berlin*, 1958; *Reinhart in Love*, 1962; and *Vital Parts*, 1970), a satirical saga of Carlo Reinhart's coming of age through the 1940s, 50s, and 60s. His new book, *Regiment of Women*, is a futuristic fantasy about sexual politics.

The problem that Berger grapples with in his works is that great Existential issue of our time—identity. While this is heavy, serious stuff, Berger is no brooding Ingmar Bergman. His books are perverse mockeries of the dreams and illusions on which our daily lives are constructed. Berger attacks everything—Indians, women, psychoanalysts, geriatrics, soldiers, hippies, nuns—with a cutting, ironic wit and a precision of detail so deadly accurate it hurts when you laugh. In this context, questions of identity and of psychic survival in a vile, fraudulent world become one vast, freewheeling, irreverent joke on the human condition.

Berger's black humor is best displayed in the Reinhart novels. In these books, Carlo Reinhart, the oaf, the lout, the loser, is invariably betrayed— both by his own trust and innocence and by a world that knows the rules of the game: deceit, corruption, and anarchy. Reinhart longs for his days in the Army (though he was no hero) where everyone had an assigned status and where the rules and regulations (though never adhered to) gave life some predictability and order. The Army is important in Berger's books for precisely these reasons. It appears in almost all his novels, a chaotic corrupt institution, to be sure, but in some sense a fixed point in a world of uncertainties.

There is an army in *Regiment of Women*, as the title implies, but the fireworks are reserved for another kind of caste system: the regimentation of sex roles. As such, it is a natural offshoot of *Vital Parts*, Berger's previous (and best) book. *Vital Parts* satirically presents the doings of the swinging sixties—the awakening of the counterculture, the drug scene, and the ambiguity of sex types—especially as evidenced by unisex. *Regiment of Women* extrapolates some of these elements from *Vital Parts*, stretching them out and distorting them in the fun house of Berger's imagination.

The new novel takes place in New York City during the 21st century, but unlike most futuristic novels or science fiction, which bristle with advanced technology (and an implied optimism about the future), Berger's novel is a world of breakdowns. Today's concerns—urban blight, pollution, inflation, sexual politics, identity, psychiatry—have become oppressive, nightmarish monstrosities . . .

In this crisis state, a number of reversals have occurred. Women rule the power structure—the government, the military, the police, big business. Austere, authoritarian, and armed with a supply of removable dildoes, they wield power over a male population of prissy, vain caricatures of femininity. The entire cast plays out their roles as transvestites . . .

This may seem offensive to those of us serious about sexual politics, but it is precisely Berger's lack of reverence, his willingness to hold nothing sacred, that provides the hilarious absurdity of the book. For this reason, to read *Regiment of Women* solely as a comment on Women's Liberation (or on male chauvinism for that matter) is to misunderstand Berger and to underestimate his irresponsibility. True to form, Berger spares no one. This book is no more antifeminist than it is antimale; Berger is not arguing any one political line. His anarchic imagination exaggerates all sexual stereotypes into ludicrous postures, perhaps to show how they rob us of our freedom.

Most of the novel focuses on the trials of Georgie Cornell, a man, as a revolutionary hero in the Sperm Service and as the recipient of various "modern" methods of psychiatry. These range from simplistic Freudian analysis to psychotherapeutic love treatment, which is, of course, anal penetration by dildo. Conventional sexual intercourse is a forbidden and an almost forgotten act here, and punishable by castration. But in the last pages, Georgie triumphs over all and "with one supreme thrust . . . reign[s] as absolute tyrant of the world."

This victory is not to be taken literally, as a fantasy of restored male dominance, but rather as a satire on just such a fantasy. As in all his work, it is Berger's use of language that reveals his satiric intent. Berger intends no return to "normalcy" when he writes: "His power was ever rising, he was adamant, invulnerable, brutal, and masterful beyond any dream."

For the reader and for Berger, the absurdity of anyone fucking their way to power, real or imagined, turns the *coup* into a joke and a wry mockery of today's politics, sexual and otherwise. Berger states his case pointedly (italics mine) in *Vital Parts*: "In a society in which a Kennedy could be murdered this adolescent [Reinhart's son] grew to legal manhood with a conviction to the effect that all existing institutions were at the same time moribund and insanely malignant, rotten at the foundation but in the superstructure terribly efficacious for evil purposes. And everybody knows a dying tyrant is the most wanton."

If Hammett and Chandler Were
Written by Perelman
[Review of *Who Is Teddy Villanova?*]

LEONARD MICHAELS

Thomas Berger's fifth novel is mainly a parody of detective thrillers; his well-known "Little Big Man" was a parody of Westerns. According to the jacket copy, in "Who Is Teddy Villanova?" we will recognize the familiar "seedy office," "down-at-the-heels shamus," "procession of sinister, chicane, or merely brutal men and scheming, vicious, but lovely women" and a "sequence of savage beatings." All this is true. The novel contains much that is conventional in detective thrillers. Still, one needn't know the books of Dashiell Hammett or Raymond Chandler in order to appreciate Berger's witty burlesque of their characters and situation. . . .

Berger's style, which is one of the great pleasures of the book, is something like S. J. Perelman's—educated, complicated, graceful, silly, destructive in spirit, and brilliant—and it is also something like Mad Comics—densely, sensuously detailed, unpredictable, packed with gags. Beyond all this, it makes an impression of scholarship—that is, Berger seems really to know what he jokes about. This includes not only Hammett and Chandler, but also Racine, Goethe, Ruskin, Elias Canetti, New York and the way its residents behave. Essentially, then, Berger's style is like itself insofar as it is like other styles. And his whole novel—in its wide ranging reference to cultural forms both high and pop—is like a huge verbal mirror. Its reflections are similar to what we see in much contemporary literature—hilarious and serious at once. . . .

On some occasions in the novel, the vulgar material slightly overwhelms Berger's wit, but this is inevitable. The book deals with certain well-known and oppressive banalities; now and then it must descend to mere seriousness. . . .

It should be said that Berger's detective hustles about Manhattan from one highly offensive personal experience to another, and this is a little reminiscent of the plot of another novel, Saul Bellow's "detective novel,"

Reprinted by permission of *New York Times Book Review*, 20 March 1977, 1, 25–26.

"Mr. Sammler's Planet." Mr. Sammler, like Berger's detective Russel Wren, is a literate anachronism, a hero who reads books and, by his very nature, too much suffers the life of the mind. . . .

Berger intends to be ridiculous, not ironically lyrical, yet he seems as impressed as Bellow by the horrifying decline in amenities and manners. Both novelists also notice murderous violence, Manhattan's dog-zoo of excremental streets, ubiquitous and matter-of-fact sexual perversity, and other features in the gruesome apocalypse of New York. Naturally both novelists make their theme the staggering insufficiency of an educated intelligence to such modern circumstances. Berger's detective, while investigating the mystery in this novel, stops to analyze events and clues. He is meticulous and exceedingly logical. As a result, he never understands anything until, at last, everything is merely explained to him by the master criminal who then blithely gets away.

But the mystery in Berger's novel is nothing anyone ever really explains. For example, there is no real reason to explain why Russel Wren is beaten up viciously in his own office just as the narrative gets started, and then, shortly after leaving his office building—which is accomplished after about forty pages of riotous complication—goes home and is not only beaten up again but intellectually humiliated while standing among his precious books. Again for no real reason. These are funny scenes not simply because they lack justification, but because they are also brilliantly written. They should remind us of the great delight we take in gratuitous, ugly, sadistic *frissons* which have become conventional in recent movies, not only in detective thrillers.

As for the mystery itself—the thing this book is about—it seems to lie exactly in Russel Wren's own literary head, his only office, the place where he lives and works. It is a place full of words, but it can neither effectively communicate with the world nor understand its deeply criminal nature. If the novel is hilarious, it is also sometimes a little sad in the sweet, strangely amazing way of Charlie Chaplin. In one scene Russel Wren, deeply beaten in body and mind, discovers a great pile of furniture in the street, including a Barca-Lounger. He sits in it and leans back. . . .

The scene is poignant and humorous, and the little reflection with which it ends—like many other reflections in the novel—is interesting and true. But of course no reader could confuse this fantastic novel with life. After all, who ever heard of someone being sodomized at a public phone in Manhattan? Any child could tell you that hasn't happened yet. Still, the novel has an important connection with life, because aside from the pleasure you take in reading it, you will have the wonderful pleasure of reading parts of it aloud to friends and watching the effects in their faces. Terrific comedians always make us "die laughing." Given the alternatives today, we should be grateful.

Home Folks at One Another's Throats
[Review of *The Feud*]

ANNE TYLER

Thomas Berger has been constructing various dark worlds for some 25 years now, but he continues to draw a surprisingly specialized audience—a kind of secret society composed of those who delight in his gleeful, mordant view of things. He is not a man to repeat himself. The stark power of "Neighbors" has little in common with the cheekiness of The Reinhart Series. But there is a certain sharp edge to his vision that identifies all he writes. He appears to see his subjects in a uniquely clear, hard light.

"The Feud," his 12th novel, focuses upon the startling speed with which events can develop into something more than themselves. At one point in the novel, a small-town police chief arrests a boy for scaring people with a pistol. It's only a starter pistol, though, as another man argues, and it's probably not even loaded. As if to demonstrate otherwise, the police chief takes a gun from his desk drawer. The other man protests: What he's pulled out is a .22 automatic. It's not the starter pistol at all.

"I never said it was," the police chief replies. "I am just showing you what kinda weapons I've took away from kids. You could kill a man with this. I took it offn some kid who had it down the dump, shooting rats. Now the slug from one of these can travel a mile or more and kill or maim. Or suppose it was to hit the head of an engineer of an express train going to the city: he'd fall down on the controls, and the train'd keep going when it got to the terminal downtown and plow right into the building and kill everybody on board and a whole lot of innocent strangers who just happened to be there at the time."

That paragraph—proceeding from empty starter pistol to mass mayhem in the blink of an eye—is a sort of miniature of the novel as a whole. The plot of "The Feud" is a gigantic sprawl of disasters triggered by the smallest of events: a discussion as to whether a customer in a hardware store should get rid of his unlit cigar before examining a can of paint remover. The customer is Dolf Beeler, a factory foreman from the little town of Hornbeck. The hardware store, in neighboring Millville, belongs to Bud Bullard. Horn-

Reprinted by permission of *New York Times Book Review*, 8 May 1983, 1, 24.

beck and Millville are within walking distance of each other, but by the time the two men's quarrel is in full swing, it seems perfectly logical that a Hornbeck boy who's tangled with the law in Millville believes that the Millville police need extradition papers to arrest him.

Feuds abound, of course, in fiction; some Hatfield or McCoy is always fascinating some writer, from Shakespeare on down. What makes Thomas Berger's version so fresh is the innocent bewilderment of most of the people involved. Neither Dolf nor Bud enters the feud by intention; neither man takes pleasure in prolonging it. It somehow just happens—set off in the first place by a third party, a marvelously drawn crank named Reverton who walks around with a pistol meant for his imaginary enemies and who spends his spare time in the library researching "the extraction of gold from seawater, Asiatic techniques for training the will, magnetism, and the Pope's secret plan to introduce into the non-Catholic areas of the world an army of secret agents whose mission it was to poison the public reservoirs."

Equally well drawn is Eva Bullard, a busty 14-year-old Juliet who ruins her elopement with 17-year-old Tony Beeler when she eats his share of jelly doughnuts. Tony has been pining for Eva for months, but it takes only an evening to see she's not yet old enough to have any personality. . . .

The humor in "The Feud" is the kind that arrives in a rush; it doesn't feel set up. This is remarkable when you consider the extremeness of some of the events—Tony's smashing a lemon meringue pie in a policeman's face, Reverton's Three Stooges-style fight with a couple he's caught "corpulating" in a body shop, the endless complications caused by the fact that the two towns' police chiefs are also feuding. There's a temptation to read the best bits aloud to everyone within hearing—which would be a mistake because, like all truly funny moments, these are part of the very fiber of the story.

The novel is set during the late 1930's, a time when a six-bit haircut is a scandal and an order of Coke and potato chips costs 10 cents. Reading of the two little towns you imagine the road between them to be the gentle, winding, untrafficked road of fairy tales. Even the local bad girl seems touchingly naïve. And there are ingenious details tucked in everywhere. It's a mark of class, for instance, that a man takes just one toothpick instead of a handful from the shot glass beside a luncheonette cash register. When Harvey Yelton, Hornbeck's none too ethical chief of police, slides out of his car, he holds on to his holstered pistol so it doesn't catch on the steering wheel—an act that somehow defangs him; it makes him seem homely, intimate, almost lovable.

Perhaps because of that homeliness of tone, "The Feud" is a warmer book by far than Thomas Berger's others. The earlier comedies—"Regiment of Women," for instance, and The Reinhart Series—were so acidic that we weren't sure we wanted to laugh. And "Neighbors," perhaps his most effective novel till now, was more rigid in its design, more obviously calculated.

"The Feud" has no such faults. When Thomas Berger pokes fun at his characters here, he does it fondly, with inspired perception. When he describes an event, it seems the event is taking place almost of its own volition; it fairly tumbles out. As a result, "The Feud" is both endearing and surprising—a comic masterpiece.

It's All Greek: Berger Perfects
the Slow Burn
[Review of *Orrie's Story*]

BILL MARX

Wielding a whoopie cushion instead of a tomahawk, novelist Thomas
Berger, best known for 1964's *Little Big Man*, a scintillating send-up of the
old West, has snuck, quietly and stealthily, into the company of our country's
indispensable comic writers. Unfortunately, the novelist has crept in so slyly
that no one seems to realize he's there, getting the drop on the slapstick
foibles of Boobus Americanus. He's as sardonic a satirist as H. L. Mencken
and as inventive a pyrotechnician as S. J. Perelman.

For more than 30 years Berger has been fashioning a magnificently
madcap oeuvre whose stylistic sleights of hand, wry absurdity, linguistic
limbo games, and satirical buckshot have taken dead aim at our cankered
heart of darkness. The newly published *Orrie's Story*, Berger's 17th novel, is
his leanest and most melancholy work to date, lacking the slam-bang language and pop-eyed sadism that marks his other randy ruminations on our
national life. But in a deeper sense the book typifies the restless experimentation that has marked Berger's career, a progression of intelligent, skeptical,
and voracious comedies that should be recognized as substantial achievements
in contemporary American literature.

Maybe it's the sleek, sophisticated cut of Berger's prose that explains
the relative neglect—his pen slices through the American psyche without
leaving a drop of blood behind. When it comes to black humor, American
readers tend to like their guffaws burnt to a crisp by the heavy-handed likes
of John Irving, Kurt Vonnegut, and Joseph Heller. But from the very
beginning of his career in the late '50s, with the first volume in the Reinhart
series, *Crazy in Berlin*, Berger's cooked with a slow burn rather than a flame
thrower. Berger's elegant prose maintains a resolutely ironic distance from
his characters' gross though exhilarating obsessions with class, sex, and
violence, the triumvirate inspiration for Berger's tragicomic tales of cheap
dreams and even cheaper revenge.

Reprinted with the permission of *The Boston Phoenix*, Literary Section, October 1990, 6.

No matter how gross or seamy their desires, the author's collection of grasping clowns, private dicks, used car salesmen, and hardware store owners are decked out in snazzy verbal tuxedos. With its poetic/pathetic images of a fortyish Reinhart grappling for the American dream in the swinging '60s while eyeing nubile teenage flesh through a pair of binoculars, 1970's *Vital Parts* deserves to be put alongside *Lolita*. ("When she moved, with a subtle rearrangement of globed bottom and soft lavender shadows below, bisected by lights' wanton yellow finger, pointing between the slim thighs, when her hair shimmered, her slender shoulders rose and fell in some transitory teeny mirth, Reinhart discarded all control and exhorted the Devil to make her turn.")

A prim God gazing down upon a primal mess, Berger lends order to an America that's continually crumbling into fragmented farce; his exultantly caustic take on our native propensities for carnage and vulgarity gives his slapstick a jaundiced flair, the exhilarating pull and jerk of gallows humor. After all, this is a country where someone can get shot if he steals a parking space from an earlier claimant. Maybe Berger isn't appreciated because his world is genuinely nasty—there's plenty of yuks but not too much sentimentality. To paraphrase Groucho in *A Night at the Opera*, Berger often writes about big bullies beating up little bullies. As failed playwright and erstwhile private investigator Russel Wren puts it in 1977's *Who is Teddy Villanova?*: "in point of mundane fact, most human beings have no vocation worth the name, no deity, ideology, or discipline. They breathe, eat, defecate, sleep, and die—to name only the essential activities. As to their aims, I believe it was the Stagirite who put it succinctly: men pursue pleasure and avoid pain." The chaotic energies lurking underneath the blank surface of American life has remained a constant in Berger's work, but he has evolved two different, but complimentary, comic styles to survey our hedonistic society.

Sometimes his writing is a jaunty roller-coaster ride through American slang, trash culture, and highbrow literature, a spry junket that makes *Who is Teddy Villanova?* one of the best lampoons of the hard-boiled detective novel . . . and 1975's *Sneaky People* a masterful rag on the back-firing lusts—sexual, material, and culinary—of small town bourgeoisie. . . .

In these satires, as in the Reinhart series and 1985's *Nowhere*, Berger reveals in his verbal fantasias on American desire, whizzing off into daunting flights of linguistic fancy. Generally, these books dissect the kinky itches of schlubs stuck in a rut, terminally horny maniacs mired in mediocrity. Two of his more recent novels, 1987's *Being Invisible* and 1989's *Changing the Past*, are gently scathing fables about caspar milquetoasts who receive miraculous powers that give them a chance to escape the dry ordinariness of their lives.

If some of his best work has the insouciant vernacular panache of the zany Hollywood comedies of the '30s and '40s, other novels restrain the whizbang wordplay, replacing it with an icy wit which first appeared in

1967's *Killing Time*, a chilling peek into the mind of a killer. He exaggerates our propensity for meaningless hostility and destruction by turning it into absurdist burlesque, watching us grind each other up with blithely disdainful impartiality. Spying the flailing foibles of middle-class antiheroes through the deadpan eye of eternity, Berger takes up the breakdown of equanimity in a trio of hilarious books (1980s *Neighbors,* 1983's *The Feud,* and 1988's *The Houseguest*) about the homicidal anger that lurks beneath our pathological version of the social contract.

The Feud, a comic masterpiece set in the '30s, takes Berger's vision of village warfare—escalating acts of guerrilla vengeance triggered by some minor infraction—into apocalyptic acts of foul play. What unites us all is our heartfelt wish to smash any sense of comradery. . . . Throughout the mounting violence, Berger calmly peruses wolfish minds obsessed with thoughts of murder. It's Social Darwinism come home to roost. . . .

All three of Berger's sardonic farces spot the dementia beneath the domestic with the pitiless precision of scientific observation, the deeds of mayhem following one another with the inexorable logic of a silent film gag, the destined bull's eye of a pie sailing through the air.

In *Orrie's Story,* Berger applies the stripped-down technique of *The Feud* to literary pastiche, a genre he's taken up before in *Little Big Man's* loving swipe at Westerns and 1978's *Arthur Rex,* which makes an erratic stab at goosing up Malory. The inspiration this time around is Aeschylus' *Orestia,* the grandaddy of all internecine squabbles. . . .

Sliding from the mythic to the minimal, downgrading cosmic catastrophe into understated farce, Berger sets his terse replay of Greek tragedy into an America just traumatized by World War II. . . .

Berger doesn't go for the operatic Freudian updating of Eugene O'Neill's *Mourning Becomes Electra,* nor does he use the archetypal grandeur of the Grecian past to put an elitist kibosh on the barbarous modern world, as T. S. Eliot does in *Sweeney Among the Nightingales.* Certainly there's a sense of drastic diminishment: the chorus comprised of the good old boys and gals of the Idle Hour Bar and Grill, and Esther and Erle drowning Augie in the bath after a futile attempt to electrocute the guy with an electric fan whose cord proves too short to reach the tub. And the author's as pointed as ever about the eventlessness of small town life. . . .

Orrie's Story, with its tight-lipped, almost stingy surface, is one of the author's most frightening books, a stinging amalgamation of faint farce and diluted tragedy that dreamily flits between the two radically different visions of existence.

It's a juggling act that may help explain why Berger is so unappreciated—in his best work he discovers the dark in the daffy, muddying up the neat boundaries between serious intentions and frivolous tomfoolery. The writer has garnered his share of critical hosannas, but the title "comic novelist" seems to undercut the huzzahs. For many literary sophisticates, laughs are demeaning unless you lace some impressive-sounding ideas in with the chuckles. Berger's taken a handful of fecund notions, energized by his love/hate for American culture, and developed them into a series of superbly constructed, iconoclastic funhouses. What's more, in his best work Berger refrains from offering the glib humanist sops that are guaranteed to please those who like the bitter bane of humor sprinkled with sugar. For these readers, the cuddliness of a P. G. Wodehouse is more life-affirming than the grouchiness of an S. J. Perelman.

But as Nietzsche, German philosophy's greatest stand-up, wrote, "Man alone suffers so excruciatingly in the world that he was compelled to invent laughter." There's real anger and desperation, not just liberal discontent, underneath Berger's creamy comic surfaces. Like Ambrose Bierce and Mark Twain, who also excoriated the vulgar underside of American idealism, Berger's writing about our native rot, the suffocating sprawl of spiritual and cultural debris, the anarchic death wish, the overgrown Id, that bites at the heels of American optimism and complacency. An admirer of the early movie comedians, his satire draws on the anarchistic spirit of farceurs like the Marx Brothers, Chaplin, and Laurel and Hardy. By combining fables of yahoo malaise with roughhouse farce, the writer gives the wisecracking, slapstick tradition of American humor a deliciously nihilistic edge. Now in his mid-sixties, Berger's led a shadowy career that itself has taken on the quirky shadings of a black comedy. After at least five or six great books, what does a comic author have to do in order to be taken really seriously—throw a pie in his own face?

ESSAYS

◆

The Schlemiel as Humanist: Thomas Berger's Carlo Reinhart

Douglas A. Hughes

Despite the critical applause and popular success of his *Little Big Man* (1964), Thomas Berger remains one of our most neglected contemporary novelists. *Little Big Man* is manifestly a great novel—it has been called the greatest novel ever written about the American West[1]—but Berger's achievement as evidenced by six other novels, especially in the Reinhart trilogy, has yet to be acknowledged by those critics who have effusively praised the work of his less gifted contemporaries. For the critic Berger is difficult to categorize, and in their efforts to fit him into the various movements and literary schools, critics have often applied misleading labels to his work. Berger is simply a unique talent, and Richard Schickel did not exaggerate when he wrote that Berger possesses "one of the most genuinely radical sensibilities now writing novels in this country."[2]

In general discussions of the contemporary novel Berger, when he is mentioned at all, is invariably classified with the so-called black humorists, whom he resembles only superficially. Berger himself vigorously rejects the label black humorist and has declared unequivocally that he feels no affinity for the somber visions of Barth, Vonnegut, Pynchon and the rest. His comic imagination, though consistently ironic and sometimes sharply satiric, does not evince the characteristic horror and foreboding that are intermittently present in black comedy; nor does it disorient or threaten the reader with apocalypse as black humor usually does. "The laughter that greets black comedy," Walter Kerr has written, "is sporadic, uncertain, often ill at ease,"[3] but the laughter Berger evokes is bright, humane, and never bitter. However zany his fictional world may sometimes be, the comic vision that animates Berger's work is closer to that of Dickens and Twain than it is to the black humorists. Gerald Green has written that Berger's novels "are wild comedy, but they are not the facile, anything-goes surrealism of the black humorists. . . . They are funny in the way *Don Quixote* or Rabelais is funny—the laughter of a wise humanist, experiencing the world in all its absurdity: tolerant, pleased, saddened—and *involved*."[4]

Reprinted with the permission of St. Bonaventure University from *Cithara* 15, no. 1 (1975): 3–21.

Berger's Reinhart trilogy, begun in 1958 with *Crazy in Berlin* and followed by *Reinhart in Love* and *Vital Parts* in 1962 and 1970, focuses on how a singular individual maintains his integrity and humanity in an increasingly nihilistic, collective, and compulsively commercial world. The protagonist's quest throughout the three novels is not power or success but freedom. The world Berger depicts is filled with a tension between appearance and reality; what appears to be real often turns out to be spurious and the authentic is usually hidden. Ihab Hassan has pointed out that "Power and Fraud rule that world, distorting appearances and realities, pressing man to the limits of his sanity, and pressing on him the guilt-ridden role of victim or aggressor."[5] Like Bellow, whom he reminds one of in some ways, Berger is a highly intellectual novelist who is less concerned with the traditional development of character than in exploring in a comic mode certain ideas and situations which render life in America what has been called "the incredible reality." Thus behind the patently comic situations and ironic style of the trilogy lie a palpable intelligence and genuine seriousness.

The Reinhart trilogy is touched throughout by satire but Berger lacks the acrid temperament of the true satirist. He does not evince the intense fervor or earnestness required of the genuine satirist. He does, of course, expose affectation, hypocrisy, and other foibles, but he refrains from unrelieved ridicule based on an implicit absolute, that is, that idealism or certainty on which the satirist draws his strength. There is a pervasive sense of the absurd in the novels and the reader is encouraged to laugh openly at the foolishness of the characters. But although these characters deserve laughter, the most unsympathetic figure demonstrates some human quality which prevents the reader from wholly rejecting him. For example, Schatzi, the mendacious Soviet agent, Claude Humbold, the deadbeat realtor, and Bob Sweet, the power-hungry businessman all possess several ingratiating characteristics in spite of the fact that they are dishonest, thoughtless men. Berger's criticisms of men and institutions remind us of the intolerable stupidities with which we live, and yet the narrator communicates a feeling of compassion and tolerance for human weakness.

The Reinhart novels, though somewhat different in theme and tone, are bound together by an unforgettable central character, one Carlo Reinhart, a Candide-like witness to recent social and cultural history. The trilogy follows the misadventures of this gentle giant from his loss of innocence at age twenty-one as an American soldier in war-ravaged Berlin through his many failures as husband, father, friend, and businessman between 1946 and 1969 in southwestern Ohio. Reinhart is an intelligent, complex, morally sensitive man who remains remarkably open to experience and other people in spite of repeated setbacks and tricks of fate. Something of an American Leopold Bloom, especially in *Vital Parts* which presents his middle years, he is a disarmingly goodhearted man in an indecent world, a victim sometimes of his own virtues in the venal, corrupted society Berger depicts. What Splendor Mainwaring, his black friend, says about him suggests the root of some of his problems: " 'I don't know,' said Splendor, 'when I ever met a man before of whom I could say he. . . . is so characterized by *justice*, a term I infinitely prefer to *reason*.' "[6] Reinhart, though far from acting without reason, possesses an abundance of imagination, the ability to project himself beyond his own concerns. In a world in which people think almost solely of themselves, Reinhart is the peculiarly responsible man who truly cares about others. As he tells his Army psychiatrist. " 'But you see, someone must care' " (C, 424). Although Berger is not Jewish—he is German and Irish—Reinhart clearly belongs in the tradition of the Jewish schlemiel-hero, the wise fool whose very real shortcomings are mitigated by his essential goodness. In examining some of the important moral questions of our time Berger employs his central character, despite his obvious weaknesses, as an embodiment of those humanist values the author wishes to celebrate. And it should be emphasized here that the Reinhart trilogy, for all its ironic criticisms of man and society, is a joyous yea-saying work.

In *Crazy in Berlin* Reinhart, just twenty-one years, is forced to come to terms with moral and philosophical problems peculiar to our time and he attempts to comprehend an awesome evil, the enormity of Nazi crimes. Although he fails in this effort, he gains from his experiences in Germany a deep appreciation of the unresting realities of the world and a better understanding of his own character. Berger's first novel is an impressive examination of the implications for the individual and society as a whole of the Nazi atrocities. In this novel Berger was interested in more than just Reinhart's experiences and therefore, though Reinhart is the central character, portions of the novel swirl around major characters such as Schatzi and lieutenant Schild and ideological questions only peripherally related to the protagonist. In *Reinhart in Love* and *Vital Parts* Berger limited himself strictly to telling Reinhart's story.

Searching in the moral rubble of postwar Berlin for clues to the problems of nihilistic violence, for the reasons for Auschwitz and Dachau, Reinhart comes to understand from his own experience that injustice and bestiality are very real, that Nazism is a state of mind to which all men are vulnerable and not an aberration of Germany only. He discovers that he himself is infected with the microbe of nihilism, but this very recognition is a partial innoculation against yielding to the temptations of destruction and nothingness. His strange experiences with some of Berlin's grotesque characters sweep away his high schoolish innocence, forcing him to mature far beyond his years. Events temporarily overwhelm him and he is hospitalized in a psychiatric ward for six months of therapy. When he emerges from the hospital and into civilian life he is emotionally a middle-aged man, but he leaves for America with, surprisingly, much of his innate idealism still intact.

Berger's schlemiel-hero demonstrates remarkable resiliency and, despite the countless frustrations and failures he endures in the years after his discharge from the Army, Reinhart always resists the temptation of cynicism.

" 'You are a fool, a good fool, a kind fool,' " Lori, the German-Jewess says to Reinhart, who decidedly is a fool insofar as he feels compelled to mitigate the wrongs of his world, but this is the kind of admirable foolishness on which decent societies are based. When he returns to America from Germany he tries unsuccessfully to curb his quixotic tendencies and to act like other socially detached persons. "For a time he backslid to an earlier conviction which six months' therapy was supposed to have obliterated: namely, that his purpose on earth was to rectify life's dirty deals" (R, 18). Although he cannot reclaim the dead from the crematoria, Reinhart feels morally responsible for understanding why the Germans, his people, brutalized defenseless Jews and he persists in trying to cut through the myths surrounding the Jew to a clearer appreciation of these universal victims. Throughout the trilogy Berger again and again takes up the question of victims and oppressors or, as Reinhart puts it, "the hurters and the hurtees."

Reinhart's interest in the horrors of Nazism and the destruction of European Jews grows out of his own diffuse guilt, partially based on his pure German ancestry, and he even believes some of his kin may still be living in Berlin. "He at last understood that the complement to his long self-identification with Germanness had been a resolve never to know the German actuality. Knowledge had exhausted his options; he now had no choice but to seek out, if still they existed, his links to what, a brief half-century after Gottfried Reinhart took ship for the New World, had disintegrated in murder and betrayal" (C, 176). Reinhart's guilt is not wholly unfounded. Being a man of uncommon imagination—he frequently thinks of himself possessed of the sensibilities of a poet—he is responsive to the promptings of conscience the typical man would never feel. He thinks, "If Nazism was a German disease of the bone, his own marrow, even at two generations' remove, could hardly be spotless. How may times had he felt within himself a black rage at existence-as-it-was and the eunuchs who prospering in it made its acceptance a standard virtue?" (C, 66) Having felt the desire to smash the existing world, he realizes that Nazism is not strictly a national weakness; it is the will to destruction for its own sake and a fascination with evil. Reinhart recognizes his susceptibility to this moral disease when, in the deserted Nazi mansions on the Wannsee, he wantonly destroys the unbroken windows and delicate glassware, emblems of civilization. "Yes, that was surely Nazism, that passion to destroy simply because it could be got away with, because one had been trained all his life to respect and abide by the constraints and then found in a crisis that they held no water" (C, 67). What Reinhart senses in his immediate experience and discerns in the workings of the Nazi mind is really the malaise of modern man, nihilism, "the absolute repudiation of worth, purpose, desirability," as Nietzsche put it. However good-natured and gentle he may be, he is able to understand and even identify with the Nazi's gelid detachment from humanity and his attraction to evil. "In almost every way but the accepted idea of common decency, he felt himself at odds with the world, a kind of Nazi without swastika, without revolver and gas ovens, without specific enemies—indeed, it was a crazy feeling, and an apparently motiveless identification, for although it did not include the trappings, it did comprehend the evil. . . ." (C, 67–68). What distinguishes Reinhart from the Nazi savage, however, is the American's refusal to act against other human beings and he knows that only by effort and vigilance can the negative forces in man's spirit be controlled. The young Reinhart is an example of the confused but faithful modern humanist who senses that traditional values can no longer find philosophical justification, that there are *no* absolutes, but who remains loyal to these values in the name of decency and civilization.

Berger confronts his unworldly protagonist with two intellectual Germans, Bach and Otto Knebel, survivors of the war who argue shrewdly against Reinhart's simple humanism. The discussions in Bach's unreal cellar, which are a significant part of Reinhart's experience in the novel, are richly imagined and filled with logical and metaphysical contradictions, underscoring Berger's insistence on the deceptive character of what we call reality. Bach is an improbable anti-semite and recounts his love-hate relationship with German Jews. Bach, who risked his life to save Lori, his Jewish wife, from the Gestapo, fabricates a story in which he was a member of the S.S. Reinhart is confounded by Bach's convoluted anti-semitism and incredible arguments. The culmination of the ironic German's argument is the curious contention that the Nazis erred in attempting to annihilate the Jews because they become stronger, truly indestructible when faced with persecution. Reinhart understands the thrust of Bach's argument and forms an ironic rhetorical question: " 'You want to kill the Jews with kindness?' " (C, 156)

Otto Knebel, a Jew and blinded victim of Nazi and Communist ideology, attempts to undermine Reinhart's humanist faith by recounting the terror and suffering he has endured at the hands of absolutists. Mocking the young American, he expresses contempt for any form of altruism and his remarks are not without a certain credibility. " 'One must love himself,' said the doctor. 'The men who killed my family did not. What are totalitarians but people who have no self-love and self-respect? . . . ' " (C, 333). Reinhart cannot accept this and says, " 'But isn't selfishness the terrible crime of the modern era, selfishly being concerned with oneself and therefore thinking the other fellow is garbage?' " (C, 342). Doctor Knebel displays the inherent strength of the cynic and his remarks are a real test of Reinhart's beliefs. In another representative exchange, Knebel says:

"If you prick (a sofa), will it not bleed? But that is not necessarily true of a man, who may spit in your eye, or, having a taste for pain, beg you to prick him again, only harder. And what might he not make of it as a moral act? That by taking his life you have confirmed his conviction that you are inferior to him, and for some men life is a small price to pay for such reward. Or that by causing him to die well you have relieved him of the need to live well, for any victim is willy-nilly a success. Or that by divesting him of everything but the naked self you have made it possible for him to accept that self. In the end he may have used you as you believed you were using him, and who can say who was the victor?"

"Oh no," cried Reinhart, even though he thought it likely he had misunderstood, "you cannot build some elaborate theory that in the end Nazism did good. That sounds like the idea of those old fellows in Neuengland. . . . Rolf Valdo Emerson, *und so weiter*, who wore frock coats and walked in the woods and never cared about women, and therefore had this dry belief that evil was only the servant of a greater good." (C, 334)

The novelistic success of these intellectual discussions lies in Berger's decision to challenge Reinhart by granting several convincing arguments to Bach and Knebel and by showing the young American rethinking ideas that at first glance appear beyond doubt. The reader feels an authentic tension in these exchanges and appreciates that Berger is not sermonizing or utilizing the characters surrounding the protagonist as mere straw men.

Following his disconcerting meeting with the cynical doctor, Reinhart explains to his friend Schild his idea of man in an imperfect world, clarifying some of the points made with Bach and Knebel. Reinhart vividly expresses himself by carefully describing and interpreting the well-known etching *Ritter, Tod, und Teufel* by the German master Albrecht Dürer. In the picture a knight in armor rides his charger through " 'a gully full of junk, lizards, skulls, tree-roots, etc.; it looks something like Berlin today.' " On one side of the scene is the devil with mad eyes and a wolf-like face and on the other side sits death who " 'has a long white beard, a hole for a nose, and wears a crown of snakes, holds an hourglass.' " These ugly figures stare at the moving knight. In the background rises a castle. Reinhart suggests that the remote castle represents heaven from which the knight cannot be aided " 'because he would not be a knight unless he served his time in the gully of death and the devil.' " For Reinhart the knight symbolizes not mankind but the truly *human* being who views the often repugnant or impenetrable reality of the world with steady eyes, knowing he must endure with dignity the presence of disorder, evil and death. The ideal man knows that the conditions of life are sometimes hateful or absurd, but he knows man may transcend the given world. Because the knight is secure in his own strength and worth, he refuses to be oppressed and requires no victims. He is a free agent. As Reinhart expresses it to Schild:

"Neither are the Death and Devil relevant. The Knight rides through the gully as if he doesn't see them. Of course he does. . . . but he walks on. And

I tell you, they look pretty squalid. If you glance quickly at the picture you won't see anything but the Knight. . . . (He moves on) looking not at the airy castle, or . . . Death or the mangy Devil, because they'll all three get him soon enough, but he doesn't care. He is complete in himself—isn't that what integrity means?—and he is proud of it, because he is smiling a little." (C, 360–61)

Berger maintains a controlled, ironic style in *Crazy in Berlin*, preventing his easily bruised material from being damaged by sentimentality, and his wit and verbal mischievousness are, for the most part, kept in check. Thus the tone of his first novel is a curious combination of restraint and playfulness and the humor is subdued, coming in flashes which quickly fade into the narrative, as for example, "He brought forth one of those American fountain pens that profess to last a lifetime—Reinhart wondered if he had owned it in Auschwitz: 'Mr. Schatzi of Berlin, Germany, used this Superba Everlasting Master-writer for three years in the living death of a concentration camp. Yet when he was liberated it still wrote good as new!' " (C, 275) In contrast, the tone of *Reinhart in Love* is unmistakably comic, full of exaggeration, caricature, and extravagant imagination.

Reinhart's return to and life in America is a hilarious comedy of errors as the protagonist impotently tries to cope with the baffling values and manners of his rapidly changing society. The second novel might well have been titled *Crazy in America*. Only one year has passed in Reinhart's life between the first and second novel in the trilogy but he now thinks and acts older than his twenty-two years. Reinhart is essentially the same character we saw earlier; we just get to know him better. What has changed significantly is his environment and the kind of characters he encounters. Reinhart is faced with the problems of adjusting to civilian life, determining what he wants to become, and establishing his own family. But most important he must confront all the crude and subtle pressures connected to the American dream of success, social and economic. Rust Hills has written that Berger really re-creates "Sinclair Lewis' Midwest, bringing it up to date with our bizarre times,"[7] and thus is an important interpreter of the way we live now. In the second and third volumes of the trilogy Berger does frame for our attention and laughter a remarkable number of absurdities that are part of American life.

Reinhart is destined by character to fail in America. Perceptive but impassive, morally tough but weak before figures of authority, Reinhart lacks the audacious, slightly dishonest quality Berger suggests is often necessary for success. In many ways Reinhart is a poet before a roomful of insensitive philistines and is forced to play the fool. But the reader finds himself laughing less at Reinhart than smiling with him at the follies of other characters because Berger permits the events to be viewed from the protagonist's perspective and the reader, appreciating the intelligence and awareness of the central character, tends to overlook his sometimes inept actions. Unlike *Crazy in Berlin* the second and third novels in Reinhart's adventures are narrated entirely from his point of view, allowing much of the story's irony to emerge from the protagonist's perception. Whereas almost all the characters in the novels, including the central character himself, regard Reinhart as something of a schlemiel, the reader knows this is only apparently true. The fundamental irony of *Reinhart in Love* and *Vital Parts* turns on the reader's appreciation that most of Reinhart's failures are actually moral successes, that the schlemiel is in fact a hero.

Reinhart returns from the Army and six months in a psychiatric hospital fearful of "America, people, and life—not really but poetically, which was worse" (R, 11). He regrets having left the Army where "the petty decisions were provided for and the majors ones ignored," in other words, where one was free to contemplate the big burly questions of life without feeling one was unproductive, a social malingerer. Although initially he feels lonely and without purpose in Ohio, Reinhart cannot bring himself to act with the cynicism he believes civilian life demands. Because he embraces experience enthusiastically and without discrimination, he realizes he is supremely vulnerable to life and the powers of others. *"Reinhart was in love with everything"* (R, 112). He knows that accepting everyone and believing the best of each stranger is foolish, but this is the man with the pure *(rein)* heart. "His personal folly was that he liked almost everybody" (R, 83), which stands in contrast to the typical character in the trilogy who mistrusts just about everybody. With an innocence that must be distinguished from naiveté, Reinhart views with fascination the spectacle of human life, knowing well that all is not sweetness and light. He says, " 'Perhaps we should try loving even that dreariness and it wouldn't be so bad, or at least we can see that, in its own way, life is interesting. After all, there it is' " (R, 136).

In one of the funniest scenes in recent literature, reminding one faintly of the Golden Day episode in Ellison's *Invisible Man*, Reinhart is dragooned by his irrepressible black friend Splendor into presenting a philosophy of life in the name of Dr. Lorenz T. Goodykuntz to an audience of black whores, pimps, criminals, and derelicts. Forced to speak extemporaneously on a serious subject to a collection of misfits, Reinhart discerns that his absurd situation is analogous with life:

> He addressed a roomful of pariahs who had been bribed, threatened, or tricked into coming. The very light that shown down from above was neither his nor theirs; the building was condemned, its late proprietor in durance vile, its latest lessee in flight. The whole situation, indeed, was just like life, and at the same time that it didn't matter, it was very serious. Though not sober (R, 132).

His speech is a delightful mixture of wisdom and nonsense. " 'I'm not here to bury life but to recognize it' " (R, 133), he says. His half-serious celebration of life is lost on his audience, but Reinhart appears to enjoy the opportunity for its own sake.

"We all," Reinhart said, "are in a world we never made, to use a necessary cliché—and what cliché isn't necessary?—but long as we are in it, we might as well make the best of what may be a mistake. I don't mean we *have* to love anything or anybody—I discussed that just after the war with a fellow in Berlin, Germany: in fact, haha, he was German; and decided that necessity and love don't mix. I just mean that it might be nice if we do . . . if we love something, that is. Otherwise life is inclined to get pretty dreary, the electricity is turned off for nonpayment of the bill, the telephone never rings except when it's people who want to swindle you, drugs fall from the medicine cabinet, friends let you down, and you never satisfy your parents, nor they you. . . ."
Stony Jack looked over a dirty Band-Aid on his right cheekbone, then spat on the floor. "I was wrong afore. This here is the foolest thang I ever heard."
"But you have to admit," said Reinhart, "that if it is the foolest, then it is interesting, because it never happened before. And did you ever think of this: that *each new minute is occurring for the first time*" (R, 136).

Here Reinhart expresses the "as if" philosophy or attitude of the modern humanist; "it might be nice" if the world were a decent place to live but there is no necessity, no support for the idea. However that may be, the world is also a great, marvelous potential for the man who is able to remain responsive, unjaded. But the speech is not without its light, ironic twists:

"Ah," he shouted, "how grand it is to be a Negro! Wonderful, just wonderful, you people have more fun than anybody . . . What is the synonym for 'exciting'? *Colorful*!" (R, 135)

However interesting life may be, Reinhart's problem is what to do with his own life beyond the mere observation of events. "The only trouble at the moment was what he wanted to be" (R,5). He is understandably haunted by his experiences in Germany and begins by doing nothing but just lounging about his father's house, trying to acclimate himself to civilian life. "Civilian life had more terrors than even he, who seldom knew a sanguine anticipation, dreamed of. Add to this the distinct impression he had that in America it wasn't serious, either—because all tragedies here seemed to be specific rather than generic; mad little private hopelessnesses and you had his dilemma" (R, 19). At first he lives uncomfortably with his parents who are outrageous caricatures of the irascible, domineering mother and the self-effacing, ineffectual father. Maw greets her son just home from the war with, " 'Here comes six more shirts per week' " (R, 16). At heart an optimist, Reinhart waits like Micawber for something to come his way. "Reinhart yet always had a feeling that something would turn up, from nowhere would come money or women or adventure and even an old friend, that is, an *opportunity* . . ." (R, 20). The opportunity appears in the form of a position in real estate and Reinhart reluctantly agrees to work with Claude Humbold. That he fails is no surprise.

A caricature of the slick, fast-talking businessman, Humbold is a wonderfully vivid character brought to life by Berger's comic use of language. Humbold's rhetoric is exaggerated and cliché-ridden, and yet thoroughly convincing, and Reinhart, who for years had hated Humbold, feels a grudging respect for the effectiveness of the older man. A greedy, hypocritical charlatan, Humbold is made almost endearing by his engaging speech and mannerisms. Giving Reinhart avuncular advice, he says:

> "There's one thing I won't stand for," Humbold asseverated. "And that is a foul mouth. Clean it up, bud, or you're out of a good opportunity. No taking of the Lord's name in vain; no friendship towards the King Brothers; no suggestiveness about the fair sex. Just listen to your Dutch Uncle Dudley. Remember you wouldn't be in this world without your dear old mother. Write to her frequently, boy. Worship your God in your own way, and go to the church of your choice this Sunday. I say so even to a Jew, for in the eyes of the Big Boy upstairs we are all even as children. He's the greatest bidnissman of them all, bud, and knows a bad property when he eyes one. Don't forfeit your Big Commission" (R, 99).

The excessive "your Dutch Uncle Dudley," combining the expression Dutch Uncle and Uncle Dudley, is typical of Humbold's improbable rhetoric and the righteous tone of his remarks contrasts comically with his values and actions. When Reinhart, defending himself against the charge that he is an innocent, says that he has been through the war in Europe, Humbold replies, " 'Yes, but this is serious, bud. That's what you just can't get through your coconut. This is bidniss, not them silly games like plugging Fachists, or Commonists . . .' " (R, 151). Reinhart is introduced to the seamier side of business and the collusion of businessmen and politicians, and he discovers that those who ostensibly are successes are running on boldness and appearances. In Humbold Reinhart believes he discerns that what motivates the "bidnissman" is not power or money but love. "Money? Ah no, it wasn't money which your true businessman lusted after. Reinhart all at once knew this and became a professional in one fell insight. It was love" (R, 102).

Reinhart himself fails both at real estate and love, though his relationship with Genevieve Raven, Humbold's predatory secretary, is a qualified success: he marries her. Reinhart's ludicrous courtship and marriage is a gentle satire of the erotic relationships among young people and few readers would not recognize something of themselves in the conflicts and absurd misunderstandings of the couple. The title, *Reinhart in Love*, is really ironic because the protagonist, for all his tenderness, cannot love such a superficial woman who has almost nothing in common with him beyond sexual need. "Did Reinhart really love Genevieve? He would have put his hand into the fire for her, but did he find her *interesting?*" (R, 239) Because he is trusting and straightforward, Reinhart is no match for the empty-headed but aggressive Genevieve who dupes him into marrying her by a false pregnancy. The reader laughs at the folly of a brash, hopelessly ignorant father's girl manipulating Reinhart, an experienced man of the world who reads *Paradise Lost* and *Anna Karenina*, and one is again reminded of how in Berger's fiction irony is generated by juxtaposing the authentic and the boldly bogus. The marriage is a travesty. Reinhart is ultimately cuckolded and, in *Vital Parts*, Genevieve takes a lover twenty years younger than herself.

Berger, however, does not allow the reader to feel much sympathy for Reinhart and the author holds his character responsible for the failed marriage as well as his many other failures. Constantly stumbling over his idealism, Reinhart often cannot find the reality of his situations and acts either too late or not at all. His compassion and goodness combine with a weak will to render him strangely ineffectual at critical moments in his life. Berger clearly indicates that the weakness which repeatedly causes Reinhart pain, as in the case of his marriage, is his unjustified deference to people like Genevieve and her fascist father who assume a facade of authority. Reinhart, permeated with self-doubt, becomes powerless before any person who can say or do anything, however outlandish, with certainty or assurance. "No, Raven [Genevieve's father] derived his authority from a conviction that he was *always right*. Thus, he truly was an aristocrat, whether or not he stemmed from a good family" (R, 259). Berger dramatizes what Yeats observed in "The Second Coming": "The best lack all conviction, while the worst/Are full of passionate intensity."

Before temporarily leaving her husband, Genevieve accuses Reinhart of being a failure, blaming it on his impracticality and lack of ambition. From a conventional point of view she is correct. She tells him, " 'You do twice the required amount of college homework, but could do half and get farther if you had a direction—which you don't. Who cares if you read all the *Iliad* or whatever old book? Why don't you study accounting or something useful?' " (R, 252–53) Here Genevieve speaks for the American tradition of anti-intellectualism and pragmaticism, and Reinhart, for his part, is incapable of that success which is obtained by propelling oneself forward by pretense and dishonesty. Although he does not respond to his wife's philistine remarks, Reinhart is not without an idealistic ambition: to combine business with culture, to become an intellectual businessman, or in Reinhart's words, to become "The cultivated realtor, the practical intellectual, Carlo de' Medici" (R, 300). For those who find humanist studies valueless and the road to success marked by business alone, Reinhart is the failure his wife believes him to be, but Berger obviously does not support this and grants Reinhart the last word: "true freedom is found only by being consistent with oneself" (R, 254). Unfortunately for him he does not always act consistent with reality.

In a crazy twist of plot Reinhart is induced by circumstances and pressures to betray his ideals for a time and he accepts the sinecure of president of the phony Cosmopolitan Sewer Company established by Humbold, the mayor, and the chief of police to defraud the city. Instantly Reinhart becomes an executive and an apparent success, enjoying the fruits of having made it economically: an expensive wardrobe, luxury car, and pretentious house, but most important he wins back his dissatisfied wife. Suggesting that power and the feel of success may subvert even the most independent individual, Berger shows Reinhart beginning to assume the role of executive, imitating the speech and almost the attitude of Claude Humbold. Speaking to Splendor Mainwaring, who has been named vice president of the sewer company, Reinhart speaks in what appears to be a foreign vocabulary:

> "Mainwaring," he commanded, "put your coat back on that hanger or I'll have you shot. As I recall, you maintain your Army court-martial was unjust. Here's a chance to clean the blot from your shield. Damn the torpedoes till you see the whites of their eyes! Full speed ahead and send us more Japs!" (R, 353)

Social outsiders—Jews, blacks, American Indians—frequently influence Berger's protagonists and Splendor, an eccentric black, here goads Reinhart into returning to his true self and together they determine to build the sewer system with the funds being embezzled by Humbold and his political associates. Reinhart declares, " 'We shall build an honest, efficient sewer . . . because we have contracted to do so. We will restore the value of man's word!' " (R, 365) Reasoning that his executive power sets certain obligations which, when fulfilled, lead to honor, Reinhart is willing to forego his shallow success to regain his freedom and integrity. But though Splendor applauds the decision to build the system in the black district, he candidly tells his friend, " 'You are a man of good will but little faith, and thus more gifted in the critical area than the creative. . . . You are like the present day English, who cannot be defeated and at the same time never win' " (R, 382).

When we return to Berger's schlemiel in *Vital Parts*, twenty-two years have passed and Splendor's observation no longer appears to apply to Reinhart. As the novel opens Reinhart in 1969 has reached a dead end. Physically deteriorating and spiritually despondent, Reinhart is all but a defeated man, at least in his own mind, at age forty-four. His youthful dreams have evaporated and there is an unmistakable weariness or lack of will about him.

He is jobless and poor, having failed at several independent business ventures, and he must endure the chagrin of being supported by his estranged wife. His marriage has dried up and Genevieve is planning to leave him for a younger man. Reinhart has been reduced to a prostitute for sexual release. Blaine, his twenty-one-year-old son, is an intolerant hippie-type who loathes his father and espouses ideas anathema to Reinhart, and his sixteen-year-old daughter is a loving but discouragingly inadequate child. Acutely aware of time, age, and death he struggles unsuccessfully with a chronic case of future shock.

Twenty-two years of frustration and failure have eroded Reinhart's cheerfulness and reserve of optimism and his view of life and others is now touched by disillusionment and some resentment. He is fundamentally the same man we met in Berlin, but he has seen his desire for freedom and independence frustrated and his sense of justice and decency go unrewarded, even unacknowledged; he has watched the world pass him by, scoundrels and incompetents assuming positions of power and prestige while he stood dismayed and empty-handed. Reinhart, who is no saint, cries out in exasperation at his situation. To his family and friends, who regard him as the personification of inadequacy, and the unjust world at large, he exclaims, " 'Long reflection on this state of affairs has led me to an inescapable conclusion: *You can all go (expletive) yourself.*' " And then in typical Reinhart fashion, he thinks, "Or should it have been '-selves'?" (V, 79). This voluntary outsider for the first time envies the successful and covets their success. *Vital Parts* is really an ironic re-education of Reinhart to the tragic implications of life as Berger permits his character to participate in the contemporary cultural scene, thereby fully experiencing what he has envied from his perspective of schlemiel. He must relearn what he already vaguely knew: life is decidedly unjust and the world does not invariably reward virtue; complete freedom is a dream and distasteful compromise a necessity; contemporary life is a conundrum, often overwhelming to the individual, which may be rendered tolerable by love and compassion. Reinhart again recognizes that "as we lose faith in our traditional individualism we seek, at every level of life, compensatory fantasies of power, of escape, of impractical idealism."[8]

Berger's strategy in *Vital Parts* is to confront Reinhart with many of the attitudes and manners that characterized our life-style in the frenetic 1960s, affording the author many opportunities to ridicule the the inanities we so complacently accepted. *Vital Parts* is clearly the most satiric of the three Reinhart novels, prefiguring Berger's recent novel, *Regiment of Women* (1973). Berger obviously deplores much of what he observers in contemporary society, beginning with the debasement of language. Although one may doubt whether his barbed comments are designed to change attitudes much less behavior, there is no denying that Berger demonstrates a remarkable understanding of social phenomena and the ability amusingly to weave his observations into fictional form. Partly because the pace of the novel is so swift, the reader never feels Berger's satirical jabs are distracting. As Brom Weber has observed, "The laughter threading *Vital Parts* brightens rather than obscures the depth of thought and emotion evoked by Thomas Berger's fiction."[9] This chapter in Reinhart's life is surely one of the most accomplished comic novels by an American in the last decade, a novel which demonstrates that comedy need not be either philosophically adolescent or perversely black.

In Berger's upside-down world Bob Sweet plays Mephisto to Reinhart's Faust. A caricature of the self-made man, Sweet was the ninety pound high school weakling with acne who, refusing to build himself up by heeding either Charles Atlas or Socrates, simply disguised his weaknesses and exploited his narrow strengths to become an aggressive, free-wheeling commercial wizard, what Reinhart calls "a Claude Humbold with class." But beneath his bland synthetic exterior—he wears false teeth, thick glasses, a toupee, a girdle and is kept alive by a German-speaking scientist who resembles Schatzi—Sweet is a prodigious fraud, an archetypal con man. Berger again presents us with an utterly worthless but audacious charlatan who gains respect and prominence—Reinhart watches him chit-chat with a Johnny Carson–like television host—by mastering the rhetoric of sincerity, projecting a dynamic image, and acting ruthlessly in his own interest. Unlike Humbold, Sweet is a dangerous and demonic character who, when Reinhart meets him, is promoting a scheme to cheat death by freezing human beings for future resuscitation. He is a consummate egotist who would sacrifice mankind to himself, whose philosophy succinctly stated is: " '*I would get mine.* I am what I am, and expect others to be the same' " (V, 25). Before his antipode Reinhart the humanist, who is still awed by authority, or more accurately the appearance of it, bows down, at least for a time, metaphorically selling his soul and literally his body to Sweet in exchange for two weeks of hoped for escape from his vapid existence.

Reinhart's short-lived decision to surrender his life by having it deep frozen is an instance of temporary despair, growing out of his overall confusion in *Vital Parts*. This compassionate, responsible individual stands like an anachronism in the spiritual wasteland of the novel, ignored, patronized, or denigrated by the other characters. Reinhart cannot understand what has happened to his familiar world, but gradually he comes to realize that the boldness and ruthlessness of individuals like Sweet, Raven, and others who always act as though they were absolutely right and without regard for others have been adopted on a grand scale by aggressive social groups. Although they disrupt or even rend society, these groups achieve their goals because, Berger suggests, society itself displays a passivity similar to Reinhart's. Speaking of the leader of the Black Assassins, a militant black group, Reinhart says:

"My son told me Storm was invited to address the local bar association and began addressing them as 'Scum' and said he looked forward to shooting them all and raping their wives, daughters, and mothers. He received a standing ovation. . . . There is talk he may be hired to head up the black studies department at the University" (V, 196).

Thus, from Reinhart's point of view traditional values, reason, sanity itself have been abandoned; things are falling apart and anarchy appears ascendant.

Public order would soon be a thing of the past. . . . The old beat cop was now in a car, unavailable unless you broke a traffic law. The Supreme Court freed convicted murderers on technicalities. Peace-parade marchers carried the enemy flag. Heroin users were on the relief rolls. The President pleased everybody when he said he would quit at the end of the term. The war was apparently lost but would not end (V, 311–12).

Reinhart becomes convinced that America has chosen to play everything as theater, especially street theater, and that "To get attention today you have to be outlandish" (V, 270). He tells Maw, who sympathizes with Blaine and his generation:

"I can understand what makes Communists in Latin America and Asia and Black assassins here—and it's not poverty, incidentally, but pride. . . . Who doesn't get enraged at the way things are? I always loved the Marx Brothers for that reason. But to live life like the cast of *Horse Feathers*, to accomplish nothing but to harass everybody who has—" (V, 219)

Berger laughingly deflates the simplistic ideas and bombastic rhetoric of youth that so characterized the last decade, but the only person who agrees with Reinhart in the novel is Splendor, who is dying of cancer and who will ultimately take Reinhart's place as the first man to be frozen by Sweet's foundation. " 'Carlo,' Splendor said, 'we live in a remarkable time. The phony is constantly turning into the real, and vice versa' " (V, 206). Referring to his son's association with black militants, he says, " 'He is American to the core: to *say* is to *be*. You and I make a distinction between rhetoric and reality' " (V, 370).

In the end Reinhart sidles cautiously back toward life, refusing to go through with the freezing plan. His adventures in the counter-culture with Eunice, Sweet's young secretary, have revealed how spurious are the manners and postures of the now generation. Furthermore, he has discovered that Sweet, whom he viewed as invulnerable, is a total fraud, and he uncharacteristically humbles him with a few blows to the midsection. Blaine and Genevieve are lost to him, but he says philosophically, " 'Life would not have been the same without them, but can be lived in their absence' " (V, 429). Reinhart is still engaged with the spectacle of life. Although he earlier told Eunice that "human beings are vile," late in the novel he thinks:

The only trouble was that, for good or ill, people were all that interested Reinhart. Vile they might well be, but it happens that vileness is fascinating—to a degree, of course. For example, he said to himself now, you will never find a transvestite bear (V, 429).

Berger's schlemiel appears to have extracted from his experiences a new sense of the world's reality: " 'The world is made up not of winners and losers, but of followers and leaders. The divine right of kings is a much more natural principle than that all men are equal' " (V, 429).

In the end Reinhart appears philosophically to accept the world for what it is, resigning himself to his role as schlemiel. He has come to understand that, as Ortega y Gasset wrote, to the thoughtful, honest man "Life is, in itself and forever, shipwreck." But to be shipwrecked is not necessarily to go under. One may survive, though lost and insecure in the currents of life. Berger's protagonist has spent much of his life bobbing on an uncertain, troubled sea far from a secure harbor, but the reader who has followed the comic adventures of this good man from Berlin through suburbia to the present knows he has learned to swim, that he will always remain a free, authentic individual. Carlo Reinhart and the imperfect humanism he has metaphorically come to represent are really indestructible.

Notes

1. R. V. Cassill in the *New York Times Book Review* (March 29, 1970), p. 4.

2. *Commentary* (July 1970), p. 80.

3. *Tragedy and Comedy* (New York: Simon and Schuster, 1967), p. 320.

4. "Back to Bigger" in *Proletarian Writers of the Thirties*, ed, David Madden (Carbondale and Edwardsville: Southern Illinois University Press, 1968), p. 43.

5. "Conscience and Incongruity: The Fiction of Thomas Berger," *Critique: Studies in Modern Fiction*, V (Fall 1962), p. 14.

6. *Reinhart in Love* (New York: Richard W. Baron, 1970), p. 36. Berger's first two novels were originally published by Scribner's and were reissued in 1970 by Baron which published *Vital Parts* the same year. All references in this paper will be to the Baron editions. The novel being cited will be indicated by the first letter of the title. The Reinhart trilogy is published in paperback by New American Library.

7. *How We Live: Contemporary Life in Contemporary Fiction*, ed. Penny Chapin Hills and L. Rust Hills (New York: Macmillan, 1968). p. 552.

8. Schickel, p. 80.

9. *Saturday Review* (March 21, 1970). p. 42.

Finding the Center of the Earth:
Satire, History, and Myth in *Little Big Man*

Michael Cleary

It is a Western to end all Westerns, with all the Western's clichés neatly reversed into something quite new.[1]

It is, of course, a satire on Westerns, told with high humor.[2]

Berger has in some manner put together a variety of techniques and infused them with a spirit so that . . . it is a functional and successful piece of literature. It is one of the best of American Western novels.[3]

If Buster Keaton had been a novelist, he might have written *Little Big Man*.[4]

This sampling of reactions to Thomas Berger's *Little Big Man* indicates the variety of opinions regarding the nature and success of the novel. The one area of agreement is that it has a satiric core; beyond that, criticism splinters off into theories which espouse romantic, mythic, tragic, parodic, historic, and absurdist interpretations. Such a range of responses implies a literary depth which is verified by close examination. While admitting the plausibility of the various interpretations, I will focus upon the satiric dimensions of the novel, examining Berger's parody of Western conventions, and then discussing its non-Western satire. It is this latter area which carried *Little Big Man* beyond the level of mere parody. On one level it is a condemnation of the weaknesses of human nature; on another level, it is a serious indictment of American institutions, culture, values, and even history itself.

One of the subjects of debate for readers of *Little Big Man* is the novel's interweaving of myth and history. These two elements are apparent in the titles of two essays which discuss the novel in detail: Leo E. Oliva's "Thomas Berger's *Little Big Man* as History" and Delbert E. Wylder's "Thomas Berger's *Little Big Man* as Literature." These essays and others draw attention to two facts: first, that the novel is historically accurate, Berger having researched sixty or seventy western historical accounts before starting his

Reprinted by permission of *Western American Literature* 15 (1980): 195–211.

book;[5] second, that the coincidences and exaggerations of the picaresque structure distract from the historical reality presented. Brian W. Dippie describes Berger's unique coordination of the opposing elements of western fiction:

> In *Little Big Man*, Berger is faithful to both the West of history and the West of myth. Each contributes in its own way to the aura of plausibility that so enriches the basic tale. . . . The surface accuracy, the correctness of detail, the verisimilitude that he conveys derive from a book-learned, factual knowledge. But *Little Big Man* rests upon a foundation of myth.[6]

The opposing values of history and myth are bound together by Berger's humorous narrative, which has fun with our historical and mythical expectations without denying the validity of either. As Jack Crabb, the one hundred and eleven year-old narrator explains, "I'm telling the truth here, and the truth is always made up of little particulars which sound ridiculous when repeated."[7] Crabb's narrative follows the picaresque format which is the key to understanding its satiric content. As L. L. Lee has noted, "the picaresque, with its wide range of action and of society, is another way of making a microcosm."[8] Berger has chosen his narrative structure well, for it is sufficiently broad and stylized to accommodate both Western and non-Western themes. Crabb's alternating experiences with white and Indian cultures allow him the perspective to satirize both, and in so doing, to satirize all of mankind. *Little Big Man* thus does more than lampoon the Western formula and myth: it finds fault with mankind itself.

Berger makes good use of the picaresque mode of episodic scenes and a succession of minor characters. Jack Crabb is an excellent model of the picaresque hero defined by Matthew Hodgart: the perennial outsider who "can find no regular occupation or fixed place in a stratified society. He is forced to . . . keep moving both horizontally in the novel and vertically in society."[9] It is hard to imagine a picaro who better satisfies Hodgart's definition. In the twenty-six years covered by the novel, Crabb is buffeted between the Indian and white societies. In the course of the narrative, Crabb assumes a number of familiar Western roles—adopted Indian, muleskinner, prospector, gunfighter, army scout, con man, entrepreneur, buffalo hunter, gambler, and even town drunk. He finds no permanent role in either world. His adventures share the varied nature of the picaresque, and the constant juxtaposition of the customs and values of both societies helps to achieve the tension which is necessary to satire.

Jack Crabb is no romantic Western hero along the lines of the prototype described by Kent Ladd Steckmesser—genteel, possessed of great physical courage, and worthy of epic consideration through comparison to classical heroes.[10] Crabb is only 5'4" and slight; he confesses that "I ain't big, but I'm shrewd" (p. 64). He is well aware of his physical limitations, creating an imposing figure through his choice of apparel: he wears two inch built-up boots and a Mexican sombrero which adds another six inches; he says that in outline he is six feet tall, but most of that is air (pp. 167–68).

Crabb makes up for his meager build by cultivating his cunning beyond the modest level of Western characters such as the Virginian; Crabb's cunning is far more sly and frequently immoral. In the course of his adventures he lies, steals, bluffs, and begs, as these means suit his needs of the moment. At one point he even out-cons a con man, and develops a ring trick to help him cheat consistently at cards. These devious methods occur while in the white society, but such devices are employed against his Indian companions as well. One incident shows the attempts of Cheyenne boys to outdo one another in bravery by piercing their skin with pointed sticks and tearing off the flesh. Jack admits that he never could get very interested in hurting himself, so he devises an illusory feat of even greater stoic proportions. Breaking an arrow in half, he holds the feathered end against his stomach and clenches the protruding arrowhead end between his buttocks. Apparently skewered, he cleverly gains a reputation for bravery and suffering without undergoing the uncomfortable consequences (p. 65).

The preceding scene prompts Crabb's remark that "Indians did not go around expecting to be swindled, whereas they was always ready for a miracle" (p. 66). This observation suggests one of the remarkable traits of Berger's uncommon Western hero—a garrulous nature which delights in offering humorous insights on any variety of subjects. This loquaciousness is at odds with the Western convention noted by John G. Cawelti: the taciturn hero who lets his actions speak for him.[11] Besides spoofing the stereotype, Berger uses Crabb's verbal wit to produce some wonderful aphorisms. The narrative voice of *Little Big Man* is a source of much of the book's humor and has reminded at least one critic of Twain's style, particularly in *Huckleberry Finn*.[12] The comparison is not farfetched; both writers share a delightful comic diction based upon wry understatement. Because even a casual perusal of the novel will exhibit its verbal wit, only a few samples will be given here, constituting what Delbert E. Wylder has described as epigrammatic satire.[13]

[On sincere curiosity in others:] It is a rare person in the white world who wants to hear what the other fellow says, all the more so when the other fellow really knows what he is talking about. (p. 117)

[On morality:] If you want to really relax sometime, just fall to rock bottom and you'll be a happy man. Most all troubles come from having standards. (p. 161)

[On self-preservation:] I might go on for hours relating the incidents of war, but whereas they are every one different in the actual occurrence and never dull when your own life is at stake, they have a sameness in the telling. (p. 101)

The cynical humor of such aphorisms tells us much about the character of Jack Crabb, the sole survivor of the Battle of Little Bighorn. The last example of self-preservation points out a very important characteristic of this atypical Western hero: his main interest is in survival, not advocating a moral position. For Crabb, as Kerry Ahearn has observed, life is not a matter of moral choices, but expediency.[14] Martin Nussbaum points out that the Western hero has long been the arbiter of moral law, even if it opposes judicial law.[15] Jack Crabb suffers no such burden. Granville Hicks has noted that Crabb is really just a fairly ordinary fellow who is placed in extraordinary circumstances and is bright enough and brave enough and lucky enough to survive them.[16] The key word here is "survive," for that is always foremost in Crabb's mind, more important than weighty moral considerations such as those pondered by Shane and other formula heroes. This characteristic is evidenced when, after years of living with and growing to like the Cheyenne, Crabb immediately throws down his weapon during a cavalry charge and turns himself over to the Indians' enemy. And on the eve of Custer's Last Stand, Crabb does give thought to his rightful allegiance, but even such commendable contemplation soon gives way to his concern for his own self-interest: "Well, I have spoke about my worries for the Indians and then my disinclination to see these soldiers massacred, but I have so far not mentioned my growing concern for my own arse" (p. 387).

In addition to his generous parody of the formula hero in the fictitious Crabb, Berger lampoons a number of historical figures as well. The debunking in *Little Big Man* is aimed at two separate targets: Western figures and literary figures. Berger's treatment is not totally farcical, however, and often his version of historical figures suggests the realm of probability; his creations of Western legends seem every bit as believable as the popular ones. A case in point is Berger's characterization of Wyatt Earp. Following a day of buffalo hunting, Crabb and his companions share the company of other hunters. One of the strangers is Earp, who suddenly confronts Crabb, demanding to know why Jack spoke Earp's name. Jack explains that he hadn't even known Earp's name, all he had done was belch. Kit Carson is bandylegged and foulmouthed, capable of unprovoked violence. Calamity Jane is even more foulmouthed, as well as being "the ugliest woman in the world. . . . She had a face like a potato and was built sort of dumpy." Crabb's first glimpse of Calamity Jane is during her resounding victory in a fistfight with Crabb's sister, Caroline (p. 161).

Wild Bill Hickock is an important minor character in the novel. A wary friend of Crabb's, Hickock is reputed to have killed all six members of the McCanles gang in a glorious showdown. Upon hearing this, Crabb reflects on the probability of such an event, and his thoughts tell us much about the mythification of the gunfight in popular fiction and films:

> I immediately reduced that by half in my mind, for I had been on the frontier from the age of ten on and knew a thing or two as to how fights are conducted. When you run into a story of more than three against one and one winning, then you have heard a lie. I found out later I was right in this case: Wild Bill killed only McCanles and two of his partners, and all from ambush. (p. 293)

Hickock is a fanatic on the operation of guns; his conversations revolve around holster types, cartridge loads, barrel length, and other technical matters. Crabb tells us that "Hickock was a marvelous observer of anything which pertained to killing" (p. 298). In direct opposition to Western mythology, Hickock deteriorates into an overweight, jowly owner of a sleazy Wild West Show.

General George Armstrong Custer is an even more important minor character. He is shown to be a foolish tactician whose arrogance demoralizes his troops (they call him Hard Ass). Custer directs the massacre of peaceful Indians and over eight hundred horses. In Crabb's version of the Last Stand, Custer is spared the expected scalping and Crabb assumes that this is in deference to his valor, but he is told that it is only because "the long haired darling" was going bald (p. 372).

The second type of debunking in *Little Big Man* is directed at literary figures; in many ways, this suggests the technique found in reactionary Western satires such as H. Allen Smith's *Return of the Virginian* and John Seelye's *The Kid*, where contemporary writers take pot-shots at preceding Western writers as well as their peers. In addition to the humorous dimension it allows, this device develops another dimension of character. For instance, Custer's comments on James Fenimore Cooper accurately describe the romantic fantasy of the noble savage which *Little Big Man* spoofs. At the same time, it reveals Custer's mental instability—his remarks are addressed to no one and come while he and his men are being overrun at the Little Bighorn.

Characterization is also revealed in Crabb's opinions of literary figures, disclosing both his sense of propriety and naïveté about literature. He describes learning about his sister Caroline's crush on a male nurse during the Civil War, a genuinely cultivated man who writes poetry of burning passion in his spare time. Unfortunately, Caroline learns that the man's passion is for a drummer boy. Crabb's gentlemanly refusal to name this writer of "robustious verse" only draws attention to Walt Whitman and his sexual preferences.[17] While journeying up the Missouri River on a steamship piloted by a Captain Marsh, Crabb recalls that "there used to be quite a body of legend about riverboating . . . and Marsh was part of it, not having been hurt any by being a friend of an author named Mark Twain who wasn't noted for understatement" (p. 359). In another scene, Jack displays his innate courtesy and desire to please Mrs. Pendrake when she reads some of Alexander Pope's poetry. Young Crabb pretends to be impressed by the verse, but inwardly feels that it sounds like the trotting of a horse. He does not really understand the lines, but what he "did savvy seemed right opinionated, like that fellow had the last word on everything" (p. 133).

This kind of spoofing is directed only to stereotypes of the white world; however, through techniques of exaggeration and reversal, *Little Big Man* mocks Indian stereotypes, too. His all too vivid descriptions of such Indian practices as scalping and mutilation may, in fact, be realistic and not exaggerated, but his objective reporting of the thwacking sounds and oozing gore which accompany these acts results in a sense of absurdity which at least appears to be exaggerated. One example of Indian humor is when Younger Bear, a lifelong rival of Crabb's, offers Jack his hand at the end of a battle. Unfortunately, the gesture is literal, for Younger Bear has pulled his own arm up his sleeve and when he walks away laughing, Jack is left holding the severed hand of a soldier. In another scene, the convention of the uncanny Indian trackers is concealed by an apparently realistic treatment which gradually moves from the believable to the exceptional to the improbable to finally, the ludicrous. The scene Crabb describes is a familiar one—an Indian brave squinting across the plains:

> One time when . . . us boys was out hunting prairie chickens, we saw some moving objects a couple of miles off that I took for buffalo, but Little Horse, with his Indian eyes, said no, they was white men, that one had yellow hair, was armed with a shotgun and rode a bay that was slightly lame in the left forefoot, and the other wore a beard and was mounted on a roan with a saddle sore. Also, they was lost, but he could see that the bay had got the scent of water and shortly they would strike the river and know where they was. (p. 78)

The second technique for parodying Indian stereotypes is reversal, a device that Berger uses to good effect. Readers long accustomed to the inscrutability and quiet menace of the Indian brave are surprised by the initial description of Old Lodge Skins, the Cheyenne chief:

> The fellow in the plug hat was their leader. He wore one of those silver medals that the government give out to principal men at treaty signings; I think his showed the image of President Fillmore. He was older than the others and he carried an ancient musket with a barrel four foot long. (p. 31)

Berger's parody of Indian stereotypes extends beyond the treatment of character traits to include the Indian environment as well. In most cases, the Indian camp suggests a proximity to nature which is lacking in the civilized white world, a view which traces back as far as the *Leatherstocking Tales*. Indians do not intrude upon their environment with permanent dwellings, but live in harmony with it. There has always been something pastoral about the Indian camp in Westerns. Berger discounts our preconceptions, however, through Crabb's revulsion upon seeing his first Indian camp:

> At the first sight of an Indian camp the stoutest heart is likely to quail. . . .
> You tend to think: well, I see their dump, but where's the town? And the smell alone is very queer, it isn't precisely a stench as white people know one, but a number of stinks melding together into a sort of invisible fog that replaces the air, so that with every breath you draw in all the facts of life concerning mankind and the four-footed animals. Right now it had a principal odor, owing to our pony stalling under us at that very moment. Except in the case of such a particular event nearby, no smells predominated. (p. 50)

Moments later, Crabb discovers that he has not yet suffered the worst. The inside of a teepee is even more unbearable, "like trying to breathe underwater in a swamp" (p. 52).

It is apparent that one of the purposes of *Little Big Man* is to spoof Western conventions which have grown up around both white and Indian societies. However, Berger's novel transcends Western parody alone, encompassing universal human traits. In commenting upon this aspect of the novel, William T. Pilkington says that "while it often depends for its effect on the absurd and the grotesque, it sheds revealing light . . . on the human condition as well."[18] The method that Berger uses to satirize mankind's limitations is to locate the same weakness in both white and Indian societies, thus testifying to its human, not cultural origin.

Perhaps the overriding human weakness attacked in *Little Big Man* is the propensity for violence in both societies. The Indians happily mutilate the bodies of their victims; the whites conduct a dispassionate extermination of an entire race. For the Indians, fighting is an integral part of life; for the whites, it is an expedient solution. This basic difference in the two cultures is complicated by the fact that neither side has any conception of the enemy's motives, nor do they really care to learn. This results in an absurd cycle of violence which is never directed at the guilty party. Crabb explains that the circle of violence commences when some well-meaning but confused Indians come into a fort to apologize for the murderous actions of other Indians. The soldiers proceed to punish those who apologized, never the ones who committed the outrage. The Indians retaliate by revenging themselves on white people who have no connection with the soldiers; and so on. Because neither side is really interested in stopping the cycle, *Little Big Man* is, as Ahearn put it, a testimony to the essential unity in violence of all men.[19] This unity is brutally evident in the parallel massacres at the close of the novel. At the Washita, Custer's troops annihilate an unsuspecting tribe; the situation is then reversed at Little Bighorn.

Man's propensity for violence discloses another universal flaw, one which sometimes accounts for violent acts—both Indians and whites display the commonly tragic flaw of pride. In battle, the Indians' pride is evidenced by the practice of taking scalps and counting coup; one counts coup by engaging with the enemy, but only touching him with a harmless object instead of killing him. This takes great courage and gains considerable glory for the successful brave. Custer shows a different kind of pride in the white man's approach to the violence of war. Custer's mad monologue on the Little Bighorn is in part due to his incredulity that others, especially Indians, could be capable of courage in the high degree. Even as he is being destroyed, Custer praises his ability to compute disparate information coolly and effectively. The dramatic irony of the scene is emphasized by the knowledge that Berger has taken the obnoxious remarks straight from Custer's self-serving autobiography, *My Life on the Plains*.[20] The General's arrogance is both comic and pathetic.

It is Berger's insight into two universal themes which distinguishes this comic novel from novels of pure parody: man's sense of history and the dilemma of modern man in a "civilized" world. In describing the debunking of Western heroes (Wild Bill Hickock, Calamity Jane, etc.) and literary figures (Mark Twain, Alexander Pope, etc.), we saw that in *Little Big Man* the "legends and the romanticized history of the West are comically disassembled like Hamlets seen from backstage."[21] As Crabb is fond of observing, we have been lied to so often and so well that the facts appear strange and sound ridiculous when we hear them. Besides his assault on our clay-footed heroes, Berger also satirizes the interpretations of historians who have peddled their erroneous theories as fact. Charles B. Harris states that *Little Big Man* thus debunks man's methods of recording and ordering his past. And although Crabb's version of history is not necessarily the correct one, it casts doubt upon the official version.[22] Berger's spoofing of history is mainly directed at white history, but there is evidence that the Indians' approach is every bit as faulty. Cheyenne history is inseparable from its myths, tales, and legends; it is always interpreted in such a way as to make the Cheyenne the handsomest, bravest, and best people on the earth. An example of this subjective history is found in the scene when Crabb, an adopted Indian brave, throws down his weapons and turns himself over to the cavalry. When he returns to the tribe years later, he finds that his actions have become mythologized to the degree that he is now a greater hero than ever.

The white man's history is equally inaccurate. One example of its questionable veracity is found in the historians' insistence on finding ulterior racist motives and a grand scheme in the actions of the buffalo hunters. Crabb, who had been such a hunter, envisions the task as just a job, not some Machiavellian scheme to abolish an entire way of life. Crabb's account is less imaginative than the historians' hindsight, but it rings true. His explanation suggests the simple motives of the daily worker, not those of a mad genius bent on genocide.

The most prominent example of Berger's satire of historical truth is the continuing absorption with solving the mystery of the events at the Little Bighorn, an interest which historians share with novelists, film makers, and television producers.[23] This sustained attention to the Custer legend makes Crabb's simple interpretation somewhat anticlimactic, but nevertheless more plausible than heroic versions: the Seventh Cavalry was destroyed by poor reconnaissance, lack of modern communication methods, and difficult terrain. Custer's madness at the end, his inability to comprehend being outnumbered more than a hundred to one, is only an interesting sidelight to the event which has no bearing on the outcome.

Berger's multi-level attack on claims of absolute historical truth is given another turn of the screw by his initial persona, Ralph Fielding Snell (the middle name is an obvious giveaway of Berger's satiric intent). A self-proclaimed "man of letters," Snell appears in the foreword and epilogue to introduce Crabb and this "major document of the American frontier" (p. 12). In the epilogue, Snell points out historical inaccuracies in Crabb's account which he has checked against available references. He prides himself on being able to personally dispute Crabb's claim that Crazy Horse did not wear a war bonnet. In the tradition that has given us many titleholders to the Brooklyn Bridge, Snell betrays his gullibility and unreliability: "As to Crazy Horse's not wearing feathers, we know that statement to be erroneous—his war bonnet . . . presently reposes in my own collection: the dealer who sold it to me is a man of the highest integrity" (p. 447).

By using Fielding and Crabb as a persona within a persona, Berger adds a new dimension to *Little Big Man*. As narrator of the "frame," Snell is removed in time and space from the nineteenth-century events described by Crabb. Stanley Kauffman contends that the foreword and epilogue only distort Crabb's tale into an unbelievable fantasy.[24] However, when viewed as a satirical representation of twentieth-century America, and even the human condition, the frame device proves to be an effective technique.

L. L. Lee has perceptively suggested that Snell and his father may be caricatures, but they are living symbols of America's changes between the Sunday afternoon of 1876 (Custer's Last Stand) and 1963 (when Snell presents the final manuscript). Although never actually appearing in the story, Snell's father is depicted by his son as a rich, powerful, insensitive figure—an entrepreneur strongly suggestive of the robber barons of the nineteenth and early twentieth centuries. Bold and determined, these men carried the single-mindedness and ambition of a Custer into the battlefields of the corporate world. The next generation finds everything a bit easier, producing offspring such as the younger Snell—an affected intellectual, "a bit of a coward, a fool, an obvious decline from the older type of American."[25] Trundled about like a child by his medical nurse, the morose victim of his loquacious housekeeper, Snell feels compelled to defend his bachelorhood and heterosex-uality to the reader, even giving assurances that he does not own a dressing gown (p. 12). Beset by a deviated septum, weak lungs, migraines, and nightmares, incapacitated for ten years by the death of his father and the discovery of a bastard half-brother, Ralph Fielding Snell is a model for the collective neuroses of the twentieth century. In spite of his obvious failings, the dilettante Snell thinks of himself in grander terms. The foreword is filled with his smug recollections of petty victories over the bureaucrats of Crabb's nursing home.

Although Berger illustrates again and again that the Cheyenne and the whites are bound by identical flaws, he does not assess equal guilt to both cultures, an assertion made by Ahearn who maintains that *Little Big Man* exposes the absurdity of both societies. There are, after all, degrees of guilt, and Berger's novel is not simply a nihilistic condemnation of all human potential. In a number of ways, the white society is shown to lack the moral base which supports Indian society. Through ironic contrast, Berger satirizes the "superior" moral standards of white civilization without obscuring the failing of Indian society. An examination of the moral integrity of both cultures will reveal Berger's predilection.

One of the traits which runs through the white society, and not the Indian one, is hypocrisy. The white man's hypocrisy in dealing with his own kind as well as the Indians is shown when Crabb describes the fate of the Hang About the Forts, the Indians tamed into submission by treaty promises. The Indians lie about the fort in a drunken stupor induced by a ready supply of alcohol. They prostitute their women to pay for whisky, and subsist on government handouts which are half the legal allotment. The other half is withheld by Indian agents who sell it to white settlers or the Army. The Army has need of the Indians' share because its supplies are often embezzled by the Eastern dealers or the officers at the fort. Berger finally ends the cycle of greed and hypocrisy, but not before the reader is aware of the shameful results of the white man's promises to the Indian and to his own people. The Indians fall more easily to the white man's legal trickery and decadence than they do to his bullets. It should be noted that it is in the white culture that Jack Crabb is bankrupted by cheating business partners, rewarded for his gambling dishonesty, and driven to alcoholism.

In describing Berger's satire, Guy Davenport has observed that the "satire, like that of Aristophanes, Rabelais, and Chaucer, needs a hard moral base from which to flail all that wobbles and stinks."[26] It is ironic that one of Berger's prime targets of satire is the white man's arbiter of morality—the preacher. The first religious target encountered in *Little Big Man* is Crabb's father, an illiterate preacher. His religious beliefs are unorthodox: indulging in "a shot or three" of whiskey while conducting services in a saloon, the senior Crabb tolerates gambling and womanizing. In fact, the only evil he recognizes is that which "makes a man into a mean skunk who will cuss and spit and chew and never wash his face" (pp. 25–26). As long as a man was clean, he could indulge in any pursuit he desired. Killed after foolishly giving whiskey to the Indians, Crabb's father dies believing that he could have converted his murderers if he had been able to speak their language—Hebrew.

At the other end of the religious spectrum is the Reverend Pendrake, a staunch clergyman whose doctrine is as stringent as Mr. Crabb's is lenient. Engulfed in religious dogma, the obese Pendrake is comfortable only when devouring enormous quantities of food. Unlike the tolerant Crabb, Reverend Pendrake is very precise in labeling sinful enterprises which consist of all works of the flesh and sundry others: "adultery, fornication, uncleanness, lasciviousness, idolatry, witchcraft, hatred, variance, emulations, wrath, strife, seditions, heresies, envyings, murders, drunkenness, revelings, and such like" (p. 140). So intent is Pendrake on avoiding sexual sins that he abstains from relations with his wife, resulting in her adulterous affair. Of course, Pendrake's colossal gluttony removes any semblance of righteousness from his dictates.

In direct opposition to Pendrake's prohibitive, joyless religion, is the Indian's acceptance of all things human. There are only two crimes in the Cheyenne culture, and Crabb tells us that they are very seldom committed: adultery and the killing of one's kinsman. This contrast between the Indians' humanity and the white society's stultifying religion is pointed out when Pendrake enumerates the many sins which comprise his faith. Jack remarks that except for envy, the list of faults perfectly describes the character of a successful Indian.

Despite their lack of a structured religion or a legal code such as that of the whites, the Cheyenne gain our admiration in ways that the corrupt white society fails to accomplish. The reason for Berger's preference for Cheyenne values lies in the two overriding principles which rule Indian life—individualism and dignity. L. L. Lee has noted that the major positive theme of the novel is that "the truly worthy man is the individual—individualism, for Berger, meaning to have the courage and strength to live one's own life."[27] This observation is supported by the fact that the only admirable white man in the novel is General Custer, a fiercely determined individual who remains true to his convictions. He is brave and goes his own way— two qualities which would have served him well had he been an Indian.

It is significant that Crabb has no success when he attempts to explain Custer's sense of independent spirit to Old Lodge Skins. The reason for the Indian's lack of comprehension is central to the virtues promoted in *Little Big Man*: to the Cheyenne, independence is the rule, not the exception. Custer is an exception because the white society suppresses independent action. Crabb does admit that this quality in the Cheyenne can sometimes lead to chaotic action, for if "you give an Indian a choice . . . he is sure to take the reckless alternative: he is inclined to let anybody do what they want" (p. 86). Nevertheless, compared to the white man's submission to authority and conformity, we admire the Cheyenne's independence.

In addition to the Cheyennes' high regard for individualism, there is a corresponding concern for the dignity of each person; this quality is expressed in an unbounded loyalty between tribe members, and even in the treatment of their enemies. The fact that there is no concern for the dignity of others in white civilization is evidenced when Crabb recalls his period as a drunk, singing and dancing to a jeering crowd in exchange for a drink of whiskey: "the Cheyenne would have been depressed to see a fellow tribesman gone to rot; they would have believed it reflected discredit upon all Human Beings. On the contrary, an American just loves to see another who ain't worth a damn" (p. 209).

The contrasting regard of the two societies for the individuality and dignity of their members is represented by the Cheyennes' treatment of their homosexuals (heemanehs). They are understanding of the heemanehs and value them as welcome and contributing members of society. The Indians' consideration of human rights is nowhere more obvious than in their treatment of this traditionally abused minority. In a society where dignity is earned, not granted, there is no need for one person to humiliate another. Even in war, the Cheyenne acknowledge the enemy's honor. The purpose of fighting is not to "show him up or make him eat dust, but rather to kill him altogether" (p. 129). This attitude is quite different from Wild Bill Hickock's, whose life is dedicated to finding opportunities to prove that he is a better man than his opponents.

There is little doubt that Berger favors the moral tenets which the Cheyenne represent. However, it is wrong to assume that Berger is therefore launching a crusade for the preservation of the noble savage or a return to primitivism. Rather, he would have us consider what it means to be a decent human being.

In *Little Big Man*, this reconsideration of human values begins with a new awareness of our Western mythology. Berger brilliantly manages to effect this new awareness without romanticizing Old Lodge Skins or the Indian way of life. However, as we get to know both in the course of the novel, our opinions change considerably. This is illustrated by Jack's changing view of Old Lodge Skins. Initially, he sees him as a farcical buffoon; as he gets to know him the image changes to that of a wise, sympathetic man whom he respects and loves. By the time he greets death, Old Lodge Skins has reached epic and tragic dimensions; his blindness, like Tiresias' in Greek tragedy, allows him greater vision than ordinary men. The same shift in perception can be seen in Jack's evaluation of the ambiance of an Indian camp. We have seen his first reaction to the suffocating stench of the Cheyenne camp, an almost physical revulsion. However, he tells us that it soon became his reality, and when he returned to white society, he missed the odor of what seemed life itself (p. 51).

In a similar manner, all aspects of the "savage" way of life are re-evaluated by Jack—and the reader. The picaresque structure allows comparisons between white and Indian societies, showing us the strengths and weaknesses of both. One of the great weaknesses of white culture is, as Max F. Shulz points out, that it is goal oriented, while the strength of Indian culture is that it is identity conscious.[28] One way that this basic ideological difference is shown is that the Indians, unlike the whites, do not wish to gain power over another's spirit, but to achieve self-fulfillment. Old Lodge Skins shows us this dichotomy when he contemplates the victory at the Little Bighorn which he realizes will mark the end of the Indian way of life:

> Yes, my son . . . it is finished now, because what more can you do to an enemy than beat him? Were we fighting red men against red men . . . it would now be the turn of the other side to try to whip *us* . . . that is the *right* way. There is no permanent winning or losing when things move, as they should, in a circle. . . . But white men, who live in straight lines and squares, do not believe as I do. With them it is rather everything or nothing. . . . And because of their strange beliefs, they are very persistent. They will even fight at night or in bad weather. But they hate the fighting itself. Winning is all they care about, and if they can do that by scratching a pen across paper or saying something into the wind, they are much happier.
>
> They will not be content now to come and take revenge. . . . Indeed, if we all return to the agencies, they probably would not kill anyone. For killing is part of living, but they hate life. (pp. 441–42)

Little Big Man is a comic novel grounded in satire, but the satire is only an instrument by which it measures the limits of human striving. It accomplishes more than other satiric Westerns because it attempts more: *Little Big Man* is a serious consideration of what it means to live well. Crabb tells us that twice while he was with the Cheyenne he was "at the center of the earth," a Cheyenne concept which expresses one's awareness of the circular nature of things, the unending unity of things past and present, life and death. To be at the center of the earth is to be at complete peace with oneself and others. It is the normal condition for the Cheyenne, but it is a unique and extraordinary experience for Crabb. He is thrilled by the sense of tranquility. Berger's satire in *Little Big Man* shows us how white society, ambitiously pursuing the transformation of the world, has forgotten what it is to live, to be a human being at the center of the earth.

Notes

1. William James Smith, "In the Vein of Mark Twain," rev. of *Little Big Man*, by Thomas Berger, *Commonweal*, 20 November 1964, pp. 294–96.

2. Robert Edson Lee, *From West to East: Studies in the Literature of the American West* (Urbana: University of Illinois Press, 1966), p. 156.

3. Delbert E. Wylder, "Thomas Berger's *Little Big Man* as Literature," in *Literature of the American West*, ed. J. Golden Taylor (Boston: Houghton Mifflin, 1971), p. 74.

4. Guy Davenport, "Tough Characters, Solid Novels," rev. of *Little Big Man*, by Thomas Berger, *National Review*, 26 January 1965, p. 68.

5. Max F. Schulz, *Black Humor Fiction of the Sixties: A Pluralistic Definition of Man and His World* (Athens: Ohio University Press, 1973), p. 74.

6. Brian W. Dippie, "Jack Crabb and the Sole Survivors of Custer's Last Stand," *Western American Literature*, 4 (1969), 202.

7. Thomas Berger, *Little Big Man* (1964; rpt. New York: Fawcett, n.d.), p. 245. All further references to this work appear in the text.

8. L. L. Lee, "American, Western, Picaresque: Thomas Berger's *Little Big Man*," *South Dakota Review*, 4, No. 2 (1966), 35.

9. Matthew Hodgart, *Satire* (New York: McGraw-Hill, 1969), p. 218.

10. Kent Ladd Steckmesser, *The Western Hero in History and Legend* (Norman: University of Oklahoma Press, 1965).

11. John G. Cawelti, "The Gunfighter and the Hard-boiled Dick," *American Studies*, 15, No. 21 (1975), p. 50.

12. Smith, p. 294.

13. Wylder, p. 73.

14. Kerry David Ahearn, "Aspects of the Contemporary American Western Novel," Diss. Ohio University 1974, p. 108.

15. Martin Nussbaum, "Sociological Symbolism of the 'Adult Western,' " *Social Forces*, 39 (1960), p. 27.

16. Granville Hicks, "Paleface in the Cheyenne Camp," rev. of *Little Big Man*, by Thomas Berger, *Saturday Review*, 10 October 1964, p. 40.

17. This seems to be a rather vicious attack on Whitman; but there may be another purpose, in light of Berger's extensive research into the topic. Perhaps Berger is so critical of Whitman because of his opportunism. According to Paul A. Hutton ("Custer's Last Stand," *TV Guide*, 26 November 1977, p. 40), within twenty-four hours of receiving news of Custer's defeat, Whitman had mailed his poem, "A Death Song for Custer," to the *New York Tribune* with an enclosed bill for ten dollars.

18. William T. Pilkington, "Aspects of the Western Comic Novel," *Western American Literature*, 1 (1966), 217.

19. Ahearn, p. 110.

20. Dippie, p. 199.

21. "Jack Crabb, Oldtimer," rev. of *Little Big Man*, by Thomas Berger, *Time*, 16 October 1964, p. 128.

22. Charles B. Harris, *Contemporary American Novelists of the Absurd* (New Haven: College and University Press, 1971), pp. 129–31.

23. The Custer massacre has never lost its intrigue to novelists or film-makers. There are dozens of novels which take up the subject, perhaps the best being Ernest Haycox's *Bugles in the Afternoon*. As recently as 1976, Douglas C. Jones broached the topic in his "what if" historical novel, *The Court-Martial of George Armstrong Custer*. Television took its turn with the short-lived 1960s series, *Custer*. But the film has been the most significant contributor to the legend of Custer, portraying him as everything from national hero (Raoul Walsh's powerful *They Died With Their Boots On*, 1940) to mad egocentric (Arthur Penn's screen version of *Little Big Man*, 1970). Still other Custer films include Thomas H. Ince's *Custer's Last Fight* (1912), Louis Weiss' *Custer's Last Stand* (1936), and Robert Siodmak's *Custer of the West* (1968).

24. Stanley Kauffman, "O'Hara and Others," rev. of *Little Big Man*, by Thomas Berger, *New York Review of Books*, 17 December 1964, p. 21.

25. Lee, p. 36.

26. Davenport, p. 68.

27. Lee, pp. 36–37.

28. Schulz, p. 77.

Reinhart as Hero and Clown

GERALD WEALES

I

Carlo Reinhart, like his creator Thomas Berger, was born in 1924 of German-American parents in or near Cincinnati, Ohio. Like Berger, Reinhart served in the army during the second world war and, home again, took advantage of the GI Bill of Rights to go back to college although, unlike Berger, he never graduated. There are probably a great many other similarities between author and character including certain attitudes, habits of mind, a preoccupation with the paraphernalia of daily living. Reinhart's eye for detail is evident in Berger's non-Reinhart novels, and both the ruins in which he sets his sexual/social fantasy *Regiment of Women* (1973) and the small indignities that beset the hero of his private-eye burlesque *Who Is Teddy Villanova?* (1977) reflect a continuing response to surroundings that he had already characterized in *Crazy in Berlin* (1958): "What was extraordinary was that America could be so ugly-dull." Berger, like Reinhart, is concerned with the dangerous uncertainty of human relationships, familial, sexual, collegial, with the problem of identity, with the slipperiness of truth, with the inefficacy of language, with the authoritarianism of self-righteous idealism, with aging and death, but, like Reinhart, he can easily be distracted by the petty annoyances of restaurant decor, advertising slogans, television programing. The quotation above is presumably Reinhart's insight, brought on by a juxtaposition of a remembered Ohio and the Europe in which he finds himself, but the accompanying list of negative (and clichéd) responses to the surface of American life go beyond Reinhart's experience. Faced with some phenomena, Berger and Reinhart work as a double, but sometimes Berger seems to elbow Reinhart offstage as in the lengthy and gratuitous parody of a Scandinavian art film in *Vital Parts* (1970) or the description of a ladies' magazine story in *Reinhart in Love* (1962), a routine joke lacking both the vigor and the dramatic force that Tennessee Williams gave it in *The Glass Menagerie*.

Carlo Reinhart was born, after all, not in 1924, but when Thomas Berger first put the character on paper. Whatever autobiographical elements,

Reprinted by permission of *The HOLLINS Critic* 20, no. 5 (1983): 1–12.

statistical and spiritual, go into the Reinhart novels, the creator and the created are not one, as the slippage cited above indicates. "I write to amuse and conceal myself," Berger said in *Contemporary Novelists*, amusing and concealing himself in the comment. I have no inclination to search out the hidden Berger in the Reinhart saga. There is an obvious tactical value in the author's sharing age and background with his protagonist; he is better able to understand his character's responses to new ideas and new modes of behavior, even when and if those responses are not precisely his. This is particularly true of the last two novels, in which Reinhart catches up with Berger, for the publication dates of *Vital Parts* and *Reinhart's Women* (1981) follow within a year or two the time of the events they recount. In the first two novels, Berger is writing in the late 1950s, early 1960s of Reinhart in the immediate postwar 1940s. It is not Reinhart as Berger, then, that interests me here—or that interests most readers, I assume—except to the extent that that identification is an instance of Reinhart as all of us. Often as infuriating as he is likable, Reinhart has a way of voicing, silently for the most part, prejudices that we pretend to have put behind us and of performing with an ineptitude to which we are clearly superior—on our good days. "You are a fool, a good fool, a kind fool," Lori Bach tells Reinhart in *Crazy in Berlin*, and twenty years later in *Vital Parts* his own accusing inner voice says, *"You're still the same old horse's ass."* The strength of the Reinhart books is that the reader keeps recognizing his similarities to the good fool, the horse's ass, when he would prefer to identify with the poet-philosopher hero that Reinhart spends so many years imagining hidden within his untidy mind and body. Dell has recently reissued The Reinhart Series, as the four disparate novels are now called, a publishing event which Reinhart would surely recognize as an artificial marketing strategy but which can serve as an occasion to take a closer look at Carlo Reinhart and the novels that tell his story.

The four books were obviously not conceived as a unit (*Reinhart's Women* could hardly have been implicit in *Crazy in Berlin*), but, as in literary series as different as the chronicles of Sherlock Holmes and Paddington, the Reinhart series just grew. Characters often reappear in later books having undergone physical or ideological changes, and there are constant references to the events of earlier books in ways that suggest a continuity without quite providing it. There is a kind of insider's coziness for Reinhart regulars when Carlo invokes a character or an event which they already know in detail, but when a reference becomes more than casual it runs the danger of turning intrusive. Splendor Mainwaring's explanation in *Vital Parts* of the preposterous ending of *Reinhart in Love* reads like a Bergerian gloss on the earlier novel and has no dramatic function except that the Reinhart of *Vital Parts*, drowning in his sense of failure, recurs constantly to the days of his youth. This extended afterthought only underlines the fact that *Vital Parts* and *Reinhart's Women*, written ten and twenty years after the first two books and with other non-Reinhart novels having appeared in between, are necessarily very different in tone. Even *Reinhart in Love*, which is Berger's second novel and in which the events follow immediately on those in *Crazy in Berlin*, is not much like its predecessor. In fact, *Crazy in Berlin* is not really a Reinhart novel in the sense that the others are. If it can be said to have a protagonist, Reinhart fills that role, but he is only one of several leading characters as the shifting point of view indicates. In the later novels, the characters exist only through Reinhart's perception or misperception of them.

II

Having insisted on the separateness of the four novels, let me now indicate what they have in common. The most obvious and the most important element is Berger's narrative method which, despite the tonal differences, remains the same for all four novels. Unlike *Little Big Man* (1964), in which Jack Crabb is allowed to tell his own story, these novels are written in the third person. Yet the presentation of character, event, idea, social situation, even the window dressing of fad is filtered through a character—usually Reinhart. This device provides the reader with a multiple prospect. He sees an event, say, through the eyes of a character whose perception is limited by his ideology, his lack of knowledge, his expectations, his longing, his preoccupation with self, but, since the reader stands with Berger, he can recognize the limitations of the point of focus. Sometimes, in fact, he stands beyond Berger and watches him pull strings, strain for effect, but usually the novelist has his narrative device well in hand. Often a third person comes between the filtering character and the material described so that, in *Vital Parts* for instance, we get Reinhart's skewered perception of his radical son's skewered perception of the world. A good example of this technique, one in which Reinhart is not the focus, can be found in Chapter 13 of *Crazy in Berlin*, in which Lt. Schild's ruminations about his Communism and his Jewishness are colored by the tension between his commitment to ideology and the humanistic impulse that led him to such political orthodoxy, a coloring that takes on another tint when he recalls his dead friend Milton Grossman, executed as a Trotskyite deviationist by his Stalinist comrades during the Spanish Civil War. Looking through Schild looking through Grossman, Berger is able, as he so often is in that book, to present abstract ideas as no more invulnerable to the individual vision that lust or greed.

To someone who comes first to Berger's technique in *Crazy in Berlin*, the complexity may initially seem confusing. When the narrator—conventionally a disinterested voice—describes the fight in the first chapter in which a drunken Reinhart protects his friend Marsala, he says of their opponent that "it was suddenly obvious that he was very dead" and "Reinhart had broken both hands at the wrist." When we realize that the man is not dead and Reinhart's hands are not broken, we have to make an abrupt shift in the way we receive information. What at first appears to be a combination of Reinhart's musings and objective reporting can be seen as a portrait of Reinhart not simply through his thoughts but imposed on people and things about him. Of course, "it was suddenly obvious" should have been a giveaway since the locution assumes it was obvious to someone, but it takes a few pages before one can sort out obviousness from factual truth. If any. Besides Berger has a use for the scene that Reinhart is not in a position to know; the non-dead dead man here is preparation for the dead dead man of the fight toward the end of the book when the pacific Reinhart does kill with his hands. The reader of *Crazy in Berlin* quickly becomes familiar with Berger's narrative device and, once a chapter identifies the point of view character, he is in a position to receive both the material and the particular bias by which it is presented. In the later books, with Reinhart as the sole focus, matters should be simpler. The hangups there are likely to be as much the reader's as the character's. The vividness with which Berger presents material can trigger a reaction in the reader which causes him to slip his aesthetic gears and blame Berger for a view that is Reinhart's. I know that that occasionally happened in my case. At the beginning of *Reinhart in Love*, when Dad drives him home from the Cincinnati station (it is unidentified, but easily recognizable), there is a paragraph in which men in bars, a waitress in a chili parlor, teenagers under a street lamp, a man leaving a library, a man at a mailbox are described in such an ugly fashion that the city street becomes a hellish vision. Oh, come off it, Berger, I found myself muttering, I could describe the same scene and make it ordinary, perhaps even amiable. So could Berger presumably, although amiability is hardly his stock in trade, but the paragraph is not really about the street that Berger has peopled for Reinhart; it is about the young man's reluctant homecoming. Later, when Berger writes, "He was going down, down, down in the quicksand of suburban faces: your only real horror, making concentration camps and secret police a sport," my first reaction was annoyance at the obscenity of the comparison. It seemed a vulgarization of an idea that was effective in *Crazy in Berlin*, in which Reinhart's discomfort at his presumed bland normality made him fascinated by and a little envious of those, victims and victimizers alike, whose existence set them apart from the ordinary. The vulgarization is real, but it is in Reinhart, for in the second book, he has already begun the descent into the self-pity that will be at the center of *Vital Parts*.

Although Reinhart's likes and dislikes may color Berger's presentation in the novels, it is safe to say that the comic extravagance of all the books—the bizarrely overstated characters, the ludicrous scenes, the complicated and overtly artificial plots—belong to the author as well as his protagonist. In

Crazy in Berlin, characters like the helpless giant Bach with his fantastic web of words, Lori's blind brother Otto and the insidious Schatzi, who despite his nickname is nobody's sweetheart, are grotesques that, perhaps because of the ruined city in which the novel is set, suggest *The Tin Drum*. Yet the American figures are also larger than life, stereotypes—the "dumb but lovable buddy" Marsala, the *zaftig* nurse, the hospital commander cutely named Colonel Fester—that burst the conventional lines in which Berger and Reinhart at first set them. In the chapter in which Lori's brother tells his story of how, as a German Communist exiled in Russia, he was sacrificed by his comradely hosts to the Nazi-Soviet Pact, Reinhart is disconcerted by the way he slips into the trivia that interests him more and asks about American movies. In an attempt to bring seriousness back into the conversation, Reinhart answers Otto's question by discussing the presumed immaturity of American film audiences and the consequent misrepresentation of Nazism in which the Nazis are either "monsters" or "ridiculous buffoons." Otto's response: "*Also,* this was an error: too realistic. I agree with you, this theme should be dealt with as fantasy." With this exchange Berger has nicely sidestepped the possible criticisms of his method of characterization. Either his grotesques are real or his themes are too serious to be treated except in fantasy. Judging by the later Reinhart books, I would go for the second of these two possibilities, for—particularly in *Reinhart in Love* and *Vital Parts*—most of his characters have become cartoons that suggest not Günter Grass, but the comic strip (*v.* Maw and Dad in *Reinhart in Love*) and movie farce at its broadest. Streckfuss, the scientist in *Vital Parts* who reminds Reinhart of Schatzi, manages to suggest the Nazi medical experimenter while he remains a comic figure, a cross between the mad scientist of horror films and the burlesque doctor in the old crazy-hospital routine, as Berger/Reinhart admits when he says "He held aloft an enormous syringe, of the kind used by veterinarians on people in movie comedies." The trick, which is to say the controlling aesthetic, of the comic strip and movie farce is that their characters have a realistic base beneath the hugger-mugger. Berger knows that realism and fantasy provide a single approach to phenomena that alters according to the vantage point of the observer.

III

Berger uses a standard plot in all the books, one in which Reinhart passes through confusion and sometimes despair to a mild triumph—at least, to a positive action or an almost accidental rescue. These endings are muted, not so much a winding up as a running down when one considers that the complications, the heavy play of chance, the disguises and the misidentifications (used philosophically in *Crazy in Berlin*, more nearly as device in the later books) suggest a kind of pop-culture comedy plot which conventionally comes to an unmistakable here-comes-the-cavalry, worm-turning, good-guys-always-win finish. The set comic scenes, like Reinhart's evangelistic takeover of the strip show at the end of *Reinhart in Love* or the slapstick with the goat in *Vital Parts*, suggest movie sequences, and the briefer bits recall similar analogues. Reinhart's surrealistic struggle with the contents of the bathroom closet in *Reinhart in Love* may have been intended as satire on American consumerism, but when I read it, I found myself thinking of Fibber McGee's hall closet which he opened with such graphic sound effects every week on his radio show. Berger and I are of an age. " 'Tain't funny, McGee," Molly used to say, and, although Berger is celebratedly hilarious, I was regularly more fascinated by his transformations of conventional comic sequences and characters than I was by the antics themselves. The outrageous Maw aside (I have a taste for coarseness), it was the surprise juxtapositions, the unexpected throwaway lines that made me laugh in the Reinhart novels. In any case, it is a response more complex and more painful than laughter that Berger wants to trap in these books.

The novels share not only narrative techniques and devices of plotting and characterization but verbal play that is clearly one of the ways Berger amuses himself in his writing. Take all those quotations, for instance. From the opening of *Crazy in Berlin* when the name of the titular city "opened magic casements on the foam of seas perilous" for Reinhart, who, like Berger, had read his Keats, the book is filled with quotations, in the dialogue or in the narrative, quoted correctly or telescoped, fragmented. Often the usage is of no more importance than the tag-ends that crop up in the conversation or the minds of all of us, particularly those of us who, like Berger, went to school in the days when students still memorized poetry. Occasionally one wants to say, with Dynamene in *A Phoenix Too Frequent*, "You needn't/ Labour to prove your secondary education," and then a bromidic line is used in a way that reinvigorates the original. In the scene in which Captain Bernstein manages, simply by the fact of his Jewishness, to quiet the sardonic Cronin, Reinhart, musing as he so often does on what it means to be a Jew, considers "Bernstein's too-solid flesh which, if some ambitious or perhaps merely desperate forebear had not shipped the Atlantic, would have by his fellow Germans been resolved into a dew." At first glance, this seems simply an instance of Berger/Reinhart's playing cute games with the Holocaust, but then the line turns back on itself and reminds us that the familiar rhetoric of Hamlet's somewhat self-indulgent speech has death at its dark center. The quotations are used to such little purpose in *Reinhart in Love* that the novel acknowledges the fact when Reinhart "began to perceive events through the filter of various old quotations." There is the same casual usage in *Vital Parts* until the scene with the accusatory guard on top of the skyscraper in which, as the two of them discuss a quotation book the man has found, Berger comes up with some lines from Dryden's "The Hind and the Panther" that marvelously encapsulate the mixture of loss and newborn expectation in Reinhart and his conviction that he was "such by nature." Little wonder that in *Reinhart's Women*, where the protagonist has a firmer sense of himself, the quotations all but disappear.

Berger's other verbal games are almost as pervasive as his use of quotations. From the first page of *Crazy in Berlin*, when Reinhart pisses on a statue of "Friedrich der Grosse" and admits it was "a gross thing to do," his and Reinhart's sometimes foolish fondness for the sound of words is obvious. In *Reinhart in Love*, Berger names the English instructor Pardy so that Reinhart, watching brown-nosing fellow students follow the man to his office, can think of them as "Pardy and party," both words having the same pronunciation in Southern Ohio. Names can be obvious jokes (Colonel Fester) or they can work by contraries: Bob Sweet who isn't. Sometimes they seem to exist simply for the sound of them—Blaine Raven, Splendor Mainwaring—or why else would Reinhart have named his daughter Winona? Not surely for a town in Minnesota. Berger seduces the reader into playing with names himself; I found myself wondering if the psychiatrist at the end of *Crazy in Berlin* was named Millet because Reinhart, in his teasing inteviews with the man, was going against the grain. Berger knows that there is something preposterous about the serious use of significant names, so he lets the elegantly allusive Bach explain to Reinhart: "The name, of course, means 'pure of heart,' *Hart* being the Low German variant of *Herz*. But I have a feeling that you, like so many Americans, have no great interest in etymology." Yet, that definition is central to our understanding of Reinhart, at least in the first novel. On the other hand, names are not only untrustworthy indicators of character (Schatzi), they are mutable, subject to the whims of those who receive them and those who possess them. Thus, Reinhart becomes Reingart in the Soviet intelligence files and both Steinhart and Reinkoenig in the mouth of Colonel Fester. In *Reinhart in Love*, Maw gives a ludicrous explanation of how Reinhart came by an Italian name like Carlo, but in that book he becomes Carl, which he remains until *Reinhart's Women*, in which, as a professional chef, he is about to revert to Carlo once again. In *Vital Parts*, Splendor admits that he invented his own name ("Does Sylvester Gordon Mainwaring sound like me?") and his son Raymond, who is Captain Bruno Storm, a black militant, in that book, becomes the born-again Brother Valentine in *Reinhart's Women*.

The voices in the Reinhart books, like the names, like the characters, stake no claim for a place in the realistic tradition. The intricate intellectual discussions in *Crazy in Berlin* turn into mini-lectures and often one speaker cannot be told from another; even Reinhart, the learner, sounds like Bach or Schild or Otto when he begins to worry an idea to death. The less exalted language is closer to ordinary speech, but it is often the stereotypical speech of popular drama, polished to reflect a single aspect of a character—Marsala's angry affection for Reinhart, say. In the later books, the artificiality becomes more obvious, as in Homer A. Blesserhart, who, obscenity aside, is a Kentuckian with one foot in *Snuffy Smith*, the other in *The Beverly Hillbillies*. Berger uses identifying tags with the tirelessness and tiresomeness of eighteenth-century playwrights. Thus, Claude Humbold, who has no other mispronunciation, always says "bidniss," presumably because he is the very model of a modern crooked bidnissman. Genevieve Raven, who traps Reinhart into marriage in *Reinhart in Love* and throws him out in *Vital Parts*, is given to garbled cliches ("You bring up such dumb things a person would think you didn't have any bats in the belfry"), a mannerism that Berger works relentlessly in *Reinhart in Love*, with less assiduity in the later books. Since I am a restrained admirer of the original Mrs. Malaprop, Genevieve's twisted sayings, like the malapropisms in the mouths of Splendor, Dad, the Maker, the Honorable Bob J. Gibbon did not send me rolling in the aisles. They seem pointless unless they have some dramatic or satiric purpose; Sheridan understood that.

All this is simply the playful surface of Bergerian speech which, at its most effective, tends to be artificial in manner, accurate at its heart. People may not really talk as Berger's characters do, but they certainly communicate in that fashion. The quarrels between Reinhart and Genevieve and the confrontation of Reinhart with Blaine, both the radical son of *Vital Parts* and the prudish square of *Reinhart's Women*, are excellent indications of the disintegrative nature of the family, as Berger sees it, and the rhetoric of the various conmen with whom Reinhart deals are reflections not of their persuasiveness but of his needs. Among the best scenes in the canon are those between Dad and Reinhart in *Reinhart in Love* in which the father always responds obliquely to the son's remarks as though the two men shared space without being able to touch. "And thanks, Dad," Reinhart says toward the end of the novel. "In your own way, you always tell me what I want to know, though never what I ask." The irony in the line is that Reinhart cannot listen. One of the major themes of *Crazy in Berlin* is the intractability of appearance so that Reinhart spends much of the book trying to sort through preconceptions and first impressions in search of truth. In the later books that search becomes a habit of speech for Reinhart; in trying to give verbal shape to a situation or a state of mind, he talks through attempts to reach him. "The possibility that he might be turning into a garrulous old bore suddenly suggested itself" to him in *Reinhart's Women*, but here he simply wants to talk about cooking while his earlier garrulity, in search of understanding, was a contribution to obfuscation. Even Berger's most frivolous verbal games are signals to indicate that this wonderfully articulate novelist does not trust language. "I write to amuse and conceal myself."

IV

In my attempts to illustrate the techniques that Berger carries from novel to novel, I have necessarily given some indication of the character of Reinhart. Beset by changing circumstances and his own aging, he is obviously not the same in each of the books. Yet, there is a core Reinhart on whom Berger rings the changes. "If you have blond hair and blue eyes, and in addition are big," he says in *Reinhart in Love*,—well, you'll find a number of people who doubt you have much upstairs." Schatzi in *Crazy in Berlin* describes him as "that oaf" and a "great lout" although he holds his own among the most arcane intellectuals, but Schatzi is correct to the extent that Reinhart continues to see imprecisely (but then who in that book does not?). In later books, Schatzi's labels seem more appropriate. Reinhart is a man who sees himself as superior to the family and the society in which he was raised, a rough diamond waiting for discovery; yet, he doubts that there is anything special about him. He certainly does not attempt to package his presumed superiority, to peddle it in a market that puts a premium on aggression. More an observer than an actor, he is constantly subject to the manipulations of others and the mercies of chance. In two of the novels he invokes Aunt Betsey Trotwood's advice to David Copperfield, "Never be mean, never be false, never be cruel," first to describe his father in *Reinhart in Love*, later to describe himself in *Vital Parts*, although he has trouble getting the quotation out in the latter instance because he doubts its applicability. Although he can be all those things young Copperfield is warned against, it is not a bad description of him because his impulses carry him toward kindness and loyalty. He is likely to accept things at face value; yet, he distrusts characterizing generalizations (although he uses them, particularly about women) and the dismissive and dictatorial results of thinking in narrow categories. That makes him a reluctant liberal in the 1940s (*Reinhart in Love*) and a bemused reactionary in the 1960s (*Vital Parts*). Faced with a person who seems to deserve a physical or verbal attack, he often finds himself seduced by blemishes of body or soul that emphasize a shared humanity and that render him helpless. Although he is "pure of heart," he refuses to identify with Sir Galahad (except in an argument with Gen in *Vital Parts*); Sir Launcelot, the flawed hero, is his favorite among King Arthur's knights.

The knighthood motif is a major one in *Crazy in Berlin*. In a long, rambling discussion with Lt. Schild, Reinhart recalls the Dürer etching, "Ritter, Tod, und Teufel," in which, of course, he identifies with the knight. The ruined landscape of the drawing is the landscape of ruined Berlin, and Berger describes the fight in which Reinhart tries and fails to save Schild in a way that suggests Dürer's picture. Reinhart's invocation of Dürer makes Schild remember his Malory, and Reinhart later tells the psychiatrist, "When Schild was a boy he read the King Arthur stories. And he still believed them up to the time he died." This is true in the way that things are true in *Crazy in Berlin*. Schild's Arthurian longings follow him to his death, as his diversionary attack on the giant Hans indicates, but he goes to that fatal meeting as a Communist who has assessed his failure and accepted the consequences, not a knight of the Round Table on a quest, but a dangerously soft-hearted ideologue, like the Young Comrade in Brecht's *The Measures Taken*, rationally ready to sacrifice his life to Party discipline. However incomplete his awareness of the conflict within Schild, Reinhart is on surer ground when he goes on, adding to the sentence above an admission that he thinks proves him truly crazy in Berlin, "Because so do I. Really." But this allegiance to the King Arthur stories has its own complexities. All through the novel, Reinhart tries in large and small ways to protect others from large and small hurts, but a knight for Reinhart is not a do-gooder. He sees his behavior as in his own interest, a way of discovering what is special about Reinhart. "Well, the Knight—there he is in the foreground, on his splendid charger walking stately through the crap," he says of the Dürer. Later, having tried a little homemade therapy on a bedwetting para-trooper, he contemplates studying psychology: "True, like knighthood, this profession gave you a permanent upper hand." That he continues to believe in the possibility of Sir Carlo in *Reinhart in Love* and *Vital Parts* is clear not in the direct references to the King Arthur stories but in his conviction of his own specialness despite the rain of failure and humiliation that keeps him from "walking stately through the crap." He develops an ironic stance— already present in *Crazy in Berlin*—which allows him to condescend to others by underlining his own deficiencies. Most of his auditors fail to hear the irony. That stance and any mention of King Arthur disappear from *Reinhart's Women*, for in that novel he no longer sees his actual self as an impostor inhabiting and inhibiting his ideal self.

V

"Yes, life is merely several long stories laid end to end," Lori says in *Crazy in Berlin*, and Genevieve, complaining about Reinhart's truth-seeking in *Reinhart's Women*, plays a variation on that statement with, "It ought to begin to occur to you that life is just a collection of stories from all points of self-interest." Now, having for so many pages ignored the separateness of these novels that I laid down at the beginning of this essay, let me look briefly at the four stories that make up Reinhart's life. *Crazy in Berlin*, in so far as it is Reinhart's novel, is a coming-of-age story. It begins on Rein-hart's twenty-first birthday and ends with his acquiring some sense of his own identity, one at least firm enough to allow him to act with deliberation. He is not innocent after the fashion of the protagonists of such stories, knowing something of sex and death before we meet him, although he does not kill with his own hands until the end of the book. He spends much of the novel wandering from one lying or misinformed truth-teller to another— a listener, an absorber, an observer, even when he talks or when he acts. In the former instance, words are sometimes forced out of him (and he often takes another's story as his own) by a need to deflect a statement that may hurt someone else. In the latter, he responds to stimuli rather than initiating action. The teen-aged Trudchen seduces him, and Veronica Leary commandeers him as friend, escort and non-sexual sex partner. He uses his great strength to defend Marsala and Schild, but he is drunk in the first case, totally at sea in the second. It is only at the end of the book, presumably cured of some madness or other, that he can expose Schatzi, an act that in itself and in the way it is performed is uncharacteristic of the hesitant, self-doubting Reinhart we have known.

Reinhart in Love is broadly comic, more given to slapstick than philosophical rumination. Splendor's pretending to have written "Bartleby the Scrivener" gives us a chance to see that story as a comment on Reinhart's attraction-repulsion toward his black friend. Although Berger's use of Melville and less well-integrated use of *Anna Karenina* remind us that *Reinhart in Love* was written by the literary gent who did *Crazy in Berlin*, most of the time the novel suggests that its author found his sources in old movies, the funny papers and television. When Reinhart, walking on air in his first (and only) success as a real estate man, came to give the good news to Dad, *"Reinhart was in love with everything."* He is in love with Gen, the idea of marriage and impending fatherhood, although the marriage began in Gen's lie about her pregnancy and hangs on the uneasy thread of material success. He has been converted to the romance of business although his job with Claude Humbold is a fake (his father pays his salary) and his exalted and profitable position as head of the sewer company is an assignment that depends on the real profit-taker's need for a patsy in case the swindle falls through. Despite his expectant sense of his own potential achievement, he is regularly manipulated by Gen, by Splendor, by Humbold, even by Maw and Dad, and he acts only in disguise. As Dr. Lorenz Goodykuntz he orchestrates the carnival orgy in which he does not take part ("I'm going home. I'm a married man") and, as an unnamed college chum of Blaine Raven, he manages to get his drunken father-in-law back to his house. These events never have the implications of the simple scene with Schatzi at the end of *Crazy in Berlin* for, despite the positive force in them, Reinhart is finally rescued at the end by accident when the disaster of Splendor's attempt to dig a sewer in the black neighborhood turns out to be profitable to Humbold. In *Reinhart in Love*, the incipient knight of *Crazy in Berlin* has become a comic butt although he does not know it.

In *Vital Parts*, he knows it, which is why that novel, despite some scenes as broad as the comedy of *Reinhart in Love*, is more somber than the one that precedes it. Now forty-four, he has a history of business failures and a marriage that has gone to pieces. Gen, the bread-winner, tosses him out when, in love and anger, he cuts the shoulder-length locks of his hippie son. Abandoned by his family (except for the hapless Winona), disowned by his mother (Dad is now dead), he is taken in, in both senses of the phrase, by Bob Sweet and his Cryon Foundation (cryonics and cry-on, obviously). "What interested Reinhart was not eternal life itself. . . . But a second chance, another start, was most attractive." Finally, unsuccessful even as a suicide, he agrees to allow himself to be frozen. To get to that point in the novel, we are forced to follow Reinhart through one indignity after another, great and small torments, most of them gratuitous, and the accumulation is so relentless that I found myself becoming as impatient with him as everyone in the novel is. Perhaps that was Berger's intention; let the reader stick it to him, too. I rescued Reinhart and myself by making a jump not signaled by the novel itself, by seeing that Reinhart is cousin to those characters that W. C. Fields used to play in the 1930s—in *It's a Gift*, for instance. Everyone and everything conspires to prove he is a cipher. When a young woman spills some oranges from a shopping bag, "Reinhart retrieved them, and the woman thanked Sweet, who had not even noticed the incident." To make matters worse, Reinhart is awash with self-pity through much of the book. There is a suggestion of the fantasy happy endings Fields used to tack onto his movies when Reinhart takes his reward for agreeing to be frozen and becomes a parody of the rich, aggressive, swinging success he always imagined he might be. Then, Berger pushes his way through Reinhart's fake triumph to let his protagonist make a real decision—to remain alive, unfrozen, to protect Winona, whose goodness makes her vulnerable in the cannibal world Reinhart knows too well.

In the scene in the disco men's room in *Vital Parts*, in which Blaine tries to buy drugs, Reinhart thinks, "He had rather been father to the pusher, who at least was working for a living." A typical Reinhart reaction to Blaine and his generation, but there is irony in the line. In none of the Reinhart novels do we see the protagonist working; he is perennially waiting for the manna of material success to fall into his lap. In *Reinhart's Women*, he is finally doing something—cooking and keeping house for Winona, now a successful fashion model. Reinhart has done these chores before—when Gen is pregnant in *Reinhart in Love*, before he is thrown out in *Vital Parts*— but now the cooking is an art, the doing a pleasure in itself. At fifty-four, he has become comfortable with himself, shed his guilt and self-pity along with his great expectations. Appropriately enough, the novel that presents the physically and spiritually slimmed-down Reinhart is lean, spare, almost conversational. The flamboyance of the earlier books is gone. According to one literary tradition (v. the Yeats of *The Land of Heart's Desire*, the Synge of *Deirdre of the Sorrows*) there is loss in such domestication, but *Reinhart's Women* has the feel of quiet triumph about it. The knight in Reinhart, the poet, the philosopher, the special person was always ill-at-ease in the American setting in which the "good fool," the "kind fool" tried to be the husband, father, lover, businessman convention dictated, even though everyone he dealt with violated those conventions. In a world that rejects Aunt Betsey Trotwood's virtues, Reinhart's best bet is to put King Arthur to rest. Not that Berger leaves him there. Having let Reinhart withdraw into the private contentment of *oeufs en meurette* well and truly made, Berger rewards him with the promise of celebrity as a TV chef, the hint of success as a restaurateur and the gratification of the love of an adoring young woman.

Is that the end of the Reinhart saga? or a new beginning? Will he still need us, will he still feed us, when he's sixty-four?

Berger, Burlesque, and the Yearning for Comedy

MICHAEL MALONE

"My intention is not to satirize or make fun of the various genres I undertake, but to celebrate them. I think you're right when you say my contributions are not parodies. My intention is to *add to* and not *take from*."

—Thomas Berger, letter[1]

For novelists, two paths have led traditionally to the Parnassus of popular acclaim, and Thomas Berger has travelled neither. As a consequence, and to our disgrace, this major writer has so far garnered few of the prizes the literati bestow on one another, and (apart from the film-fed celebrity of *Little Big Man* [1964] and *Neighbors* [1980]) remains far less well-known to the reading public than he has long and eminently deserved to be. One path has been through the groves of academe: Authors, like Joyce, whose works overtly solicit, indeed insist on, critical exegesis, are naturally enough championed by literary scholars who need texts upon which they can visibly exercise their craft, just as analysts need patients who want their dreams deciphered, and lawyers need clients of litigious disposition. Critics, wary in general of works not already safely validated by Time, and suspicious besides of fiction as opposed to fictivity, are likely to shy away from any but the most "textual" of contemporary novels.

In the so-called "school of black comedy" in which Berger has been rather haphazardly placed, the last American novel to attract a thick swarm of academics was Thomas Pynchon's *Gravity's Rainbow* (1973). Pynchon, already the subject of full-length scholarly studies, announced his "significance" by modernist techniques, a polysemous allusiveness and periodic lyric flight. Berger, for all his perceived "cerebral brilliance" (not to mention the range of his canon), appears more accessible, and therefore is not taken as seriously. As yet, his work has received nowhere near the critical attention given even Joseph Heller, his contemporary, and author of the most popular of the World War II "black comedies," *Catch-22* (1961). Berger's first novel, *Crazy in Berlin* (1958) came too early to gather the college cult that Heller

Reprinted by permission of *Studies in American Humor* 2, no. 1 (Spring 1983): 20–32.

and Vonnegut were to win in the sixties—and win with it places on reading lists in college courses. Besides, Berger's characters are insufficiently adolescent—Carlo Reinhart, for example, being neither fetchingly nuts like Yossarian or Billy Pilgrim, nor shiny with fey innocence like Holden Caulfield or Garp or Tom Robbins' heroines.

Another contemporary of Berger's, cometed into Manhattan's literary firmament by a first novel on the war, is our major living example of the alternative path to Parnassus: the Romantic route. Norman Mailer's books are variations on a personal mythology; as with a movie star, his writings are fused in the public's mind with the publicized myth of the man. The great triumvirate of this Byronic variety—novelists more read about than read, more written about than they wrote—remains Fitzgerald, Hemingway and Wolfe, all of whom were brought to fame, significantly, by the also mythologized editor, Maxwell Perkins. There is nothing of this personal nature in Berger's work. It is language, not self-expression, that absorbs him; voices, not Voice. He has never shown the slightest interest in broadcasting either youthful melancholia or middle-aged angst. If the hero of his Reinhart "Quartet" may in any sense be said to speak for his author (and I should think this a dangerous assumption), Carlo is in any case far too wry a man to keep romantically awash in the poignant disenchantment that popularized a Jake Barnes or Dick Diver.

Nor has Berger any public myth, unless it be the recent, and to him amusing, efforts to depict him as an unreachable recluse. While it is true that he takes no part in the New York flashdance (having concluded long ago that it is our sad fate to live in an age when "the Philistines are the intelligentsia"), he is by no means a social misanthrope, but rather as warm, ebullient, and charming a hermit as anyone is likely to meet. We are unlikely, however, to meet him on a talk show. Berger is a writer (a private act), not a Writer (a public art), nor an Author (a critical cult). In analyzing why Thornton Wilder never became a star, Malcolm Cowley pointed out how different from one another all his works were, how various in social setting, in time, in form and theme. We can observe in Thomas Berger's novels the same variety, with the same results, for this kind of decentralized range and impersonality, coupled with readerly accessibility, make it difficult for critics (or fans) to "get a fix" on a writer. A sensibility, choosing freely among disparate styles and structures, is less readily extracted than a forefronted persona or overriding myth. *Arthur Rex* (1978) is a chivalric romance; *Regiment of Women* (1973), anti-Utopian science fiction; *Killing Time* (1967), a *roman policier* with the sharp flat sheen of a 1940s *film noir*; *Little Big Man*, a picaresque frontier epic in the national Twain vein; *Sneaky People* (1975), smalltown social comedy in the tradition of fellow Midwesterner Booth Tarkington; *Neighbors*, domestic Beckett in farce form.

Morever, narrative style (monochromatic, and so immediately identifiable, in writers like Vonnegut) changes from one Berger comedy to the next.

Not only are the first-person narrators highly varied, each of the omniscient narrators is distinctively idiosyncratic: The style of lyrical whimsy and heroic sentiment peculiar to the chivalric, carnal, Christian author of *Arthur Rex* is no more like the ironic, detached author of *Killing Time* than Jack Crabb's hyperbolic humor in *Little Big Man* resembles detective Russel Wren's dead-pan literary wordplay in *Who Is Teddy Villanova?* (1977). They do all, of course, share Something—Berger's unique sensibility—but of what it might consist has never been satisfactorily explained, or even explored. And it is unique sensibility. Berger remarked once, in a discussion about editors, that in twenty-five years of publishing, he had had almost nothing to do with them: "My vision is so peculiarly my own that another human being has a hard time getting his foot in the door." As for himself, he has little interest in making distinctions among his books, except to say that *Villanova* was the easiest to write, and *Crazy in Berlin* the hardest (because first), and that he liked them all, and would "in any case never admit to disliking any."

Reviewers have sensed from the beginning that Berger is "One of a small group of important American writers," but they have remained uneasy about defining why. Since he writes comedies, and aligns himself with traditional narrative genres (romance, picaresque, mystery), and since the only high-fashion literary relation to comedy and genre today is parodic and satiric, these reviewers, in order to take him seriously, have toppled into the perfunctory collective habit of calling him a satirist: a modernist offering a "bleakly comic account of the world's malevolent absurdity" (Kenneth Graham), a parodist "sending up" traditions, and so ranked, by the *New York Times*, with Philip Roth "among our first-rate literary wise guys." It is occasionally added that he is a nihilistic satirist, so flippant "he cannot resist drawing almost anything he happens to know into the circle of his ridicule" (Leslie Fiedler). To call Berger a joker "without moral earnestness" is preposterous, but the charge underlies the equally false conclusion that books like *Arthur Rex* and *Little Big Man* are parodies; *Sneaky People* and *Neighbors*, social satires.

Berger is not only not a satirist, he keeps saying he is not a satirist. He wrote shortly before *Neighbors* was published, "Those who believe my *intent* is to criticize society, to satirize, to write spoofs and send-ups, to be that most humorless of scribblers, the so-called comic novelist, are utterly misguided. I write for the purpose of providing myself with an alternative to reality. Nevertheless, be prepared to read many reviews of *Neighbors* that confidently announce my success or failure at holding the mirror up to suburban society." Now, fiction writers cannot always be relied upon to admit (or to know) what they're doing, but in this case, Berger knows better both his own texts and the conventions in which they are founded. Satires are by tradition works intending to reform our vices and follies by ridicule (gentle or bitter) and by moral judgment (urbane or indignant). Berger might well agree with Juvenal that it is difficult *not* to write satire these days (he jokes that he will join an amateur theatrical society of which I'm a member if we agree to cast him as Timon of Athens, Thersites, or Tom O'Bedlam), but he feels no compulsion to vex the world in print with his moral disapproval—at least not in any hope of teaching it a lesson.

Perhaps Berger views the world as past remedy, but I rather think he suffers fools so gladly in fiction because he delights in the creation of their folly. Once when I fairly idiotically asked him what he meant by saying "In my own work I have tried to compete with that reality to which I must submit in life," he replied, "My interest is in creation, not in commentary." Of the writers he told me were his "tutelary masters," only Kafka would seem to fit the typical view of Berger's tone and style. The others were Dickens, Shakespeare, Melville, Balzac and Proust, all great creators of characters, who never sacrifice depth of individuation to belletristic play. What first struck me about Berger's novels was the delight he takes in *writing*, in literary forms themselves, and in the particular world of language (the stylistic system) each intrinsically inhabits. (The sensitivity to dialect in the 1930s Midwestern *Sneaky People* or *The Feud* is as much a linguistic tour de force as the medievalness of *Arthur Rex*.) By talking about a delight in literary forms, I do not mean fictions about fictivity, or writing about writing, but instead the wide-ranging way in which (with the exception of the Reinhart novels), it is Berger's pattern to generate fiction by the fusion of his "peculiar vision" with strongly defined, traditional narrative modes— like the Western "biography," the Arthurian chronicle, the mystery. This is experimental writing, but because modern critics tend to limit their perception of "experimental" to violations of conventions like syntax, diction, or typography, and to the evaporation of "story," Berger's extraordinary technical and verbal virtuosity has gone largely unremarked, even by enthusiasts. Most often, he's acclaimed for being "funny," as if he were Peter de Vries.

He is, of course, not the only writer of comedy (as opposed to comic writer) to have his novels indiscriminately praised as "outrageous satires," "hilarious farces," burlesques and parodies. Nathanael West's *Miss Lonelyhearts* (as perfect and painful a novella about salvation as *Wise Blood*) was called by Edmund Wilson a "comic epic" and by Erskine Caldwell "a good satire on life and living in this area." Terms for comedy have long been a hodgepodge of jumbled misuse, tossed about as loose synonyms for tone. Barth's *The Sot-Weed Factor* (which bears a relation to the eighteenth-century British picaresque similar to that of *Little Big Man* to the nineteenth-century American) was called a "boisterous farce," a "bareknuckled satire," an "historical novel," and (by its author) a "moral allegory."

Unfortunately, mislabeling leads to misreading. Parody and burlesque are caricatures; the first, a ridiculing imitation of a work or its author's style (*Shamela* of *Pamela*, Hemingway's *Torrents of Spring* of Sherwood Anderson);

the second, a comic disjunction between style and subject matter (as in Pope's mock epic, *The Rape of the Lock*). To call *Arthur Rex* a parody or burlesque, rather than a twentieth-century adaptation of the "Matter of Britain"—as Tennyson's *Idylls of the King* is a nineteenth-century adaptation—is to misread the novel. In fact, both in its earthy texture and elegaic wistfulness, in the elaborate weave of its vast interlace structure, Berger's version comes closer to the Gawain poet and to Malory than most of the interpreters in between. Mark Twain's *A Connecticut Yankee in King Arthur's Court* is a burlesque. *Arthur Rex* profoundly participates in, as it reinterprets, the values of chivalric romance. In a letter about a screenplay he'd read on the Arthur story, Berger spoke jokingly of his own preparation for his novel. The scriptwriter had apparently read "none of Malory, Chretien de Troyes, Wolfram von Eschenbach, Alf Tennyson, Dick Wagner's *Tristan* and *Parsifal* and the many other forerunners whose works I ransacked (including two books for children which were my principal sources). This unbelievable trashy practitioner had *invented* his own Arthurian narrative!" The comment is indicative of Berger's respect and familiar affection for the legend and its tellers, and his serious claim to a place among them.

Arthur Rex is not spoofing the unattainable dream of rightness, harmony and goodness for which Arthur stands, nor the splendor of heroism like Lancelot's, nor beauty like Guinivere's, nor love like Tristram's. The fall of Camelot is not mocked, but sorrowed over: ". . . some say he will return when the world is ready once more to celebrate honor and bravery and nobility, but methinks that is a long time yet." The book's bawdy comedy is no more anachronistic than Chaucer (in fact, Berger interpolates the Wife of Bath's tale into the plot), nor is the narrative style an antiquarian joke; it has the wit and whimsical charm of a Celtic illumination. In short, *Arthur Rex* is whole cloth—a twentieth-century weaver at work with medieval threads on a tapestry, not a cartoon.

It might seem that an easier case could be made for defining *Regiment of Women* as a social satire, despite Berger's claim that he doesn't write them. But considering that some readers have thought it a spoof of the women's movement, and others a feminist assault on chauvinism, if it is a satire, its social target is extremely ambiguous. A comparison with a straightforward satire like Orwell's *Animal Farm* reveals a fundamental difference in both intent and methodology. Both take the traditional satire form of the anti-Utopia: *Animal Farm* (like the fourth book of Swift's *Gulliver's Travels*) uses zoomorphic fable. *Regiment of Women* (like Butler's *Erewhon*, Huxley's *Brave New World* and Orwell's own *1984*) focuses on the struggle of a human sexual love against a futuristic totalitarian government's desexualizing, dehumanizing control. Orwell's target, in his parable of the rise of Napoleon the pig from revolutionary to tyrant, is as clear as a party slogan: Freedom good, totalitarianism bad. He tells us so. "Every line of serious work that I have written since 1936 has been written, directly or indirectly, against totalitari-anism." It is difficult to imagine Berger stating such an ideological credo, though I'm certain he is as opposed to dictators as he is to demagogues.

The comedy of *Animal Farm* derives from the substitution of animal for human stereotypes (the proletarian workhorse, the mob of sheep). In *Regiment of Women*, it is male and female sex role stereotypes that are reversed. The humor comes from incongruities that expose how inculturated these stereotypes are; transposed pronouns and adjectives shock: "You never knew when you might meet a sex criminal or, perhaps worse, a junkie desperate for funds with which to support her habit." The hero, once a very "masculine" that is, obsequious, love-hungry, weepy, frigid, and mechanically inept receptionist, who loves to cook and read books like "The Gentle Man's Guide to Needlepoint," who wears babydoll nightgowns and "very virile earrings," suddenly reveals an "effeminate streak of brutality" and strikes back at the thuggish women cops who've arrested him for putting on corduroy slacks and a plaid shirt. Berger extends this reversing conceit from attire to psychol-ogy and social position. Women are the generals, surgeons, lawyers, politi-cians, artists, athletes, and criminals. They are considered more intelligent, more aggressive, and less emotional: they run the world and create its art; they also start wars, rape, and aren't in touch with their feelings. All they talk about is "work and politics and sports and their bank accounts."

Men are secretaries and sex objects. They are considered charming, personal, sensitive, chattering, jealous, passive incompetents. Ultimately, the hero is brought to the realization that men have no power because they have penises, which make them vulnerable. "This and this alone is why men are basically inferior," why they need dolls and pets and can't play sports, why "men are made to be manipulated and penetrated." The ironies move in every direction, undercutting every position. It is absurd for women to behave like men; it was absurd for men to have behaved that way. It is absurd for men to behave like women; it was absurd for women to have behaved that way.

From their Huxleyish incubator hatcheries to the need for gas masks against a constant Pollution Alert, the regiment of women has made as much a botch of their brave new world as did any patriarchy. In describing that world, Berger turns to his anti-Utopian predecessors like Huxley and Orwell; in fact, his futuristic society is in many ways a comic version of the dreadful, loveless, mirthless Oceania of *1984*: The economy has collapsed under infla-tion; the cities are rotting (Central Park is a rubbish heap of compacted garbage beneath buildings); the caste system subjects all but a few elite to crowded dingy slums, harassment and deprivation; government control and censorship are pervasive (possession of photos of women nursing or of Hemingway's *Men Without Women* is illegal, Men's Libbers are subject to castration), and are thwarted only by computer breakdown; the doublethink Newspeak jargon of the Female Establishment is used to enforce orthodoxy and control the past. History is rewritten to delete all reference to any period when women were not considered superior to men—artists like Thomasina Gainsborough and Leonarda, painter of the *Mono Liso*, are glorified. It is possible that even the name of Berger's hero (Georgie Cornell) is a (subliminal at least) reference to George Orwell's influence.

Like Orwell's unwilling hero, Smith, Georgie joins the Underground. "The Brothers" indoctrinate him to see himself as a slave of a power structure which must be brought down, without, however, men taking on the brutal natures of their oppressors. Like Smith, Georgie learns that the Underground is a handy, harmless Establishment tool. Like Smith, Georgie is brought into war against the State first by circumstance, then by affection for a women; in this case, Harriet, a gentle F.B.I. agent committed for treatment as a recidivist after confessing that as a child she preferred dolls to guns. If Berger is "saying" that power corrupts—whether men or women hold it— he is also "saying" that collective protests against those systems of power are not only futile but ridiculous. The sadistic establishment psychiatrist (who charges Georgie $300 an hour for her anal rape therapy) and the tender liberal psychiatrist (who wants to help raise his Basic Awareness) are equally inane. Government and Underground are both ludicrous. The sweeping zaniness closes round into a self-contained whole, dissipating our indignation; social satire, while pervasive, is finally coincidental. Our responses are instead those elicited by all of Berger's comedies, whatever the generic model they have incorporated. One, we share the aesthetic delight he himself has in the traditions of form and their capacity to release characters and language. Two, we are brought comically, as with Beckett, to confront our *metaphysical* (as opposed to our social) bewilderment. Three, we share the emotional yearning for human love, harmony and nobility that is persistently drawing Berger towards those romance elements of his tradition that help make his novels true comedies, always a much more serious (and moral) business than burlesque.

This third response is evoked, for example, by the end of *Regiment of Women*. Unlike the defeated lovers of *1984*, Georgie and Harriet are not destroyed or coopted by the system, nor do they defeat it. Instead, they leave it—to flee to the Maine wilderness; and there, by a series of mishaps that burn up all their supplies and clothes, they literally begin the race anew; each "a blank tablet on which anything might be inscribed," as they stand naked in the Edenic lake. They will cultivate their garden, and raise a family, and presumably take turns "being boss." The retreat to the "green world" is the impulse not of satire but of comedy, at least of the branch of comedy that replaced the satirical conventions and societal setting of classical comedy with the romance conventions of comedic writers from Chaucer and Shakespeare to Dickens and Joyce. The impulse is a strong one in Berger, as well as a complex and ambiguous one. The comedic movement is towards communal harmony (usually symbolized by the sexual communion of marriage that ends the novel or play). The commitment of comedy is to the triumph of life (Falstaff leaps up from the dead, Tom Jones is cut free from the noose, Molly Bloom says yes). In addition to the technical opportunities that traditional comedic narrative modes give Berger to explore his verbal craft—comedy, being social, is always in some sense "about" language— these earlier modes draw him as well by the pull of the earlier *values* of comedy: communion, order, and harmony. So high is his esteem for these values, so low is his estimation of the modern world, that he cannot locate his comedy in a contemporary setting, but chooses forms that give him generic access to such themes. It is as if the further he sets his stage from "modern civilization" (in his view, a misnomer, anyhow), the more room his characters have to feel "the old verities" (the nobility with which Old Lodge Skins dies, the graced courtesy with which Sir Gawain lives); the more place there is for them in the circle of comedy's dance.

The circle is Berger's persistent metaphor for the "at-oneness" into which comedy invites us, and against which—in life—disorder and estrangement have almost inevitably triumphed. Camelot's Round Table of chivalric knights is broken by the forces of the serpent Mordred. The Cheyenne of *Little Big Man* are "doomed as knights in stone castles." For the Indians, "time turns in a circle, present and past, living and ghost, for the Mystery is continuous." This "mystical circle" is "the round of the earth and the sun, and life and death too, for the disjunction between them is a matter of appearance and not the true substance." The Cheyenne, who see "no power in a square," are destroyed by the white race of "powerful death lovers," who have turned the earth into a dead "world of sharp corners." Theirs is the race that "progressed" from covered wagons to the cars that Buddy sells in *Sneaky People*, and that Buddy's descendants ultimately drove to those dead-end, isolated cul-de-sacs of suburban developments where Earl Keese runs afoul of his *Neighbors*, where all is absurdist disjunction between appearances, (substance, long lost), where communion is impossible because "communication" is a maddening dialogue of non sequiturs whose terrible inconsequentiality has even more terrible consequences.

And so Berger returns to chivalric Camelot, to the Iliadic Old West, to the codes of honor of 1930s detective fiction, to the 1930s small towns of his childhood's midwest, in both *Sneaky People* and *The Feud* (1983), where sidewalks curve, connecting life to life, and if there are families of Montagues and Capulets feuding, there are also Romeos and Juliets. In saying that the conservatism intrinsic to comedy is congenial to Berger, I should quickly add that he is no sentimentalist, nostalgically afloat in a prettified past. Compare, for instance, the whore-with-a-heart-of-gold-who-beautifully-initiates-the-young-boy in Faulkner's *The Reivers* with the same character in Berger's *Sneaky People*. Faulkner's character marries her simple, noble knight, and they name their first child after that young boy; Berger's character realizes her knight is a cad, considers entering a convent, finds it closed, and returns to prostitution. Nor is Berger a romantic primitivist. Jack Crabb

(*Little Big Man*) honors the Indians as noble, natural, vital, well-mannered, sane and heroic; he also finds them crude, nasty, smelly, barbaric, and ignorant. His story of the harmonizing "magic circle" in which the tribe captures 1,000 antelope is followed by the story of Indian women and children exuberantly scalping and disembowelling dead and wounded enemies after a raid. If Jack has the all-American Huck Finn itch to escape ("I got to go off now. . . . The trouble is I don't think I can ever be civilized"), he also admires the white "triumph over the empty wilderness" and all the artifacts and aspirations of white civilization. He both hates and glories in General George Armstrong Custer. So does Berger, just as he thinks Lancelot is both a magnificent hero and a dangerous idiot. That is also Guinivere's opinion, but then Guinivere is as wise and irrational (and as incomprehensible to the narrator) as the Lady of the Lake, with her true magic, is to Merlin, with his wizard's tricks. Almost all Berger's women live in this sealed, ineluctable universe, baffling and alarming to the men around them, and if Berger could be said to have single social leitmotif, it is probably Freud's ultimate question: "What is it that women want?"

What Peggy Tumulty in *Who Is Teddy Villanova?* wants is the hero, Russel Wren; that she gets him, and the book ends with their first embrace, is another example of Berger's move towards comedy; in this case, against the grain of his literary model—the hard-boiled detective novel. *Villanova* is as close as Berger has come to parody (which may be why he says it was the easiest book to write), but, again, the parodic elements are ultimately coincidental to the comedic core. All the conventions are here—the Chandler/Hammett private-eye, the intricate (if not undecipherable) plot, the eccentric cast, the continual beatings, sudden corpses, the sexuality, the grimy urban world; everything from Sam Spade's loyal, tough secretary and fat man villain to Marlowe's stained washbowl and Lew Archer's sagging couch. The opening line, "Call me Russel Wren" is an echo of the "My name's Marlowe" style. However, it is also, of course, a paraphrase of the opening line of *Moby Dick* ("Call me Ishmael"). And when we immediately learn that detective Wren is an out-of-work English literature teacher and a playwright, whose polysyllabic diction and erudite references bespeak his lost profession, and whose interrogation by a policeman named Zwingli (partners—Knox and Calvin) takes the form of a literary oral exam, we are prepared for something other, and more than, a stylistic send-up of the melancholic machismo sentimental cynicism at the core of the American detective genre.

What we have is not a parodic exaggeration of the style, plot and characters of this narrative tradition, but their celebration, and their interpolation into a typical Berger comedy: its coupling of romance (the relationship between Russel and Peggy; the fanciful adventures and chivalric codes of the detective) with metaphysical humor. By the last, odd phrase, I mean that the comic troubles of Berger's characters are likely to be epistemological in nature. The answer to the question, Who is Teddy Villanova?, is not to be solved by Joe Friday's "just the facts, ma'am." Wren (like Earl Keese in *Neighbors*) is frantically trying to sort out what he can know to be "real" from what proves to be "fictional," a mere appearance, and trying to come to some conclusion about *how* to differentiate the two—if, indeed, it is possible, or meaningful, to do so. Whereas the plots of the detective novel unravel to reveal the real threads that connect them, *Villanova's* labyrinthine plot unravels to reveal its utter fabrication. All the events (arrests, conspiracies, murders) prove to be totally "false," as it were, a literary creation of one Sam Polidor (a better playwright than the hero), who has hired actors and staged scenes entirely for the purpose of persuading Wren to vacate his Manhattan office so that Sam can sell the building. In other words, Sam is a master plotter in the Prospero vein, and the story of Berger's novel is Sam's creation.

The fabrications through which Earl Keese doggedly gropes for the "truth," despite the constant lesson that seeing is not believing, nor words immutable, reveal more profoundly the epistemological roots to Berger's comedy, and lie behind his comment that *Neighbors'* "morality is metaphysical and has no social significance," although critics were likely to think it a social satire. (And indeed, Christopher Lehmann-Haupt was to sum up: "*Neighbors* parodies all the rituals of neighborliness.") The abundant burlesque elements in Berger's work (the avalanching hyperboles and incongruities, the sudden plummets from sublimity to slapstick) are not there to mock his literary progenitors, or to lash society for its own betterment; they are there because "the world" makes no sense, and innate (and comic) in the human condition is the desire that it should make sense.

There is a wide gulf between those comedic circles of harmony, order, courtesy and honor for which Berger has an undeniable attachment, and the existential disjunction from "Reality" in which he perceives us necessarily to live. (We cannot be, nor would we choose to be Old Lodge Skins, for whom the universe is "self-explanatory.") Fiction is Berger's bridge across the gulf. He is careful to insist that the bridge cannot reach over into the world. Nearly all his comments about fiction emphasize its self-containment, its distinction from life. It is "an alternative to reality." Arthur Rex "was never historical, but everything he did was true." The "editor" of *Little Big Man* (whose middle name in this picaresque comic epic is, significantly, "Fielding") worries whether Jack Crabb is history's "most neglected hero or a liar of insane proportions." His concern is irrelevant. The Preface to *Killing Time* tells us that "a work of fiction is a construction of language, and otherwise a lie."

Thomas Berger goes about comedy's business of choosing life, by killing time. The "hero" of his book of that title is an insane idiot (in Dostoevski's sense), and an artist. He murders three people. He does so to kill Time. "To kill Time is to know God." By killing these people, he "Realizes" them, creates their eternity. "Realization," he explains to his disturbed lawyer, is the culmination of art, and the transcendence of Time. "Realization" is the function of fiction. The achievement of the best fiction-makers, like Thomas Berger, is to triumph over Time, not by the mocking murders of their predecessors, but by continual re-creation. Prefacing *Who Is Teddy Villanova?* is a line of Baudelaire's: "We are all celebrating some funeral." Berger is not announcing here the death of a narrative form, nor his plan parodically to dance on the grave. The celebration is a commemoration. The ceremony is a new work of art. Baudelaire's line is from "On the Heroism of Modern Life." The heroism of Thomas Berger as a modern novelist—the risky and as yet insufficiently acknowledged or rewarded heroism—is to honor the traditions in whose line he takes his place, and whose forms he makes uniquely his own, to go about the act of writing without either self-heralding or the trumpets of the academy, and to keep on quietly creating fictions.

Note

1.   Unless otherwise noted, quotations from Berger are taken from his letters to the author.

Crazy in Berlin as Ethnic Comedy

MYRON SIMON

> There is no native American but the redskin; we others are something else at
> a slight remove, which cannot be changed; our names and looks and surely
> some complexion of the corpuscles themselves are to some old line peculiar,
> else we should blow away without identity. So [Reinhart] believed.[1]

To praise a novel as national or universal in its appeal is, of course, the
conventional way to make a claim for the range and endurance of its meaning;
whereas to call it by some regional or ethnic name constitutes just as obviously
a smaller estimate of its importance. So I preface my reading of Thomas
Berger's first novel as the richly comic extension of a German-American
literary tradition that includes Dreiser's *Jennie Gerhardt* (1911) and Ruth
Suckow's *Country People* (1924) with a few distinctions meant to suspend, at
least for the space of my reading, so arbitrary and overly simple a judgment
of ethnic writing.

    Crazy in Berlin (1958) is not by another of the Jewish-American writers
who gained prominence in the 1950s, although some of its early readers
may have supposed that it was; it is the work of a German-American. Berger's
unmistakably deep sense of compound nationality doubtless has behind it a
long and complicated history of feeling foreign in America and Germany—
and yet somehow at home in both places as well. In its general outlines,
such a life is common to all hyphenated Americans; but the *qualia* of each
ethnic community's experience come to embody something like species of a
generic foreignness, making each immigrant tradition unique in certain
respects. Such lives contain resonances that may elude even the most acutely
sensible of outside observers. Despite their ethnic subject matter, neither
G. W. Cable's *Old Creole Days* (1879) nor Willa Cather's *My Ántonia* (1918)
is really ethnic literature. In both it is *place* that matters most and is so
brilliantly evoked, not a specifically ethnic sensibility through which events
are given their special character. Clearly, good books about an ethnic-group
experience in America have been written by non-group members like Cather
and Cable; and writers from the immigrant communities have sometimes

Reprinted with slight adaptation by permission of *Studies in American Humor* 2, no. 1 (Spring 1983):
33–44.

written books in which there is little or no discernible evidence of their ethnicity. Nevertheless, a useful distinction may be drawn between the author of a novel about a German-American who *is* what he writes about and the author who is not, although it cannot be assumed that the book issuing from ethnic experience itself—as distinct from observation of it—will be the better one.

Further, any labeling of a writer's work must be partial, must be qualified and expanded when measured against all that it purports to describe. Shifts in a writer's public and fictive lives, motives, and contemplated audience inevitably alter his angle of vision and style. *Sister Carrie* (1900) and *Jennie Gerhardt* derive ultimately from closely related events in Dreiser's early life, but only the latter took the form of an ethnic novel through Dreiser's detailed emphasis upon the deficits accruing to Jennie from her membership in an impoverished, fragmented, and socially inferior immigrant family. Similarly, *Crazy in Berlin* and *Neighbors* (1980) proceed alike from a moral intelligence continually at war with most of human nature and nearly all of modernity; but the label "black humorist" so often applied to Berger is more applicable to the author of *Neighbors* than it is to the muted idealist who has faithfully summoned Carlo Reinhart into being. Like Dreiser before him, Berger is an ethnic American who has written both ethnic and non-ethnic stories, as well as stories only incidentally or impurely ethnic.

Understandably eager to assert Berger's true eminence as an American comic novelist, his defenders usually attempt to rescue him from neglect by calling attention to his stylistic complexity and parodistic skills, to his mastery of black humor and possession of a postmodern sensibility by means of which he has penetrated the deepest existential reaches of the human condition. These claims—each with its demonstrable basis in Berger's large and strikingly varied body of work—are clearly intended to elevate his ranking among contemporary American novelists and to make the case for the permanence of his achievement. So oriented, Berger's admirers—from Harvey Swados to Brooks Landon—have minimized and frequently overlooked entirely the ethnic dimensions of *Crazy in Berlin* and the novels that succeeded it.[2]

If certain of Berger's novels have gone unnoticed as ethnic literature, that is surely not because he has masked their ethnicity. It is the case, rather, that German-American writing is not one of the commanding or urgent categories of American ethnic literature, if one may judge from representative anthologies and scholarship. With the exception of Dreiser's humorous dialect story "Old Rogaum and His Theresa," I find no German-American writing in the anthologies of ethnic literature. And Wayne C. Miller's *Comprehensive Bibliography for the Study of American Minorities* (1976) mystifyingly omits from its short list of German-American writers any reference to such valuable work as the Jacoby's Corners pastorals of Jake Falstaff and the popular dialect verses of Kurt M. Stein. Since the Germans were among the largest and most literate of America's immigrant communities and possessed the most extensive immigrant press, it seems odd that more attention has not been given to the German-American literary tradition.

Perhaps this near omission of the Germans from contemporary surveys of American ethnic writing reflects the fact that, like other participants in the pre-1880 "older" immigration from Western Europe, they have been sufficiently assimilated into mainstream working-class and middle-class culture to no longer register convincingly as an ethnic community. For example, Reinhart's parents—in *Reinhart in Love* (1962) and *Vital Parts* (1970)— betray in a steady flow of malapropisms not the confusions of their German-speaking parents or grandparents but the semi-literacy of rural midwestern tradesmen and mechanics. German only in their names and in vague family memories, they are by all outward signs small-town American proletarians. Moreover, the diligence, thrift, and formidable intellectual traditions of the Germans surely earned them gradual acceptance as successful American farmers, businessmen, and professionals.

But even this "older" immigration achieved something less than the full assimilation early envisioned by the dominant nativist culture, the American Anglo-Saxons. If only symbolically, ethnicity survives the loss of distinctive language, customs, community structure in the second, third, and succeeding immigrant generations; for, as Glazer and Moynihan have noted, ethnic groups "are continually recreated by new experiences in America."[3] For example, the wartime hatred of Germans, which reached one climax in the hysteria of 1917–1918 and another with the concentration-camp discoveries of 1945, brought the experience of being a German-American closer to that of the "newer" immigrants, the Southern and Eastern Europeans and the Asians whose vast admissions beginning about 1880 aroused so many misgivings about both the practicability and the desirability of full assimilation.[4]

Reinhart has grown up between the wars, when "nobody, least of all the boys of German stem, served willingly on the Kaiser's side in war games" (p. 31). An imaginative boy, he finds in his grandfather's German origins— preserved only in a letter from Berlin and a book of Nuremberg scenes redolent of medieval times—a desirable alternative to "ugly-dull" suburban Ohio. He sadly finds nothing to appropriate from his parents' vacant and defeated lives, nothing of value transmitted through them to him. Thus, he is culturally starved and anomic, a classic third-generation product of assimilation in his sense of loss and consequent reaching back to an ancestral tradition. Fair and blonde, his size and strength are also—by association with his grandfather—confirmations of his older nationality. He chooses the more European weightlifting over American football as his high school sport, and dreamily pursues the study of German at college. When he reaches Berlin as a twenty-one-year-old corporal in the Army of Occupation, Reinhart is overwhelmed by "the sheer grandeur of his geographical position" and concludes that "if he had any structure beneath the meretricious American veneer, it was one he shared with" his German relatives (pp. 5, 66).

However, if at home he is not a genuine American but, rather, "a good, sturdy *German* type" (as evidenced by his consumption of German potato salad with vinegar, German cole slaw with bacon grease, German coffee cake with butter-lakes, residence in a German bill-paying home, and the observation that he was going to be a big German like his grandfather), Reinhart soon recognizes that in his "ancient homeland" too he is "something different" (p. 15). Accordingly, he acquires a singularly complicated awareness of what it means to be a reflective third-generation German-American in the aftermath of the second World War. He knows that one may be a native-born, English-speaking American citizen and yet be despised as a German; and he learns that one may be German in physical attributes and ancestry and yet remain an ineluctably American outsider fatally incapable of distinguishing the fake from the real in Berlin.

"Something different" in Germany as well as in America, Reinhart nevertheless cleaves to both. Although he is at home "as nowhere else" in the "splendid, dear, degrading society" of U.S. Army billets, a community "grounded on common inconvenience" (p. 304) and therefore suitably emblematic of social intermingling throughout America, he feels no less at home in the Bachs' damp cellar apartment where decency obscurely survives in over-civilized, ingeniously oblique arguments whose "every word, every nuance" Reinhart felt he understood, although in his Ohio college he had "almost flunked German 2" (p. 345). Holding fast to both worlds, he can be surprisingly tolerant even of their representative scoundrels. Through an ironized mixture of sympathy and satire, Reinhart acknowledges the shallowness of such American dreams as Lieutenant Harry Pound's vision of a used-car dealership as the key to a golden post-war life in Los Angeles. Similarly, with every allowable charity and a final qualified acceptance, he contemplates a far more dangerous survival artist, the metamorphic Schatzi.

There is a beast, however, that haunts these explorations of the German in the American, the American in the German *manqué*. Whether at home or in Berlin, Reinhart cannot escape the nearly universal identification of the word *German* with "a kind of foulness" (p. 15). Characteristically reluctant to injure anyone himself, he is hurt by the use of the word *German* as a synonym for unfeeling brutality. "I'm sick of being made to feel a swine because I'm of German descent," he angrily responds to his inimical friend, the Jewish-American Nathan Schild (p. 365). And he is obviously bothered by the unhesitating "liberal" opinion that Germans are inherently tyrannical, militaristic, suicidal, irresponsible, and mad (pp. 46–48). Such categorical hatred, no matter how over-generalized, obliges Reinhart to confront more truthfully the identity he seeks to repossess, the identity lodged perhaps in the very complexion of his corpuscles. A large part of Reinhart's "craziness" in Berlin is provoked by his awakening from an adolescent dream of German history "to see the terrible landscape of actuality" (p. 47).

In Berlin, he "at last understood that the complement to his long self-identification with Germanness had been a resolve never to know the German actuality" (p. 176). Here Reinhart learns to feel intermittent loathing for his German self but, simultaneously, to hate the experience of being stupidly hated as a brutal Kraut. The cruelly unfair experience of being hated abstractly, without regard either to his personal deserts or to that humanely Enlightened part of the German mind embodied in Frederick the Great and in Goethe, gives Reinhart his special relation to other ethnics similarly burdened. His attraction to Nathan Schild and, later in the "Reinhart" tetralogy, to black-American Splendor Mainwaring and his son does not arise from "liberal" piety, for which he feels only contempt. It comes from a suffering not the same as theirs but proximate, and it is expressed not guiltily but unsentimentally and sometimes comically.

In the densely plotted and sub-plotted *Crazy in Berlin*, the central pairing is Reinhart with the Communist "traitor" Schild. Given the novel's publication in 1958 when Jewish-American sensitivity to criticism was especially high (owing, for example, to the trial of the Rosenbergs and the resulting linkage of Jewish political liberalism with treason), Berger could hardly have assumed a greater risk of being misunderstood than he did in having the story turn ironically upon his searching comparison of a thoroughly decent German-American *mensch* and an arrogantly ineffectual Jewish-American traitor. Contrary to the reader's expectations, it is Schild who is the class-conscious officer demanding the respect due to rank, while Reinhart is the enlisted man with a strong instinct for democratic fellowship. They are both the children of foreigners in America and both speak German (Schild far more fluently than Reinhart); but Reinhart sifts through the ruins of Berlin in order to confront the worst in his Germanness and to determine whether anything decent has survived the *Reich*, while Schild coldly denies his history to serve an abstract Communist future.[5] Both are murderers; but the German has murdered with his bare hands to save a friend, the Jew by informing on a friend in a neurotic act of betrayal.

That they ultimately become friends tells us more about Reinhart than Schild. This German, ironically, is the man for whom Schild has been waiting all his life, the man who, knowing him Jewish, would be perfectly indifferent to the fact. It was an article of Schild's Communist faith that in the future workers' State "there will be no separations of one man from another" and that any means might justifiably be employed, any "decency" violated to bring this new, undifferentiated man into being (pp. 201–204). Comically, when Lichenko enters Schild's life as the first of these new men, he proves to be (as Schild early recognizes but cannot persuade himself to believe) a Soviet-army deserter in flight from everything Communism represents. He does not, in fact, regard Schild as a Jew; but his indifference, as Schild mordantly observes, is merely self-preoccupation:

> In Lichenko's egocentric vision he knew now that he had never been more, or less, than a host fat for the parasiting, a mere object, a thing to be used, not comrade nor ally, not even a man—*and therefore not a Jew*. (p. 202)

Reinhart, seemingly a provincial, is more universal in outlook, more comprehensive in his sympathies and understanding than Schild and other "liberal" intellectuals he encounters. His open fascination with the world in its full particularity is uncompromised by any ruling theory or impulse to exclude.

Reinhart's way of addressing the question of anti-Semitism is the same as his method of addressing the existence of Buchenwald—of dealing with those Germans who murdered and those who could be bribed not to murder: "Facts must be faced" without resort either to the simplifying rhetoric that divides humanity into good men and bad or to such historical abstractions as "German militarism" and "international Jewry" (p. 67). He perceives in Berlin that SS men are not necessarily cowards and bullies "who will fight only someone weaker" and that blackmailers may display "a strange, mad kind of courage" (p. 177). In confronting "the German actuality," he saw that "Here all the known qualities of humanity had been united with their contradictions" and, consequently, that "guilt could be confessed to only in a lie of the guiltless," *i.e.*, in the rhetoric and abstractions of the oppressed (p. 178).

Those who have been victimized come to enjoy a kind of moral leverage, so that in time they assume—in their very desolation—a commanding position. Although certain that he could break Schild in two, Reinhart feels "vaguely afraid of him" (p. 119). Moreover, while he is clearly offended by Trudchen's anti-Semitic outburst against Schild, Reinhart still recognizes, somewhat resentfully, the advantage of a two-thousand-year grievance in allowing one to feel sure that the burden of guilt always rests somewhere else (p. 129). This too is a fact that must be faced.

Schild conforms perfectly to Reinhart's observation that "Jews are sometimes know-it-alls and their manners could stand improvement, but that doesn't have anything to do with decency and is anyway a proof of their freedom" (p. 364). That is, it is true that Schild is an arrogant, untidy sectarian; but it is also true—and, for Reinhart, of far greater moment—that he finally reclaims his humanity from the Party and that he dies because he has turned his back on his adversary to save a friend. In Berger's comedy of reversals, the German is the survivor, not the Jew, who dies trying to help the German.

Such complications of perspective may seem outrageous in their implied exculpation of evil, but the omniscient narrative focus of *Crazy in Berlin* is that of a moralist steadily opposing himself to hatred and cruelty in their myriad forms and opposing himself equally to any rush to judgment. It is evident that Reinhart genuinely admires and likes the Jews as much as any person may be said to like and admire a whole community, but the facts must still be faced: the anomalies of human behavior make moral determinations difficult and unreliable when one proceeds, as any good observer will, case by case. Reinhart's running commentary on Jewishness, together with Bach's brilliant monologue on Jewish-Gentile relations, reflects an insider's knowledge of Jewish behavior; and the Berger papers in the Boston University Library indicate that he had studied Jewish culture extensively before creating Nathan Schild and, indeed, before creating Reinhart, an "unusually observant" (p. 119) third-generation German-American with exceptional empathy for those who are instantly perceived as Jewish or German before they are perceived as anyone else. When Reinhart observes that Schild is the kind of Jew who made him feel responsible for having done something nasty which he had forgotten but the Jew had not, and when this perception reminds him that "the other thing about Jews" is that "when they weren't eying you with suspicion, they never saw you at all" (p. 118), we are in the presence of life observed and understood with an accuracy that is uncanny.

Nor have these complicating details obscured Reinhart's other, and to him more important, perception that Schild is a "decent" human being who "had buried his humanness so deep that one could bring it to the surface only by outraging him" (p. 217). Berger's satire is directed not at Jewishness but at the repressive side of "liberal" attitudes and behavior. Indeed, the Stalinist mentality has never been more subtly examined, more coolly anatomized. Berger is so much more interested in and appreciative of human differences than ethnic predecessors of his like Dreiser and Mencken that there is no trace in his work of the reservations about Jews which is to be found in theirs.

It is as fitting as comic that *Crazy in Berlin* should begin with its hero's unwitting performance of a gross act—"taking a leak" on a statue of Frederick the Great—that he knows to be a violation of decency when he discovers what he is doing even as he does it, for "decent" is Berger's often repeated key word. Like the hedgehog of Archilochus, Reinhart knows "one big thing." Decency is his "single, universal organizing principle in terms of which alone all that [he is and says] has significance."[6] Bach somewhat ironically refers to the Americans as "one-hundred thirty millions of decent chaps" (p. 144), but means by that only that Americans are superficially affable or agreeable. Reinhart, however, makes decency his summarizing term for a small body of specific injunctions: a decent person does not hurt others, a decent person responds generously to others in need of help even when it is not expedient to help, and so on. He is deeply suspicious of easy "liberal" schemes for the transformation of individuals and their societies because he judges the problems and deficiencies of humanity to be unsolvable and unsuppliable by utopian means. Together with his belief in the persistence of ethnic identities ("our names and looks and surely some complexion of the corpuscles themselves are to some old line peculiar"), Reinhart believes only in "an idea of the possibility of simple decency" (p. 48). Himself a manifestly decent person, he is saddened and occasionally made indignant by the indecencies of Germans and Americans. But he also finds in both cultures signs that nourish his faith in the "possibility of a simple decency."

Berger's minimalist ethic grows out of his conviction that when the mystery is great and the creature limited, its equipment for living must be unambiguous enough to be grasped and applied, for he posits a world in which "People from different countries really don't understand each other" (p. 418). Like Henry James, Berger shows us a world filled with people from different circumstances and places talking endlessly at cross-purposes. So, as against dialectics and apologetics, Berger proposes a vocabulary of moral actions as profound as they are simple and communicable by gentle ways. Reinhart remembers his grandfather as "kindly" (p. 32), and tells his father—an inappropriate father to him in so many other ways—that he is "unique" because he has never been "mean," "false," or "cruel."[7] In specific terms, therefore, Reinhart's ancestry has supplied him with an aversion to cruelty and a disposition to kindness that make him seem a fool and blunderer at times but that make him a saving human presence as well, if only through his inherent incapacity to take advantage of or to injure others.

Separated by so much else, Reinhart and Schild are drawn together powerfully by the simple recognition of their concern for each other. When Schild says that he interferes in Reinhart's life simply because of friendship, Reinhart "dared not admit to himself how deeply he was touched," for he believes friendship to be the only good reason "for doing anything in the world" (p. 318). Although Reinhart and Schild share a common decency, Reinhart's decency operates as his single all-comprehending principle, whereas Schild's is at best a mediate virtue until the convulsive release of his humanity in the final episodes of the novel. His failure to understand at once Reinhart's motives in seeking an abortionist for Veronica effectively measures the moral distance between the two at that point (p. 319).

Reinhart is Berger's German-American embodiment of a homely, particularized idealism that turns away from what Marcus Klein has called the "terror beyond evil"[8] and from depersonalized, ultimately repressive political remedies for it toward simple acts of humanity and refusals to act inhumanely. The ambiguous ending of *Crazy in Berlin* is prefigured in Reinhart's feelings toward Schild when he angrily takes Schild to be Veronica's irresponsible secret lover and the heartless exploiter of a wretched former concentration-camp prisoner. His heart tells him that, even if Schild had "raped Veronica and murdered Schatzi," he could not raise his hand against him. "Man, man," Reinhart thought, "one cannot live without pity" (p. 308). From this vantage point, it is possible to understand Reinhart's sense of kinship to the medical officer "whose face was manifestly German-American," an

honest if naive man expressing wonderment that murderous Nazis and Communists alike are "just fellows, people like anybody else in the beginning."
This reflection, with its refusal to be vindictive or to hate oneself by association, fortifies Reinhart's slender faith in the possibility of refraining from
harming others. Reinhart will join neither the liberals nor the reactionaries,
for he perceives that fiercely partisan loyalties inescapably undermine "the
precious quality of humanness." Reinhart stood, therefore, "with the doctor,
two dense and heavy light-complexioned oafs who saw the mellow where
the bright boys detected the sinister" (pp. 244–245).

Like Saul Bellow, Bernard Malamud, and Ralph Ellison in their efforts
to transcend alienation, Berger knows that—after the unprecedented inhu-
manities revealed in 1945—"we are all on the edge of dissolution" and that,
accordingly, "plain necessity" dictates that the human community must be
made at least a bare possibility. Marcus Klein argues that such a making,
however narrowly qualified, moves beyond alienation to celebration, to an
affirmation of the possibility of "restoration and love" in at least the small,
domestic details of life. The hope of the individual must be "to make and
preserve," at least tentatively, "a home in this world . . . for lack of any
better present possibility." Klein rightly notes that the "technical term" for
this "mood" is comedy because, in pursuing "accommodation," a person
"exercises his wits and thereby lives within his dilemma, and managing to
live within it he proposes the possibility of living."[9]

It is in precisely this high, philosophical sense that *Crazy in Berlin* is
most transcendently comic. Berger's comedy is, of course, most evidently
on display in his indefatigably fertile wordplay, as in his subtle use of class
dialect and his rendering of German-English linguistic confusions. It is also
conspicuous in his mockery of American provincialism and in his yet more
savage ridicule of human meanness and low cunning on both sides of the
Atlantic. But, more affectingly, Berger broadly exposes Reinhart to the
antics of humanity—from Trudchen to Lori, from Schatzi to Bach and
Doctor Knebel, from Captain St. George to Schild. And he endows him
with enough irony "to confront the ideal with the actual and not go mad"
(pp. 247–248).

That is, Berger's loftiest comedy arises from what Kenneth Burke describes as "the methodic view of human antics," a view poised always "on
the verge of the most disastrous tragedy." In this view, we have the comic
writer chastising fools and villains but humanly realizing "that *all* people
are exposed to situations in which they must act as fools, that *every* insight
contains its own special kind of blindness." The heroic, triumphant aspect
of comic action is its continuing study of man in society, its ongoing search—
guided by realism and humility—for a perspective that is "charitable but
not gullible."[10] It is in this sense that Reinhart is most profoundly a comic
character. Sometimes taken to be a fool or clown, he is neither. Sustained

above all by decency, his own and his recognition of it in others who have never willingly hurt anybody, Reinhart wryly accepts and even celebrates the world through his material acts of pity and charity. Such a perspective lies behind the ambiguity of *Crazy in Berlin*'s ending. Reinhart has discovered the viciousness so expertly masked by Schatzi's many disguises, but Schatzi makes the imposition of justice more complicated by swiftly citing every conceivable mitigating factor. If, these arguments notwithstanding, Reinhart has "betrayed" Schatzi, the nature of the betrayal remains unclear, suspended. Nothing, then, is concluded; the celebration, a quiet one at best, continues.

Like those early American voices of democratic fellowship Hawthorne and Melville, Berger observes that "all we have in this great ruined Berlin of existence, this damp cellar of life, this constant damage in need of repair, is single, lonely, absurd-and-serious selves; and the only villainy is to let them pass beyond earshot" (pp. 319–320). In his portrayal of a "lonely, absurd-and-serious" German-American clinging stubbornly to his humanity, Berger—like Ellison in *Invisible Man* (1952) and Malamud in *The Assistant* (1957)—has written one of the few truly indispensable ethnic novels in American literature.

Notes

1. *Crazy in Berlin* (New York, 1958), p. 48. All subsequent page references are to this edition.

2. Harvey Swados, "An American in Berlin," *The New Leader* (December 15, 1958), p. 24. In a letter to Ihab Hassan dated November 4, 1962 (in the Berger papers at the Boston University Library), Berger identifies Swados as the critic who launched his career with his "eloquent and tireless" efforts in behalf of *Crazy in Berlin*. See also Brooks Landon's Twayne volume on Berger (Boston, 1989).

3. Nathan Glazer and Daniel P. Moynihan, *Beyond the Melting Pot*, Second Edition (Cambridge, Mass., 1970), p. 17. See also Herbert Gans, "Symbolic Ethnicity: The Future of Ethnic Groups and Cultures in America," *Ethnic and Racial Studies*, 2 (1979), 1–20; and Richard D. Alba, *Ethnic Identity* (New Haven, 1990).

4. In *German-Americans and the World War*, Carl Wittke points out that "The war precipitated a violent, hysterical, concerted movement to eradicate everything German from American civilization. . . . practically everything that could be labeled with the hated German name, or could be traced to a German origin, came under the ban, as the passions aroused by the war threatened to divide the American population permanently into a pro and an anti-German group. German-Americans suddenly suffered from the hatred and persecution of large numbers of their fellow Americans with whom they had once lived in harmony, good neighborliness, and mutual respect" (Columbus, Ohio, 1936), p. 163. See also John A. Hawgood, *The Tragedy of German-America* (New York, 1940), pp. 292–308.

5. A member of the anti-Stalinist left in New York during the early 1950s, Berger contributed to *The New Leader* and was a librarian at the Rand School of Social Science, thereby allying himself with the democratic socialist opposition to authoritarian Communism. He was contemptuous of the intellectualized cruelty of Stalinists who had surrendered individual will to the achievement of power, and praised both George Orwell's *Homage to Catalonia*

and Czeslaw Milosz's *The Captive Mind* for their attacks on Stalinism and their example of simple decency. The Berger papers in the Boston University Library contain much evidence of the political perspectives out of which Nathan Schild was invented.

6. Isaiah Berlin, *The Hedgehog and the Fox* (New York, 1957), p. 7. The Berger papers contain the following note in which Berger draws upon his reading of Edmund Wilson's article "The Scrolls from the Dead Sea" in the May 14, 1955 issue of *The New Yorker*: "Great rabbi Hillel . . . said to Gentile who had challenged him to convert him by teaching the whole of the Torah while Gentile stood on one foot: 'What is hateful to thee, do not unto thy fellow: this is the whole law.' "

7. *Reinhart in Love* (New York, 1962), pp. 11, 13.

8. Marcus Klein, *After Alienation* (Cleveland, 1965), p. 295. First published in 1962.

9. *After Alienation*, pp. 30, 276, 294–296.

10. Kenneth Burke, *Attitudes toward History*, Second Edition (Los Altos, California, 1959), pp. xiii, 41, 106–107, 166–171. First published in 1937.

Alien Encounter: Thomas Berger's *Neighbors* as a Critique of Existential Humanism

JOHN CARLOS ROWE

Those encounters which counteract themselves because they are organized, those encounters to which good will, busy-body behavior and canny desire for power tirelessly exhort us, are simply covers for spontaneous actions that have become impossible.

—Theodor Adorno, *The Jargon of Authenticity* (1964)

The few scholarly critics to have written about Thomas Berger have placed him in various post-World War II literary movements or schools. Berger's distinctive mode from *Crazy in Berlin* (1958) to his most recent novel, *The Feud* (1983), has been to parody well-established literary forms, including the western legend, Arthurian romance, detective-thriller, the war novel, local-color regionalism, sentimental romance, even the serial novel. Such formal variety and stylistic virtuosity as Berger's are very difficult to categorize in terms of a unified, coherent *oeuvre*, even though such literary metamorphoses do seem to belong generally to the formal experimentation in the novel that characterized the surfiction of the 1970s. Max Schulz discusses Berger's *Little Big Man* in relation to such experimental fabulists as Borges, Pynchon, and Coover; Alfred Kazin, Stanley Trachtenberg, and others compare Berger with John Barth.[1] Yet, Berger's works seem especially resistant to such identifications with the literary avant-garde, if only because Berger's own values seem to be traditional, often politically conservative, and philosophically pragmatic. In a review of *Neighbors* in the *New Republic*, Isa Kapp tags Berger "a magic realist," identifying him with the Latin American fictional mode of Borges and other early twentieth-century moderns such as Carpentier.[2] Indeed, Berger's ironic mode, dependent as it often is on the discrepancy between his own mannered prose and the banalities of his characters, seems to fit well the category of Latin American Magic Realism, in which "the world and reality have a dream-like quality captured by the presentation of improbable juxtapositions in a style that is highly objective, precise, and deceptively simple."[3]

Reprinted by permission of *Studies in American Humor* 2, No. 1 (Spring 1983): 45–60.

There are good reasons for not applying the term "Magic Realism" in any hasty manner to contemporary North American fiction—reasons based largely on the significant differences between Latin and North American social realities as well as their different literary evolutions. On the other hand, it is fair to say that the philosophical assumptions of Magic Realism are essentially existentialist, much in the manner of the existential fiction produced in the United States in the 1950s and 1960s. Roth, Bellow, Heller, Malamud, Ellison, Mailer all wrote works in this period that stressed the discrepancy between public and private worlds, the alienation of the sensitive and self-conscious protagonist, and the absurdity of contemporary social and political reality. In many respects, it was this existential no-exit in post-War literary realism that prompted the literary experimentation of the late 1960s and decade of the 1970s. From among the existentialists, writers like Roth and Mailer radically retooled their fiction and tried out what appeared to be drastically new and avant-garde forms. Writers like John Barth, Coover, Pynchon, Hawkes, and other fabulists created their own self-referential worlds and repudiated the traditional claims of the novelist to represent reality. As different and conflicting as these two basic directions in post-War American fiction may then have appeared to be, both share the fundamentally outmoded values of what we might term "existential humanism." The imaginative "freedom" of the fabulist or surfictionist was claimed as a consequence of a "reality" constructed principally in the mind from the arbitrariness and contingency of the empirical world. Confronted with the "lie" of another man's truth, the avant-garde writer romantically bid for his own palace of thought and art. Where the existential realist found contemporary man alienated, impotent, subordinate to powers he rarely understood, and thus condemned to an identity and life that were *de facto* inauthentic, the fabulist transformed such failure into self-conscious knowledge, dependence into playful rebellion, and alienation into the bravura of the isolato, the iconoclasm of the avant-garde genius. Both literary modes inclined to similar moral homilies, often repeating the popular saws that they had hoped to condemn or at least transform; art, love, care, communication, self-awareness were various and yet strangely equivalent "cures" for the contemporary malaise. Such solutions all had one common feature: the honest confrontation of man's essential predicament as an alienated, mortal, conscious creature driven by his elementary desire for being. Whether self-consciously playful or ruthlessly "realistic," such existentialist art claimed the visionary ability to see such truths even as the rest of the culture labored to bury this terrifying knowledge beneath the facades of order, respectability, and stable meaning.[4]

It is easy and even a bit unfair to treat the dominant existentialism of the post-War period in such a cavalier, even flippant, manner, but my purpose is to demonstrate that such philosophical assumptions, remnants of early twentieth-century modernism, haunt the contemporary American writer just in proportion as they are recognized as shopworn, clichéd, but still not overcome. Such, I think, is Berger's relation to this existentialist heritage. At once contemptuous of all philosophical generalities and universals, Berger is also forced to recognize that such contempt belongs to the existentialist's valorization of particularity over generality and that, before one knows it, his readers are muttering: "Existence precedes essence." The variety of Berger's formal experiments belongs with the sort of imaginative and metamorphic powers that the existentialist identifies with authenticity or what Mailer's Rojack considers sanity: "the ability to hold the maximum of impossible combinations in one's mind."[5] In this regard, the Reinhart series of novels is a good measure of the problem confronting Berger, because it consists of four novels written over nearly a quarter of a century—that quarter of a century from the mid-1950s to the 1980s in which the existential literary mode I have been describing was transformed from a rebellious rejection of bourgeois America to part of the middle-class's very equipment for living in the late 1970s and early 1980s.

Carlo Reinhart is at once a schlemiel and a survivor; his ability to survive has much to do with his gradual recognition of his anti-heroic humanity—a recognition that assumes positive value by the time he achieves the relatively confident and stable maturity of *Reinhart's Women* (1981). The young Reinhart of *Crazy in Berlin* barely survives the psychic warfare governing human (and political) relations in a world where the sheer banality of existence seems defined by its unpredictability.[6] The mature Reinhart may not be able to transcend the contingency of existence, but he has seen enough of an arbitrary world to have acquired a certain hard-won stoicism and pragmatic orderliness. Taken together, the four novels in the Reinhart series educate Carlo out of the naivete of his youth through the disillusionment and cynicism of his early manhood and the repeated failures of his early middle age (in both *Reinhart in Love* and *Vital Parts*) to the wise, even charitable, skepticism of his role in *Reinhart's Women*. The culmination of such an existential education is Carlo's discovery that the cultivation of a "genuine skill," such as cooking, provides the sort of tangible defense against the arbitrariness of existence that he had missed in his previous ventures in such abstractions as "real estate" and cryogenics. Cooking, like writing, requires a certain stylization of the material (food or words), and it is that "stylization" that provides the cook and author with some validation of their existence in an otherwise utterly arbitrary and contingent world.

This attitude toward artistic representation as a defense against existential contingency is one that Berger makes quite explicit in discussions of his work. In his interview with Richard Schickel, on the occasion of the publication of *Neighbors*, Berger wrote: "I need some rest between novels, but I never take much, because real life is unbearable to me unless I can escape from it into fiction. An exception might be made if I could experience something remarkable in actuality, but I find that the older I get the less fecund becomes my non-literary fancy: I've either done it or I don't want to."[7]

Russel Wren, Berger's literate version of the Hammett-Chandler detective, employs deliberately mixed or florid metaphors "as a willed ruse to lure me away from panic—the fundamental purpose of most caprices of language, hence the American wisecrack. . . ."[8] Like other existential humanists, Berger imagines his fictions to be defenses against those deceptions and distortions in our experience that are effected either by the sheer perversity of nature or the willful act of some other, more powerful "author": convention, culture, commerce. In his apparent deathbed letter to his son, Blaine, in *Vital Parts*, Carlo writes: "The whole of life, as we know it, is a construct of mind, perhaps of language."[9] In context, Carlo's little dictum sounds treacherously like Harry's banal philosophizing in *Neighbors* or Bob Sweet's glib counsel in *Vital Parts*. Carlo's appositive clause, "as we know it," makes his equation of life with "mind" or "language" a virtual tautology. Staring into the void that he has himself chosen, the existential hero, Carlo, counsels his alienated son. The comedy of Berger's parody requires only that we recall Carlo's "living-in-the-face-of-death" is his "choice" to have himself frozen by Bob Sweet and Dr. Streckfuss to publicize their Cryon Foundation. Despite the brilliance of such parodies, Berger's novels do seem to lead us relentlessly to the very existential platitudes for which so many of the characters are mercilessly condemned. The artist's understanding of the essential ideality of the world—its fabrication from minds and words—seems best used in Berger's terms to construct an interpersonal space, in which a particular self and a concrete other may confront each other in terms of need as basic and human as the hunger or desire served by an exquisite meal or a delectable metaphor. Like Ford Madox Ford, Berger imagines the satisfaction of hunger or the desire for being to be measured more in terms of pleasure than use. Indeed, for his own philosophical purposes Berger deliberately confuses or conflates the Kantian distinction between appetitive and artistic desires, if only to argue that in modern consumer societies most biological functions have been subordinated to psychic needs.

The defense that art provides against the intrusions of a world of chance is an existential recourse that relies on the means of literary formalism. What Murray Krieger has termed the "existential basis of contextual criticism" helps explain this relationship, in which the apparent anti-formalism of existential philosophy indirectly approaches the aesthetic values of the New Criticism.[10] For the New Critic, literary form achieves the resolution, balance, or synthesis of life's contradictions that serves author and informed reader as a substitute for the coherent and stable being unavailable in ordinary experience. Describing his own writing as a form of creative dreaming, Berger writes: "I write each novel in a trance that is peculiar to each book alone. Hence when I am forced to awaken from it I am thrown into a horror of actuality from which I find no relief until I can enter another fantasy. Has not recent research into sleep established that if a mortal is inhibited from dreaming he will go mad? Perhaps written fiction has some similar efficacy in broad daylight. But I am much more interested in the treat than the treatment."[11] "Forced to awaken," "thrown into a horror of actuality," "no relief": these descriptions are characteristic of the modernist's and existential humanist's response to an unsatisfying reality, prompting that defensive gesture toward the fabrication of some simulated, artistic control.

Berger's literary order and coherence are not explained simply by observing that his diction, grammar, and narrative tone contrast sharply with the clichés and idle chatter of his characters. Berger is not merely protecting his own narrative order, he is also *purging* those forces of disorder by the customary means of the satirist: parody, bombast, bathos, hyperbole, caricature. Satire achieves its end by *estranging* familiar and thus often unrecognized ills. Such estrangement is rarely, however, the dispassionate work of the cultural anatomist; more often, it betrays a certain fundamental fear on the part of the writer that he is particularly prone to the sins he would reform or exile. Like Pound in *Hugh Selwyn Mauberley*, Joyce in *Portrait*, and Eliot in *The Waste Land*, Berger remains within a venerable modernist tradition when he attempts to define his own artistic order and function in terms of his *denial* or even *refusal* of all that so persistently and absurdly *is*. This sort of denial—often associated with the discipline, even asceticism, of the modern artist—is an active sort of negation, a will to obliterate the actual and replace it with one's own fiction, even as the artist recognizes the impossibility of sustaining such a beautiful illusion in the face of so many competing lies. It is worth adding that this sort of artistic will assumes its most explicitly vainglorious forms in the nearly literal efforts of Proust, Faulkner, and Joyce to substitute their multi-volume worlds (Combray, Yoknapatawpha, Dublin) for the ruins of the West. Such a will-to-power, of course, re-enacts the willful, narcissistic world that Berger so accurately satirizes in his fiction. What art would escape it all too often mimics in its own form and for its own ends.

In short, Berger often seems to be struggling to deny the hip psychology and popular existentialisms that by the 1960s sounded uncannily like his own, harder won understanding of the world. In *Crazy in Berlin*, Carlo begins to take control of his existence again when he recognizes his elementary relation to another human being, the Jewish double-agent, Nathan Schild; it is a recognition that Carlo makes only after Schild has been killed and after Carlo has killed in the vain effort to save Schild. Carlo's knowledge lends itself all too easily to the jargon of the "existential psychoanalysis" popularized in the 1960s: "Existential thinking . . . finds its validation when, across the gulf of our idioms and styles, our mistakes, errings and perversities, we find in the other's communication an experience of relationship established, lost, destroyed, or regained. We hope to share the experience of relationship established, but the only honest beginning, or even end, may be to share the experience of its absence."[12] This passage from R. D. Laing's *The Politics of Experience* might serve as an adequate commentary on the "wisdom" of *Crazy in Berlin*, even as it would do injustice to the complexity of Berger's vision in that work, to say nothing of his technical virtuosity. Nevertheless, by the late 1960s, it is fair to say that such jargon threatened the basic philosophical and aesthetic values of many writers like Berger, whose work had first appeared with the bravura of the artistic rebel.

In its own way, *Neighbors* (1980) addresses this very problem and attempts to demonstrate how the internal logic of existentialism encourages such popularization. Stanley Trachtenberg has argued that one of the consequences of Berger's comedy is that "The loss of coherence between various aspects of self comically fragments the notion of identity and thus fictionalizes the existential concept of authenticity as a shaping condition of it."[13] If the self is multiple, if existence precedes and informs essence, if "I" am nothing more than the sum of my actions and choices, then the very ideal of existential authenticity is already a function of the inauthentic. The customary existential response to this charge is that the "recognition" or "self-consciousness" of such inauthenticity is the highest form of authenticity or honesty. Yet, the Marxist critique of modernism generally indicts this claim for existential self-consciousness as just one more way in which the dominant ideology rationalizes its contradictions.[14] By transforming the inauthenticity of a specific historical moment into a metaphysical condition, the existentialist claims a transcendent knowledge that unwittingly serves to conserve and perpetuate the existing order. Such an indictment of the existential notion of authenticity is, of course, indebted to such works in the critical Marxist tradition as Lukács' "The Ideology of Modernism" and Adorno's *The Jargon of Authenticity*. As Trent Schroyer summarizes Adorno's argument: "His basic thesis is that after World War II [existentialism] became an ideological mystification of human domination—while pretending to be a critique of alienation."[15] Indeed, the methodological procedures of phenomenology are transformed in the work of Jaspers and Heidegger into reified abstractions. Rather than making possible new and transvaluing approaches to existing cultural problems, phenomenology became a "philosophy" with its own stable concepts. The "jargon" of this philosophy achieves the same end as advertising slogans, popular clichés, and other degradations of language in contemporary life: "Whoever is versed in the jargon does not have to say what he thinks, does not even have to think it properly. The jargon takes over this task and devaluates thought."[16]

In *Neighbors*, such jargon is embodied in Harry and Ramona, who change personalities with the same ease that they slip into different sets of verbal conventions. Nothing but surfaces, shaped only of the clichés and verbal chicanery of "high-tech" media culture, Harry and Ramona simulate the spontaneity, vitality, and metamorphic qualities often associated with the existential anti-hero. "Harry apparently never did the expected," Berger tells us in a narrative aside.[17] This inconsistency, even contradictoriness, is finally what lures Earl Keese into the apparent adventure of the open road together with Harry and Ramona. Earl's "fatal stroke" cuts this journey short and seems to mark symbolically the difference between the Keeses' middle-class respectability and the shape-shifting lives—the pure "becoming"—of Harry and Ramona. Yet, the interest of Berger's narrative derives not from the tired scenario of the suburbanite waking to the nightmare of existential truth; rather, *Neighbors* holds the reader by means of the uncanny relationship between bourgeois stability and the contrived unpredictability of Harry and Ramona. In my judgement, this uncanny relation is analogous to the relation Berger finds between his own aesthetic values and the existential "jargon" so popular in the past two decades.[18]

Harry's and Ramona's relationship with the Keeses is properly "uncanny," in the technical Freudian sense of the term. The translation of *"das Unheimliche"* as "the uncanny" allows us to forget how intimately Freud associates the notion with home and hearth: "Among its different shades of meaning the word *heimlich* exhibits one which is identical with its opposite, unheimlich. . . . In general we are reminded that the word *heimlich* is not unambiguous, but belongs to two sets of ideas, which without being contradictory are yet very different: on the one hand, it means that which is familiar and congenial, and on the other, that which is concealed and kept out of sight."[19] Freud explains this apparent paradox in terms that are basic to his understanding of the psychic (and literary) Double; the "uncanny" is, in fact, "nothing new or foreign, but something familiar and old-established in the mind that has been estranged only by the process of repression."[20] Throughout *Neighbors*, Harry and Ramona evoke a certain familiarity from the Keeses that seems to suggest their strangeness may be a consequence of the Keeses' repression as much as it is a function of Harry's and Ramona's "alternative" lifestyle.

Up to a certain point, an existentialist reading of *Neighbors* accounts quite nicely for the "uncanny" relation Harry and Ramona have with the Keeses. Earl and Enid have taken "control" (one of Earl's favorite words) of their lives only by disguising their essential alienation and the sheer contingency of their human situation. At home neither in the suburbs nor the city, the Keeses share the "homelessness" of Harry and Ramona. Like Twain's middle class, the Keeses labor principally to disguise from themselves the fact of their own impotence and insignificance. In the midst of the farce that dominates the drama of *Neighbors*, there is a familiar narrative development: the progressive exposure of all the Keeses' values as elaborate fictions with intricate genealogies disguising their imaginary origins. Halfway through the novel, Earl suddenly realizes that: "He had no idea of what [Enid] did all day" (*N*, p. 118); early in the novel, Berger notes: "For a number of years now Keese had observed his wife only by means of what she did . . . he saw the actor only through the action" (*N*, p. 3). Earl's memories of his daughter's, Elaine's, childhood rarely agree with her own; in general, his relation with Elaine is more a product of his imagination than of any recognizable historical evolution. Even before she has met Harry and Ramona, Elaine mimics their curious blend of affection and domination: " 'I just wanted to be cruel to you for a moment. . . . Just because you're my very own dad. You're mine, you belong to me, you're my property' " (*N*, p. 108). Given the ease with which Harry and Ramona expose the hollowness of the Keeses' values, the reader expects Berger to reveal the metaphysical truths of alienation, will-to-power as the law of human relations, and a world of unpredictable changes. Earl tries to conclude at one point, in an infamous echo: "Timing was all. A minute passes and the world is changed in every respect. The landscape out the window looks the same, but every atom of it is different" (*N*, p. 170).

In such an existentialist reading, however, the *provocateur* who exposes such inauthenticity is generally representative of the philosophical truth that characters like the Keeses initially refuse to acknowledge. Harry and Ramona are hardly exemplars of such authenticity; they themselves are constructed from the fragments of the Keeses's world. Harry and Ramona represent the very contradictoriness of this particular suburban and Capitalist world; that contradictoriness has been rendered strange and "other" by means of the Keeses' strategic repression. It returns in the form of the glib and changeable jargon of these two latter-day hipsters. Harry and Ramona are "really unreal," to echo a popular oxymoron of teenagers; their "reality" is precisely a function of the studied, designed unreality by which they appear to others. Berger has assessed Earl's problem as his inability to "believe in his own reality."[21] Earl is introduced in the novel in terms of his "strange malady or gift": "Were Keese to accept the literal witness of his eyes, his life would have been of quite another character, perhaps catastrophic, for outlandish illusions were, if not habitual with him, then at least none too rare . . ." (*N*, pp. 1–2). Keese's tendency to confuse perceptual and imaginary objects is one of the sources of Berger's comedy in this novel, and this inclination helps relate that comedy to Berger's serious themes (never far removed from the wit). Berger seems to be arguing that contemporary culture discourages the exercise of the imaginative faculty and encourages the sort of literalness ("seeing is believing") in thought and language that is the human equivalent of automation. Berger turns this somewhat familiar criticism of modern times in a new way, suggesting that the repression of our imaginative capabilities allows the imagination to escape our control. Working with the logic of nightmare, the imagination produces strange epiphenomena that are, in fact, expressions of our own cultural schizophrenia. Berger takes a certain perverse pleasure in enumerating the curious twists of imagination that are everywhere evident in the advertising slogans, teen argot, and media clichés of contemporary life.

One of the functions of the imagination is the mediation of inner and outer worlds, and it is the sharp distinction maintained by Earl between public and private that provokes many of the absurd events in this novel.[22] Earl is outraged to learn that Harry is cooking spaghetti in his kitchen after he has conned Earl out of $32.00 to pay for take-out food. In existential terms, Earl gets what he deserves: his distrust of Harry is a form of bad faith that is simply repaid in kind. In another sense, Earl is not so much "paid back" as responsible for having established their relationship in terms of basic economic exchanges. Earl is shocked at the idea of paying his "neighbor" to cook dinner, but he fails to recognize that *all* relations in this society are based on such payments. When Earl accuses Ramona of blackmailing him to keep quiet about what he has done to Harry's car, she asks: " 'Wouldn't you, if you had somebody cold?' " (N, p. 42). Even before he has met Harry and Ramona, Earl tells Enid: " 'We could probably get away with giving them no formal welcome whatever. It's scarcely a true obligation' " (N, p. 1). What constitutes a "true obligation" in this society remains ambiguous, precisely because the "true" basis already involves a contradiction: a relation is determined by its exchange-value, which in "human" relations is already a denial of the "human" element. When Earl meets Harry on the latter's lawn, Earl says ingratiatingly, even subserviently: " 'We're on your property now. Now you're the boss. You can make short work of me if I get out of line . . . you have the moral advantage and . . . I'm in a subordinate position . . . that gives you a tremendous edge' " (N, p. 144). It's fair to say, even though we should be suspicious of all "origins" in such a novel, that Earl conceives of life and human relations in terms of basic master-servant relations and economic obligations long before Harry and Ramona arrive in the neighborhood. As early as the first page of the narrative, Earl and Enid agree that a "true obligation" would be " 'like giving food to a starving person,' " which is still part of the economic give-and-take on which the Keeses base their lives.

Critics of James's *The Turn of the Screw* have often observed how the Governess re-enacts each appearance of Peter Quint and Miss Jessel; this formal consistency in James's narrative has strengthened the arguments in favor of the ghosts as objectifications of the Governess' psychic anxieties. In an analogous way, most of the surprising acts of Harry and Ramona are foreshadowed by words, dreams, or acts of the Keeses, especially Earl. Ramona accuses Earl of "attempted rape," a charge later withdrawn as an apparent joke. Earl is thrilled by the brush of Ramona's breasts as she first enters the house; only minutes after her arrival, Earl is attracted by the possibility of tricking his wife into staying home while he and Ramona dine at a fancy French restaurant. Ramona certainly exaggerates Earl's idle fantasies when she accuses him of attempted rape, but her exaggeration works in the manner of every good nightmare or irrational fear. Earl is titillated by Ramona's boldness and vulgarity throughout the narrative. She may seem to be leading him on, but the sites of their near-trysts are always uncannily familiar to Earl: the bedrooms in his house, his gameroom, his front porch, his kitchen. When he does visit Harry and Ramona's house, Ramona is curiously absent—at Earl's house with Enid and Elaine, we learn later.

Earl's relations with Harry demonstrate a similar structure of *prolepsis* (the rhetorical trope of anticipation). When Earl finally sees Harry's car in the morning light, he considers how he might restore peace: "Were his car retrieved . . . and not only restored in appearance but improved—e.g., a completely new coat of paint!—he would not come away empty-handed" (*N*, p. 159). After Harry has looked at his car, he says: " 'Earl, that car needs a paint job. There's no two ways about it. Now, if you want to renege, O.K., I won't sue you. I'll make it a matter of honor. I'm saying what's right' " (*N*, p. 188). Once again, Harry calls attention to the contradictions between moral and economic values in this culture, and what he says is merely an echo of Earl's own idea of "settling up fairly" (in the current argot). Earl responds to Harry as if Harry were a cheap confidence-man, trying to beat Earl out of the money for the paint job. Earl is not just guilty of hypocrisy or of applying a double-standard in moral judgments; his behavior provokes, even "produces," the sort of exaggerated opportunism that Harry represents in this instance. In this regard, Earl and Harry are proper "neighbors," insofar as they share this uncanny relation. When Harry says to Earl, " 'Has it occurred to you that we are inevitably drawn back to a kitchen table whenever we have tried to talk all evening? Maybe that does suggest we're in some basic sympathy, like members of the same family?' " (*N*, p. 146), he may be making an observation shared by Berger.

Just what causes "Harry & Ramona" (Berger represents them this way to stress their "corporate" qualities) to materialize in the first place takes us beyond their associations with the hidden contradictions of the Keeses' safe, middle-class existence. Their uncanniness reminds us that the bourgeoisie produces its own marginal "other," its own rebellious alternatives, in part to constrain, by means of a strategic anticipation, those forces that threaten revolution. In Marxist terms, one might argue that the petty master-servant contests of these surburbanites are means by which the dominant ideology displaces (and thus defuses) the political necessity of the class struggle. Berger is no Marxist, of course, so his own reaction to this cultural "artistry," this manipulation of self and other, is to use his own imaginative powers to transgress the existing order's proper boundaries between order and chaos, coherence and contradiction. In *Neighbors*, Berger's own artistic values seem to undergo some sort of revaluation; rather than offering the protective space of controlled language, art seems more closely identified with the provocations and harassments of such minor criminals as Harry and Ramona. Yet, Harry and Ramona are themselves part of the problem; they are merely the uncanny expressions of the incoherence, superficiality, and contradictoriness the culture has produced in its specific and historical will for truth. Berger's art differs from the derivative and reactive "arts" of Harry and

Ramona, insofar as Berger's narrative represents the entire dialectic of such banality as Harry, Ramona, Earl, Enid, and Elaine collectively express. This dialect has a particularly interesting consequence for the reader's relation to the artistic act. In other novels by Berger, the text seems to direct the reader toward some agreement with the general skepticism of tone and formalism of method. In *Neighbors*, Berger seems more interested in constructing a dramatic situation involving apparent "choices," so that each reader will find his choices to be not only judgments of his values but also subversive of the formal ending of the novel.

Berger's method in this novel is similar to Melville's in *The Confidence-Man*, a work that has also attracted much in the way of an "existentialist" reputation and yet remained always beyond such readings. Melville's work is a labyrinth of different stories, all of which repeat the same semiotic law: character, reader, writer (all one) unwittingly reveal their vanities and sins in the course of telling stories they intend will shore up their identities and reputations. Writing shares with culture the tendency to hide much for the sake of what it would express. Berger and Melville develop complex means of turning the intentions of their characters and their readers against themselves—that is, of turning those intentions "uncanny." The logic of such an aesthetic requires the artist to turn its method upon his own identity as "author." In *Neighbors*, Berger uses Earl and Harry to parody the idea of art as a defense against a threatening world and to relate that aesthetic to a glib existentialist jargon. In a sort of echo of Jay Gatsby, Earl cries desperately: " *'Everything can be put back where it belongs'* " (*N*, p. 160). In the neighborhood of uncanny resemblances and uncontrolled acts, the very concept of ownership, as Earl understands it, has vanished. This very bourgeois cry for "order" is also a curious double for the modernist's claim that the form of art might redeem the waste land of the age, might give "things" those proper "places"—the neighborhood of being—where they "belong." Earl insists in the best tradition of the novel: " 'Sequences are all-important, too, . . . and timing, in general' " (*N*, p. 240). Yet, the disturbing loss of time for Earl during his hectic weekend ("a thrill a minute") reflects how Earl's ordered time and proper sequences are only simulacra of any significant history.

In his interview with Richard Schickel, Berger notes: "Harry and Ramona would certainly seem to be outlaws in Keese's scheme of things, but perhaps, taking the wider view, it is they who protect and conserve and perpetuate. Though a larger, younger and seemingly more ruthless man, Harry can usually, when the dust settles, be identified as Keese's victim; and not even with the help of Eros can Ramona prevail for more than the odd moment."[23] On a certain level, these claims seem unproblematic; Earl himself makes the same observation more economically when he claims: " 'I've given more than I've got. I don't mind admitting I'm proud of myself' " (*N*, p. 162). Only Berger's claim that Harry and Ramona "protect and conserve and perpetuate" seems troubling, given their contempt for the middle-class world of the novel. There are, I propose, two senses in which such outlaws serve such conservational ends, both of which express the transformation of Berger's aesthetic values in *Neighbors*. In one sense, their inconoclasm is borrowed from the sham spontaneity and directness of video-culture, which would have us believe the sheer immediacy of all that "is" and forget the complex weave of imagination, memory, and repression operating in every "event." Harry's and Ramona's existential spontaneity is a kind of family-room hipsterism that transforms the contradictions of middle-class America into the "real and honest" spiritualism of some popular guru. As Adorno points out, the "jargon" of existentialism "ends in a miserable consolation: after all, one still remains what one is."[24] Culture's "other," its eccentric margin, is often little more than the means by which it confirms its ideology and establishes its borders. In this sense, the artist may lead us to "metaphysical" visions that would blind us to the contradictions of our historical and social situations.

In another sense, Harry and Ramona may be turned ultimately to the task of artistic provocation, thus conserving those powers (of the imagination: subversion, skepticism, satire) that regenerate cultural vitality. As characters in Berger's novel, Harry and Ramona hardly can be made to carry such responsibility; as "figures" for the uncanny, that method whereby each will to authority reveals its own unconscious, Harry and Ramona signal the power of art to question cultural values. Berger has acknowledged his debt to Kafka as the master "who taught me that at any moment banality might turn sinister."[25] *Neighbors* demonstrates the evil of banality as much as the banality of evil in its exposure of the contradictions governing the lives of the Keeses. *Neighbors* also shows how art can share, even justify, such banality and secret contradiction when it strives to preserve itself from the corruptions of the actual and the contradictions of the historical and political situation that gave rise to it. In a playful autobiographical aside, Berger notes: "Incidentally, this narrative may have been a bit of wish-fulfillment. I wrote the book while living in Maine, where I had no next-door neighbors of any sort. Only in such a fashion is my work ever autobiographical."[26] One is tempted by such a disclosure to guess what sort of wish-fulfillment was involved: the desire to harass the neighbors or the need to be harassed? It is, of course, the dialectical—more properly, differential—relation of these two "alternatives" that constitutes the interest and novelty of Berger's *Neighbors*. The reviewers in the popular press quickly chose sides: Harry & Ramona *or* Earl Keese. In this case, to choose is to abuse. The uncanny doubles of this novel have their precedents in Berger's earlier fiction, but in *Neighbors* these doubles serve to question the very values governing Berger's art.

I shall not speculate concerning Berger's intentions in all of this, aware as I am of his contempt for those who would second-guess him. On the evidence of *Reinhart's Women* (1981), which appeared the year after *Neighbors*, I would have to conclude that Berger's existentialist and formalist inclinations are still powerful. I might qualify that judgment, however, by adding that *Reinhart's Women* works with the momentum of the three previous Reinhart novels, which may have something to do with the easy or nonchalant existentialism of Carlo in this final volume. On the evidence of *The Feud* (1983) and its return to the doubles of *Neighbors* in the larger social context of the twin towns of Hornbeck and Millville, I would conclude that Berger has worked consciously and carefully in the past several years to cast aside his existential humanism for the sake of an art concerned with a new understanding of the interrelation of psychology, language, and the development of American social values.

Notes

1. Max Schulz, *Black Humor Fiction of the Sixties* (Athens: Ohio University Press, 1973), pp. 72–77; Alfred Kazin, *Bright Book of Life* (Boston: Little, Brown and Co., 1973), p. 281; Stanley Trachtenberg, "Berger and Barth: The Comedy of Decomposition," in *Comic Relief: Humor in Contemporary American Literature*, ed. Sarah Blacher Cohen (Urbana: University of Illinois Press, 1978), pp. 45–69.

2. Isa Kapp, "*Neighbors*," *New Republic*, 26 April 1980, p. 34.

3. Seymour Menton, "Jorge Luis Borges, Magic Realist," *Hispanic Review*, 50 (1982), p. 412.

4. Richard Lehan's *A Dangerous Crossing: French Literary Existentialism and the Modern American Novel* (Carbondale: Southern Illinois University Press, 1973) studies the affinities between Continental existentialism and American fiction from such moderns as Hemingway and Faulkner to experimentalists like Pynchon and Barth.

5. Norman Mailer, *An American Dream* (New York: Dell Publishing Co., 1965), p. 150.

6. "How strange could be the most banal of life's sequences," Reinhart reflects in *Reinhart's Women* (New York: Delacorte Press/Seymour Lawrence, 1981), p. 58. Brooks Landon, "The Radical Americanist," *Nation*, 225 (1977), 153, argues that Berger "characteristically turns familiar means to strange ends." This is a distinctive feature of Berger's style, but the passage above from *Reinhart's Women* suggests that such "stylization" is for Berger a form of realism, much in the manner of those upsurges of the absurd one finds in classic works of existentialism by Sartre and Camus.

7. Richard Schickel, "Interviewing Thomas Berger," *The New York Times Book Review*, 6 April 1980, p. 1. Further references in the Notes as "Schickel Interview."

8. *Who Is Teddy Villanova?* (New York: Delacorte Press/Seymour Lawrence, 1977), p. 21.

9. *Vital Parts* (New York: New American Library, 1970), p. 351.

10. Krieger expands and develops his original observation (in *The Tragic Vision*) that existential philosophy and the New Criticism share fundamental affinities in "The Existential Basis of Contextual Criticism" (1966), reprinted in *Critical Theory Since Plato*, ed. Hazard Adams (New York: Harcourt Brace Jovanovich, Inc., 1971). It is important to note, however, that Krieger's argument in this essay attempts to subordinate existentialism to the higher aims of that literature defined by the New Criticism. In historical terms, Krieger considers the relation between existentialism and the New Criticism to be principally a consequence of their shared sources in Romantic Idealism; Krieger sees the contemporaneous development of existentialism and the New Criticism to show how those sources "persist . . . among very different temperaments that have made use of them" (p. 1230). My argument is that the

two movements are inextricably related in their historical development and the purposes they served in conserving certain values of the dominant ideology.

11. Schickel Interview, p. 22.

12. R. D. Laing, *The Politics of Experience* (New York: Ballantine Books, 1967), p. 56.

13. Trachtenberg, p. 60.

14. See Georg Lukács, "The Ideology of Modernism," in *The Meaning of Contemporary Realism*, trans. John and Necke Mander (London: Merlin Press, 1962), p. 21: "Man, thus conceived, is an ahistorical being. . . . There is not for him—and apparently not for his creator—any pre-existent reality beyond his own self, acting upon him or being acted upon by him . . . the hero is without personal history. He is 'thrown-into-the-world': meaninglessly, unfathomably. . . . The only 'development' in this literature is the gradual revelation of the human condition. Man is now what he has always been and always will be. The narrator, the examining subject, is in motion; the examined reality is static."

15. Trent Schroyer, Foreword, to Theodor Adorno, *The Jargon of Authenticity*, trans. Knut Tarnowski and Frederic Will (Evanston: Northwestern University Press, 1973), p. xiii.

16. Adorno, *The Jargon of Authenticity*, p. 9.

17. *Neighbors* (New York: Delacorte Press/Seymour Lawrence, 1980), p. 24. Further references in the text as *N*.

18. In their haste to make some sort of "decision" about the "meaning" of *Neighbors*, reviewers of the novel often ended up mimicking the sort of jargon used by Harry and Ramona. Thomas Edwards, "Domestic Guerillas," *New York Times Book Review*, 6 April 1980, p. 23, claims that Earl is headed for "a new sense of self that can survive the loss of the people and things and styles his old self had seemed to require." Isa Kapp, *op. cit.*, p. 36, insists: "We are being warned, in this . . . sparest of Berger's fictions, that we cannot count on the better side of man." In several cases, reviewers quote Harry's own exercises in banal philosophizing to make their serious points about the novel.

19. Freud, "The 'Uncanny,' " in *On Creativity and the Unconscious*, ed. Benjamin Nelson, trans. under the supervision of Joan Riviere (New York: Harper and Row Publishers, 1958), p. 129.

20. *Ibid.*, p. 148.

21. Schickel Interview, p. 21.

22. For Kant, the imagination makes possible the schematism of sensory data and the a priori categories of mind. For existentialists like Sartre and Camus, the imagination is a distinct mental faculty that facilitates our relation to the Other, whether such otherness be another person, the past, or the sensory world itself.

23. Schickel Interview, p. 21.

24. Adormo, pp. 115–116.

25. Schickel Interview, p. 21.

26. *Ibid.*

A Murderous Clarity: A Reading
of Thomas Berger's *Killing Time*

JON WALLACE

In *Consciousness East and West* two clinical psychologists, Kenneth R. Pelletier and Charles Garfield, cite Harvard psychiatrist Andrew Weil's claim that "A desire to alter consciousness periodically is an innate, normal drive analogous to hunger or the sexual drive . . . a biological characteristic of the species."[1] Pelletier and Garfield go on to note that although a number of altered states of consciousness are possible (e.g., hallucinatory, hypnotic, meditative), Western societies have generally accepted only three as normal: ordinary waking, dream, and sleep. Of course Hindus and Zen Buddhists have been experiencing ASC for centuries, but in Western culture such experiences are usually suspect. Pelletier and Garfield believe that prejudice against them

> is based more on political and social considerations than on psychological insight. Perhaps these experiences are opposed to social responsibility, individual initiative, and self-control, which are so revered in Western cultures. But these are social criteria and are distinct from the more psychological observation that these experiences are a source of profound personal inspiration and are invaluable sources of information in determining the transcultural functions of the human mind.[2]

In passages that are very much to the point of Thomas Berger's novel *Killing Time*, the authors speak of the similarity between what is considered a form of insanity in Western culture, schizophrenic psychosis, and "the seemingly bizarre but socially sanctioned behavior of the primitive shaman." On this point, they quote J. Silverman:

> In primitive cultures in which such a unique life crisis resolution is tolerated, the abnormal experience (shamanism) is typically beneficial to the individual, cognitively and affectively; he is regarded as one with expanded consciousness. In a culture that does not provide referential guides for comprehending this

Reprinted with slight adaptation with the permission of Jon Wallace from *Philological Quarterly* 68, no. 1 (Winter 1989): 101–14.

kind of crisis experience, the individual . . . typically undergoes an intensification of his suffering over and above his original anxieties.[3]

More bluntly, he is considered insane and institutionalized, often in a setting
that does little to "improve" him—or her.

In *Killing Time* Berger explores, among other things, the ways in which
language is used to write off the experiences of one Joseph Detweiler—a
man who, not coincidentally, has little use for words. As a visionary who
would, if he could, kill time and so enable all people to transcend the here
and now by moving themselves anywhere they desired "using only the mind,"
Detweiler is committed to the control of a non-verbal, extra-sensory reality.
Words to him are worth very little:

> For himself, Detweiler disapproved of writing. Words were elements of
> another kind of reality than that which claimed his primary attention. He
> would have written things if by so doing he could create actual states or
> situations, if by writing "John is happy," John would indeed be rendered
> happy. But if John was already blissful, to write that would be solely to
> describe. If John was unhappy, it would be a lie.[4]

Detweiler believes that spiritual reality is the only reality worth bothering
about, and that language is of little value since it partakes of, or can only
describe, the material reality of ordinary experience. When he does kill, he
kills to gain silence, for it is only in silence that his spiritual interests can
be served (p. 248).

Detweiler is Berger's version of Robert Irwin, who in 1937 confessed
to murdering a Mrs. Gedeon, her daughter, and a male boarder in a manner
similar to Berger's account in *Killing Time*. According to Frederic Wertham,
a psychiatrist who befriended Irwin before the murders, Irwin was a man
with strange spiritual commitments who once declared that he wanted

> "to get my mental radio running in such a way that I can get in complete
> touch with the universal mind. We are all just radios and get our mentality
> from a central broadcasting station—the universal mind. Broadcasting station,
> you know, is just an analogy. It sounds as fantastic as can be, but it isn't."
> (p. 124)

Of course Irwin was right: his analogy does sound fantastic, but the basic
idea is not. The belief that human beings can tune in to universal energy
and knowledge by means of meditation or prayer is relatively common within
both Eastern and Western mystical traditions. But no one was interested in
Irwin's spirituality as such. The following dialogue, with which Berger
was certainly familiar, occurred shortly after Irwin's arrest. He is being
interrogated by a psychiatrist named Dr. Leland E. Hinsie, then Director

of the New York Psychiatric Institute. Hinsie has been pressing Irwin to accept full responsibility for his crime. Irwin's position is that he and God are one; therefore, God is as responsible as Irwin—insofar as a distinction can be made. Replying to Hinsie's question "God is you?," Irwin offers an analogy. "In the same sense that you can say—you ask me if God is me— oxygen and hydrogen are water. They are not water and yet they are water. I am not divine by virtue of my imprisonment in this mortal state." Irwin's ideas are neither unique nor difficult to follow, especially in the light of his apt analogy. But Hinsie seems unable to get the point—and frustrated enough to resort to some unprofessional name calling:

Q: Is divinity responsible for every movement that you make, for every thought you make?

A: Yes.

Q: Isn't that a crazy idea?

A: That is not crazy at all.

Q: Who was ultimately responsible for the murder of these three people?

A: Divinity. Absolutely!

Q: Divinity may be responsible but divinity is not in the Tombs; you are.

A: No, divinity is in the Tombs, and I am in the Tombs—the two are one.

Q: Listen, I believe personally that Robert Irwin in and of himself by and with his own consent and knowledge murdered these three people.

A: Yes, but actually it is divinity that pushes it along.

Q: Therefore, you and divinity and God and the universal Mind are all one.

A: So are you, of course.

Q: Then I can only conclude or reframe your statement to read as coming from you, "I am God."

A: Yes. Absolutely! Since you limit your whole statement to me, exactly.

Q: What does the statement read?

A: The statement reads that I am God.

Q: I consider that to be a very crazy idea.

A: I made such a statement only under your persistent questioning but I will prefer to say the same thing in a different way. I am inherently divine.[5]

Hinsie appears surprisingly obtuse here despite Irwin's very sensible, and we would think helpful, qualifications. No doubt his inability to comprehend Irwin's alternative frame of reference is due largely to the fact it calls his, Hinsie's, into question, along with his status as an investigating official whose authority rests upon science, not upon Irwin's brand of pantheistic mysticism.

Hinsie's ideological deafness exemplifies the official treatment of Irwin as described in two non-fiction accounts: journalist Quentin Reynolds' in *Courtroom* and psychiatrist Frederic Wertham's in *The Show of Violence*. My intention is to demonstrate how Berger's novel may be read as a response to both Reynolds' and Wertham's reductionist perspectives on a man who truly didn't "fit," socially or ideologically. For reasons that no doubt have more to do with politics and psychology than spiritual insight, Reynolds and Wertham use journalistic and psychiatric language respectively to clarify Irwin, that is, to explain him away. Berger, on the other hand, recognizes that Detweiler is opaquely human and therefore ultimately beyond the reach of official or unofficial categories that obscure rather than describe the non-verbal human reality to which they are supposed to refer. Unbewitched by the illusive and often destructive clarity of language, Berger preserves Detweiler's opacity by dramatizing his contradictions and by constantly reminding us of the dubious, problematic relationship of language and reality. By doing so, he forces the reader to see his own fictional equivalent of Irwin, Joseph Detweiler, as a disturbed but undeniably human being.

In *Courtroom* Reynolds gives us the Irwin that the famous defense attorney Samuel S. Leibowitz had to deal with: a madman. For Leibowitz and Reynolds, there is no spiritual or metaphysical issue. For Reynolds, Irwin is a problem, certainly, but only in a legal and logistical sense. What or who he is, is never in doubt. Under the guise of straightforward, descriptive reporting, Reynolds subtly rules out a humanizing perspective on Irwin, one that could allow us to see him not merely as an "insane criminal" but as a dangerously troubled human being under the pressure of impulses and revelations that he could not resist. For example, Reynolds observes that Irwin had "the uncanny knack of inspiring sympathy in others."[6] Given the invisible (because unquestionable) assumptions that validate Reynold's discourse, what is actually a confession of ignorance appears as a description that in turn functions as argument: There is no good (that is, ideologically defensible) reason for liking Irwin, no legitimate basis for his appeal. He is as guilty, in other words, of interpersonal deception as he is of murder. After all, sane, fully human people do not transcend time and space, think of themselves as divine, or murder other people who have done them no harm. In most public discourse, most especially in "objective" journalism, such premises go without saying—and from it practically everything that happens to Irwin, in jail and on trial, follows: He is locked up without compassion and most definitely without understanding.

Notably, it is for Reynolds Irwin's "knack," not Irwin himself, that is uncanny. From the journalistic perspective, Irwin himself is "insane," "diseased" and "deluded"—in sum, not fully human and hence not so much "uncanny" as "un-human"; therefore, we need not consider the import of his revelations or spiritual goals any more than we should consider the import of a drug addict's hallucinations. They are signs of a sickness, not of some other reality. Safely enclosed within such a secure ideological frame of reference, Reynolds can write the following with little fear of contradiction—or discovery:

> Irwin always protested when any of the doctors referred to his "insanity." He denied that he was insane, although he knew that proof of saneness would mean the electric chair. Actually, he didn't care much about the consequences of his act. He had remained in the Gedeon apartment for more than an hour after the final killing . . . and he never bothered to lock the door. After he had gone from the flat he realized that he had left a glove there, but he didn't bother to go back for it. His delusions were so great by then, that he had virtually abandoned all contact with reality. His "flight" (Philadelphia, Washington, Cleveland, Chicago) was a haphazard affair and he had made no attempt to disguise himself or his movements.[7]

Within Reynolds' universe of discourse, words such as "insanity," "delusions," and "reality" pose no problem. Everyone knows what they mean; indeed, to know what "reality" is to know what "insanity" and "delusion" mean: to be out of contact with it, with that commonsense reality of time, space, and solid material objects we all know is really there, save in dreams, illusions and hallucinations. Out of contact with such a reality, Irwin was insane enough not to plead insanity, care about the consequences of his act, leave the Gedeon apartment immediately after the murder, or keep well hidden. A question Reynolds never poses is: what if Irwin had actually had an experience—a genuine religious experience not unlike those described by socially sanctioned spiritual leaders—that had transformed him spiritually but which had left him as helpless as ever to control his impulses? Thus transformed, could he not be alive to another world, and obedient to demands other than those most normal people respond to? It never occurs to Reynolds to ask because he is working within a set of assumptions that excludes such possibilities. By means of them, Reynolds is able to capture Irwin within a net of ideological certainties that render him as harmless spiritually as he becomes physically in prison.

Wertham accomplishes the same end, but more gently, offering a sympathetic first-hand account of Irwin's incarceration and trial. He also describes Irwin's difficulties as a child forced to grow up as the fatherless son of an impoverished and, according to Wertham, fanatically religious woman. Wertham contends that under such circumstances, Irwin simply had no chance to live a healthy, productive life, especially in a society that was indifferent to his plight during his childhood, and deaf to his voice during and after his trial. Compared to such brutally legalistic officials as the trial judge, the members of the so-called Lunacy Commission, and Hinsie, Wertham seems to be a competent, broadminded professional, determined to understand Irwin as a human being. But Wertham, too, has an official side—and language, which ultimately serves to explain Irwin away. In commenting on the district attorney's use of the term "motive," Wertham makes a useful distinction. *Reason*

> is the conscious explanation a man makes for himself or an outsider makes for him before, during and after a deed. *Motive* is the real driving force which is at least partly unconscious and which can be understood only as part of a continuing and developing process. In the medico-legal discussions and proceeding of this case these two terms were constantly confused.[8]

In other words, reason is linguistic, expressible and understandable only in language; motive is non-verbal, an aspect of a seamless reality that can be understood only after being divided into verbal categories. With such a distinction in mind, we recognize how difficult it is to explain why people do what they do, how they think, what they mean, and, most significantly in this case, who they are. In this passage, Wertham seems to be aware of the huge discrepancy that can exist between human individuals and systems of rational explanation, be they legal, religious, or psychiatric, that seek to define them. Nevertheless, to read his chapter on Irwin is to read a drama in which a protagonist (Wertham) succeeds in freeing an abused captive (Irwin) from the reductive, impersonal cages of officials, only to imprison him again, this time in a cage of humanistic psychology. Near the end of the chapter, Wertham captures Irwin in one paragraph:

> A case like Irwin's cannot be summed up in a Greek word. But at its minimum the designation *catathymic crisis* indicates, on the one hand, that there is a pathological condition with a beginning and a course, and excludes the unpsychological claim that Irwin was a case of schizophrenia (dementia prae-cox), ununderstandable, bizarre, and "incurable."[9]

Wertham acknowledges the limitations of his language, but he nevertheless claims understanding, despite the fact that he, like every official before him, fails to accept as legitimate, or "real," Irwin's spiritual claims—for example, that he was a "molecule that had to be liberated from the barriers of mortality," or that he had actually seen a distance of a million miles when he was sixteen.[10]

Although Pascal and Descartes describe similar mystical experiences in their biographies, literally no one takes Irwin seriously on these matters, including Wertham, who ironically enough quotes him as declaring "The only freedom I want is freedom of expression."[11] Wertham offers this line at the end of a paragraph in which he describes Irwin's artistic interests; he never acknowledges its relevance to Irwin's spiritual convictions as well. In response to Irwin's "mental radio" analogy, Wertham declares that "It would have been senseless for me to make frontal attack against these ideas"—as if any sensible reader would see how utterly ridiculous Irwin's convictions were. Thus, although Wertham does help us see beyond the all-too-simplistic and all-too-convenient explanations of Irwin formulated by various officials, he himself resorts to a single perspective, psychiatry, from which he is able to see Irwin as a "catathymic" whose visions must, be definition, be "distorted."

And perhaps they were, whatever that might mean. In any case, the issue here is not how "sane" Irwin's mysticism was, but how easily he and it were dispensed with—at least conceptually, by everyone involved. Or, to change metaphors, how easily he was absorbed into various codes (legal, journalistic, psychiatric), as if they were anti-bodies and he an invading toxin.

This is precisely what does not happen to Joseph Detweiler in *Killing Time*. Berger's narrative strategy is to dramatize Detweiler's effect on four people: Betty Bayson, the daughter and sister of two women he has murdered; Detweiler's attorney, Henry Webster Melrose; a detective named Tierney; and a reporter named Alloway. Although Tierney's and Alloway's pursuit of Betty constitutes two sub-plots of the novel, Berger is specifically interested in how language serves to protect an established metaphysical frame of reference against a character whom it cannot explain or even understand. Throughout the novel, he shows such language at work while at the same time he preserves Detweiler's complicating contradictions. On one hand, Detweiler is the brutal killer of three people; on the other, he is the man who speaks the following words to a group of newspapermen shortly after an editor has called him "son" and told him that his "philosophy" wasn't worth much:

> ". . . my sole purpose in talking to you gentlemen of the press is to disseminate knowledge of my work. Realization means not only recovering the past, making it current and thus ending the bondage of Time. It also means realization of the potential of the human race.
>
> "I don't want to insult you fellows, but have you ever thought of the futility of what you do? There is another newspaper every single day: all those that have gone before are dead. All you powerful, clever, and wealthy men are slaves to that rhythm. Do you seriously believe that the quality of existence would be changed if you suddenly one day failed to bring out an issue? Or do you write about life at all? I mean the fundamental kind of life that a snake lives, or a fish in the sea, or a bird.
>
> "Cannot what you do be seen as a game or even a dream? Does it matter? Won't there always be another inning even if any one or all of you have quit? Your own time runs out, but Time continues. . . ."
>
> "Joseph." It was the publisher who now broke in. Had the editor spoken at that point, Detweiler would probably have tried to eliminate him. He had gripped the chair so tightly that four fingers of each hand had penetrated the leather, broken through the stuffing. (pp. 176–77).

The questions are obviously sane ones. They underlie all major religions. So does the conclusion that life ordinarily lived at a mundane level is *sub specie aeternitas* a game or dream.

Although this conclusion might help provide at least a partial understanding of Detweiler, no one is interested in exploring it, in considering what it might mean to actually believe in the possibility of escaping time and thereby realizing the potential of the human race—no one, that is, except Berger, who is dramatizing Detweiler as neither heroic nor villainous, sane nor insane, but inexplicably human. In Berger's novel, Detweiler simply exists as a character capable of both murder and spiritual insight, murderous rage and profound sensitivity. However, rather than confront Detweiler's contradictions, his opacity as a human being, other characters in the novel seek to clarify him by means of the most ideologically convenient categories (e.g., "madman," "murderer," "killer"), which in fact clarify nothing but do serve to justify, within a conventional frame of reference, "an intensification of his suffering over and above his original anxieties." As an insane killer, Detweiler is no threat to the ideological status quo, to an atomistic view of the world in which individuals exist independently of both divinity and each other and exercise, or fail to exercise, rational free will in accordance with commonsense standards of decency. As an insane killer, Detweiler is also useful to the press as a sensational commodity.

Given these ideological and professional assumptions and motives, newspaper officials can dismiss Detweiler's questions as "crazy" rather than as expressive of a profound sensitivity. The publisher certainly does. In a perfectly deft—and deaf—use of defensive language, he silences Detweiler's personal voice. By using what seems to be a personalizing word, Detweiler's full first name, the publisher gives an impression of concern when in fact he is demonstrating a lack of it by denying Detweiler what he wants and, from a moral point of view, so obviously needs: the freedom to express himself, to justify his existence by conveying his message to the world.

The linguistic drama I have described, in which other characters attempt to enclose Detweiler within politically convenient categories, is implicit in the above scene and in most of the encounters between Detweiler and public officials. It could therefore go unnoticed had Berger not been at pains to foreground language as an issue.[12] In a Note that precedes the text, Berger explicitly asks us

> not to identify the characters in the narrative which follows—criminals, policeman, madmen, citizens, or any combination thereof—with real human beings. A work of fiction is a construction of language and otherwise a lie.
>
> Some years ago a notice was posted at the entrance to Sala B of the Uffizi Gallery in Florence: "Please don't touch the pictures! It is dangerous for the works of art, it is punished by law, and finally it is useless."

Berger's novel is to be sure not only a construction of language but an artful one at that. Indeed, it is through artfulness that Berger tempts us to forget the problem of reference and simply enjoy the carefully modulated sentences and the non-literal, conspicuously literary language. Here, for example, is Berger describing the problems Betty Bayson faced as a writer:

> She could say "I" with abandon, but could not inscribe it upon the nullity of the blank paper. That was the first revelation: the utter lack of community between the written and the real, when both were personal. Life had another grammar than language, though words were alive and living had its verbal features. "When I was thirteen, my father tried to rape me." This statement was as clear, as direct, as true as she could fashion it, impeccable in talking-turkey syntax and brass-tacks vocabulary, this being no subject for the obscenity of circumlocution—yet as a characterization in words of the event in time, it missed the mark. (pp. 314–15)

These are the words of a artist, not a technician or ordinary journalist. They were created in part to give pleasure, to engage our aesthetic interest, not simply to communicate information. Reading them, we cannot help but be impressed by the author's control of rhythm, syntax and diction, for instance, and the way he uses sound to reinforce meaning. Berger's novel is also a lie in the sense that it is not a mirror reflecting what we take to be the concrete particulars of our world. Joseph Detweiler, for example, is Joseph Detweiler, not Robert Irwin, and his acts are his acts, not Irwin's, and Betty Bayson is equally her very fictional self, not a real Mrs. Gedeon's daughter.

But Berger's novel, contrary to the apparent implication of the Note, is not *only* a work of art that we can choose to touch or not to touch, because to understand his words is to experience what some writers, aspiring in their art to the condition of music, seem to consider the taint of reference.[13] We cannot help but connect Berger's words to our world, specifically to our experience of language. Berger refers to it constantly and in such ways as to call our attention to its complexity—to the difference between it and non-verbal reality, to its power as a means of both revelation and deceit. Consider, for instance, the paradoxes that result when Betty Bayson tries to use it to convey personal experience. In a paragraph that follows the one quoted above, we learn that the statement "When I was thirteen, my father tried to rape me" misses the mark not because it fails to convey the horror of an actual objective event, but because it fails to convey the truth of an imaginative experience that she believed occurred in a different order of reality altogether. She recalls the night she dreamed with pleasure of a hand fondling her. When she woke, she discovered she was holding her own wrist and her father was standing above her. He had come, he said, to close the window.

The rape was implicit in this experience, though perhaps, probably, he had not even touched her. What was true had not happened; therefore to be literal was to lie. Most of the story Betty had to tell was of a like nature: the truth that had not occurred, the history of that which had no time. But she was not dishonest. She could not represent the narrative as a personal confession, autobiographical, taking its chronology from the standard calendar, recording local names and habitations. To speak truly she must invent, construct, distort, and prevaricate. (p. 316)

Which is to say, Betty Bayson must write fiction, must do what the note-writing author of *Killing Time* presumably has done: construct a novel which lies about objective facts in order to tell the truth about subjective experience.

Her sophisticated understanding of the complex relation between language, objective reality and personal experience would enable Betty Bayson to appreciate the interpretive thicket Berger obliges us to enter in his Note. To negotiate it, we would be wise to bring along a few grains of salt, gleaned in part from the text itself. [14]

Detweiler's attorney, Henry Webster Melrose, is also interested in well-crafted language, but not as means of personal expression. Winner of eighty-two capital cases and loser of none, Melrose is a supremely confident, unsentimental man who is determined to practice something beyond good and evil—a profession as austere and impersonal as any saintly calling. In order to accomplish it, Melrose resolves to separate himself from his words and his words from life, "to speak always for others, the state or the accused, and never [for himself]" (p. 200); and "to practice his trade [without confusing it] with life, and thus [remain] its master and not a servant" (p. 202).

In short, Melrose approaches law as a disinterested verbal artist whose "joy was to exploit the possibilities within the discipline, as a poet using the constricting form of the sonnet" (p. 201). For him language is a means of disguise and escape, little more than a tool he uses to accomplish legal and quasi-aesthetic ends—until he meets Detweiler, whom he immediately recognizes as a threat to his moral isolation.

Initially, therefore, he refuses to accept Detweiler as a client, but then impulsively asks twice the fee he is offered. When a newspaper publisher agrees to meet his demand, Melrose feels compelled to accept. Immediately he finds himself enmired with misgivings that foreshadow his ultimate failure. Up to this point, he had defended killers who had murdered for a reason; but Detweiler, he is convinced, is a madman, which makes him "a resident of a different universe of discourse, with no neighbors, feeling no affinity even with other maniacs; by his very existence derisive of Melrose's art, wit, life" (p. 201). Detweiler represents to Melrose that dimension of experience that cannot be translated and so made comprehensible. At the same time, Detweiler speaks a simple moral language that Melrose cannot afford to hear. " 'I know that in your profession' " Detweiler says to Melrose during one of their interviews,

> "you have to protect yourself with cynicism, being the middleman between crime and punishment. Your clients are by definition morally inferior to the rest of humanity, and are on trial for doing things that you, yourself, would never even be suspected of. To speak for them requires great irony on your part, but there must be an even greater irony that nobody understands but yourself. I mean, I suppose people tend to think of you as something of a criminal if you defend criminals, and those you defend think of you as being ultimately on the side of the law. As for yourself, you must wonder whether you chose the profession because of compassion or cruelty." (pp. 245–6)

Like Hinsie before him, and like most officials faced with questions about their legitimacy, Melrose responds to Detweiler by reverting to role, by invoking the rules of the very system whose legitimacy is being questioned. " 'You have not retained me to study my motives, Joseph' " he says, as if Detweiler needed to be reminded of the official function of defense attorneys. A few minutes later, when Detweiler asks Melrose if he thinks that he, Detweiler, is guilty, Melrose in effect speaks to the broader question: " 'Joe, what you are is not relevant. What concerns us is what you can be proved to be in a court of law' " (p. 247).

Later Melrose comes to respect Detweiler's spiritual commitments,[15] but he never succeeds in representing him in either a legal or a linguistic sense. He cannot control him in the courtroom, nor can he express him in terminology that will influence a judge and jury. All that he can do is plea bargain and, before this, learn to envy Detweiler's transcendent independence, his peculiar ability to remain untouched "by other human beings," even "by the man who had saved his life. Melrose recognized that he was jealous of Detweiler" (p. 203).

Near the end of the novel, Melrose's envy burns into anger and despair. He curses his client and confesses to being sick and tired and old. Then he tells him that " 'I labor under an awful obligation, Joe. I am obliged to look after the best interests of my client. I take this as my divine duty, the execution of which will save my immortal soul' " (p. 364). Once the proud and contemptuous practitioner of verbal art who sought to separate life from art, his own being from his own words, the defeated Melrose is reduced to expressing very conventional sentiments in very conventional and unpoetic language.

In his discussion of linguistic factors in prejudice, Gordon Allport asserts that "Most people are unaware of this basic law of language—that every label applied to a given person refers properly only to one aspect of his nature. . . . Thus each label we use, especially those of primary potency, distracts our attention from concrete reality."[16] In telling the story of Joe Detweiler, Berger not only reveals the limitations of labels, he also calls our attention to the limitations of language itself as a means of knowing, or revealing, the world—and persons. By making Detweiler entirely unclear, by refusing to offer an "official" explanation of him that in fact extinguishes him, Berger, like Allport, reminds us that persons are always something more than what we call them. As human beings, he seems to suggest, we will always remain in some shadowy, non-verbal other place—beyond the reach of language and the value assumptions that inform it.

Notes

1. Kenneth Pelletier and Charles Garfield, *Consciousness East and West* (New York: Harper Colophon Books, 1976), pp. 30–1.

2. Pelletier and Garfield, p. 18.

3. Pelletier and Garfield, p. 23.

4. Thomas Berger, *Killing Time* (New York: Delta, 1967), p. 170. Subsequent parenthetical references are to this text.

5. Quentin Reynolds, *Courtroom* (New York: Farrar, Straus and Company, 1950), pp. 135–6.

6. Reynolds, p. 122.

7. Reynolds, p. 138.

8. Frederic Wertham, *The Show of Violence* (Garden City, N.Y.: Doubleday & Company, 1949), p. 168.

9. Wertham, p. 182.

10. Reynolds, p. 134.

11. Wertham, p. 182. For an account of Descartes' and Pascal's mystical experiences, see J. Bronowsky and Bruce Mazlish's *The Western Intellectual Tradition* (New York: Harper & Row, 1960), pp. 217–18 and p. 233.

12. One never knows how to take Berger as a commentator on his own work, but he has declared that language is the theme of all of his novels. See "Works in Progress," *New York Times Book Review*, 6 June 1982, p. 11.

13. Berger himself might be such an author. "I have never believed," he has been quoted as saying, "that I work in the service of secular rationalism . . . (the man of good will, the sensible fellow, the social meliorist who believes the novel holds a mirror up to society, etc.). I am essentially a voyeur of copulating words." See Brooks Landon's entry on Berger in the *Dictionary of Literary Biography Yearbook: 1980* (Detroit: Gail Research Company, 1981), p. 12.

14. In *Middle Grounds* (Philadelphia: University of Pennsylvania Press, 1987), Alan Wilde addresses the issues I have raised here. "Berger's kind of fiction," he says, "while it also questions a traditional authorial center and power, preserves in its forms and rhetoric a referential, if not . . . a representational function. . . . It strenuously interrogates the world without foreclosing all knowledge of it and unsettles rather than topples our certainties and presuppositions by way of parody and other recyclings of fictional, cultural, even metaphysical givens" (p. 45). Which is to say, as a referential writer, Berger refers to the world but does not try to re-present it in commonsense, realistic terms. Wilde goes on to suggest that Berger writes in a spirit of openness—and uneasiness, multiplying perspectives, refusing "to espouse unequivocally a single point of view" (p. 64). In the light of Wilde's observation, we might

read Berger's prefatory note not as a separate, authoritative text of the biographical Thomas Berger who, as such, *knows* what he and his books mean, but as another biased point of view.

15.   " 'Joe' " Melrose says, after several long interviews with Detweiler, " 'you have your own theories of reality, and they are interesting, challenging, serious, so serious that you took human lives in their pursuit, and are willing to lay down your own life as well. My own philosophy does not have the magnitude of yours' " (p. 257).

16.   Gordon Allport, *The Nature of Prejudice* (Garden City, N.Y.: Doubleday Anchor Books, 1958), p. 175.

Short-Changed: Thomas Berger's
Changing the Past

PATRICK O'DONNELL

> "I wouldn't ask too much of her," I ventured. "You can't repeat the past."
> "Can't repeat the past?" he cried incredulously. "Why of course you can!"
> He looked around him wildly, as if the past were lurking there in the shadow of his house, just out of reach of his hand.
> Nick Carraway to Gatsby, *The Great Gatsby*

At the heart of "the American dream" as articulated by Gatsby in what many still consider to be "the great American Novel" is the idea that one can repeat the past and, in so doing, change it. Gatsby's desire is not simply to repeat the romance of his and Daisy's youth in Louisville, but to reinvent the uninvented past as he imagines it. Logically, Gatsby cannot repeat the past, even on his own terms, for that past never "happened"; rather, in the same stroke, Gatsby wishes both to create the past and to alter his creation at will, claiming in that moment of alteration the authenticity of the past (its "repetition") and his own status as authenticator. That Nick has completely misunderstood the assumptions that found Gatsby's ill-fated designs upon the past is evidenced in the novel's closing elegiac passage, where Nick comments with rueful self-pity upon humans' tragic condition, trapped in an intractable past subject to no human efforts at intervention or transformation: "So we beat on, boats against the current, borne back ceaselessly into the past."[1] So thinks Nick, but he has missed the point in attempting to translate Gatsby's story into the imperialistic "American" story, the story of the West, the story of the New World haunted by the specter of an irrefutable historical past. Gatsby's idea, however illusory, is that one can repeat—and only repeat—that "past" which one invents in the moment of repetition. While Nick is interested in history and the impossibility of recreating it (even if his historical recountings are given over to the kinds of fictionalizations that Hayden White argues can be found in the writing of history at large),[2] Gatsby is interested in the past as a metaphysical paradox, as something that exists only in the future of its making. In short, however incompetently, Nick wants to be an historian, Gatsby a novelist.

This essay was written specifically for this volume.

The Great Gatsby is pertinent in this context because it informs both the comic and authorial strategies of another novelist, Thomas Berger, who has always been concerned with the writing of history and the construction of the past. Gatsby, the fictional character, and Berger, the author who makes up characters, share this striking similarity: they are both formalists in the restricted sense that they both view the past as "not existing" until it is given shape and structure, until it is formed into narrative. Gatsby, of course, has no past save that conferred upon him by Fitzgerald, but given what might be called the ironic authorial freedom to make himself up (ironic because in the instant that he invents himself, someone else—Nick—reinvents him), Gatsby composes a past stitched together out of received cultural narratives proceeding from romance, the bildungsroman and the Horatio Alger story, gangster movies, tabloid journalism. So too, Berger, in this intertextual mode, has written novels that assimilate and play upon available forms and genres: the "western" in *Little Big Man*, the hard-boiled detective novel in *Who Is Teddy Villanova?*, the Arthurian romance in *Arthur Rex*, the utopian fable in *Nowhere*, the historical novel in *Orrie's Story*.[3] As Gatsby constructs a personal past out of received discourses and available stories, so Berger has constructed his own canon—he has composed an authorial "past," a list of books available to interpretation and the invocation of intentionality—out of forms and stories of "literary tradition."[4] The obvious difference between Gatsby and Berger is that one is simply trying to constitute himself as a character in a novel while the other constitutes himself as an author of novels, but for both, the self-authoring of a personal past and the authoring of a discursive past comes about as the result of an attempt to convene and use the past by inventing it. And that inventing occurs within the double-bind that Berger comically reflects upon in *Changing the Past*: one can only invent what has already been invented; to use cliché, what is past is prologue.

Changing the Past is the story of a few days in the life of Walter Hunsicker, the head of an editorial department at a commercial publishing house. Hunsicker is typical of Berger's comic bourgeois protagonists who live comfortable if unexciting lives—that is, until new neighbors move in, or a guest arrives, or a petty insult is delivered. A man who believes " 'not even God can change the past' . . . after living almost six decades in which virtually every other supposedly unassailable truth had been successfully challenged,"[5] Hunsicker only begins to change his mind about the intractability of the past when he encounters "a little man" in a dark doorway during a rainstorm. The little man, appropriately disguised as the proprietor of a shop that sells prosthetic devices, turns out to be one of those folkloric figures who can grant three wishes or, in the case of Walter Hunsicker, change the past. Driven in part by curiosity, and in part by grief over the newly acquired knowledge that his gay son has contracted AIDS (a fact of life he seeks to change), Hunsicker agrees to participate in what the little man describes as an experiment in free will. And as in the tales of three wishes Hunsicker's desires are fulfilled, but only in unexpected ways, since the desires themselves are unexamined. Successively, Hunsicker becomes Jack Kellogg, a rich and sleazy slumlord, Jackie Kellogg, a borscht-belt-cum-Vegas comedian on the skids, John Kellogg, a novelist whose first success is followed by a series of mediocre failures, and Dr. John Kellogg, a radio psychiatrist whose popularity is instrumental in getting his wife elected president of the United States, only to see her assassinated during her inauguration. In each instance, Hunsicker gets what he asks for—money, popularity, creativity, virtue—but what follows from the acquisition of ostensible talent or success in the form of a logical extension of Hunsicker's personality is out of his control, once he is placed within the confines of the narrative architecture whose construction he has initiated with a wish.

One implication the reader might draw from *Changing the Past* is that, though the circumstances of his past can be altered at will, Hunsicker's personality remains constant, or more precisely, those aspects of his personality brought to the forefront by his changing occupations are part of a thoroughly self-consistent identity that manifests itself as benevolently mediocre in one life and tragically successful in another. Almost in the manner of a logical equation, the novel suggests that "history = the constant of personality + the chance of events." It poses the possibility that a John F. Kennedy born into an impoverished family in Texas might still have been "Kennedy," but could have died at an advanced age after serving for many years as the mayor of a small town; or that, given different circumstances, Hitler would still have been the embodiment of vicious evil, but could have been one of the hoods executed in the St. Valentine's day massacre. By inverting these transformations—by positing the transformation of the anonymous Hunsicker into a public "personality"—*Changing the Past* suggests that "fate" is a complex interaction of historical accident and the collision of identities understood as integral or totalized embodiments composed of "aspects," only a fraction of which reveal themselves in any given life.

In the novel, Berger provides his protagonist with the rare opportunity to experience several lives, and thus to witness the emergence of heretofore unknown facets of a personality that, paradoxically, grows more familiar—more consistent—the greater the apparent differences between Hunsicker's "real" and "imagined" lives become. What Hunsicker experiences in each life begins in fantasy and ends in disaster; thus, it would be inappropriate to term the pasts he "re-lives" as forms of wish-fulfillment. Conversely what these "lives"—businessman, comedian, novelist, radio talk-show host— have in common involves a failure of the imagination on Hunsicker's part. As the little man says to him after Hunsicker resigns from the experiment of living alternate lives following his aborted attempt to become the first "first gentleman" of the United States, "I find it significant that you did not make *yourself* President, nor as a writer did you present yourself with the Nobel Prize, and as a performer you did not become the Dean of American Comedy, acquiring a fortune in real estate and playing golf with chief executives. . . . There was always something about you in each life that was not quite what it should have been. Perhaps it was a basic lack of imagination. But then you never had much enterprise in your original existence" (277–78).

Hunsicker experiences "anti-fantasies" in the sense that they are constricted both by his own capacity to imagine—in Wallace Stevens's phrase from *The Man With the Blue Guitar*, "[a] tune beyond us, yet ourselves"[6]— and by the fact, since Hunsicker is reimagining the *past* once a chain of circumstances is initiated, that a certain kind of fatality sets in (Hunsicker is not allowed to project himself into an open-ended "future," and mortality remains at the limit of his alternative pasts). As the little man informs him when Hunsicker complains about his inability to micro-manage specific elements either of his present life or its alternatives, specifically the fact of his son's affliction, " 'My goodness, you cannot exercise a line-item veto when it comes to these matters: you have to take the package. If you'd like a heterosexual son, you've got to take what comes with him. He could be mentally impaired, for example' " (46–47). The subtext for what Hunsicker discovers in his backward glances and reconstructions is provided by another Stevens poem, "The Comedian as the Letter C" (perhaps echoed by Hunsicker's projection of himself as Jackie Kellogg, the comedian in the novel). There Crispin, voyaging to the new world of the imagination, ends where he began with the "nota" that "man is the intelligence of his soil" (Stevens, 27), and with the knowledge that whatever alternative narratives of identity one may concoct in possible pasts or possible futures, death remains as the final note and structuring element of those narratives: "so may the relation of each man be clipped" (Stevens, 46). So Hunsicker is compelled to acknowledge after this "experiment in free will" that his imagination— the imagination—is entailed by the logic of consequences and the logic of being.

The implications of these revelations manifest themselves in a number of ways across Hunsicker's alternative pasts, but perhaps most consequentially in two aspects of the "narrative structure" of these imagined pasts: pacing and repetition. As a comic writer, and reflexively in a novel that portrays the rise and fall of a Don Rickles–style comedian who becomes successful by insulting the members of his audience, Berger knows all about pacing, or timing the joke or story so that its punch line or climax arrives when the audience is maximally prepared for it. Indeed, both Jackie Kellogg's fame and failure can be attributed to good and bad timing: he is in the right place at the right time when the regular comedian at the night club where Jackie works as a busboy becomes ill, thus providing him with the opportunity to initiate his career in comedy; on one propitious evening, he stumbles upon the technique of insulting the audience when he turns his anger upon a particularly unreceptive crowd, and is surprised by the gales of laughter that meet his affronts; he endears himself to a powerful performer (Tony Gamble, who bears strong resemblances to Frank Sinatra) and hitches his wagon to Gamble's star at the time of Gamble's greatest influence, subsequently detaching himself from Gamble at the precise moment when "another philosophy of popular music than Tony's was gaining ground everywhere, one which furthermore had Leftist connections, whereas Tony was . . . of the old-fashioned school of sentimental patriotism" (90–91).

Yet, as much as Jackie benefits from good timing and time passing, he is also defeated by the latter as his style of comedy—like Gamble's style of music—becomes outmoded as the culture moves through the 1960s and into the 1970s. Jackie's insults, founded as they are upon racist and sexist stereotypes, become increasingly unappealing in the sensitized atmosphere of the post-Vietnam era. And unlike Gamble, who transforms himself into a rock musician as times change, Jackie is too much "himself" to become a comedian of the 1980s; instead, he changes occupations altogether by transforming himself into the manager of his young wife's career as she becomes a network news star, but even this attempt at change is aborted when his now-successful wife divorces the husband who has become a drag on her career. The final blow comes when Jackie hears in a conversation with an old girlfriend that the child he thought was his has never been born: she had lied to him about being pregnant and thus had caused Jackie's immediate departure for the big city and a new life as a once-successful comedian. Jackie discovers in the past imagined for him by Hunsicker that he cannot change the past even as the past is "in process," that is, unfolding as a story within a story that can be truncated whenever Hunsicker decides he has had enough. Kellogg the comedian ascertains that while one can control the timing of the performed narrative of a comedy routine, one cannot control the timing and pacing of "life," even if (and this constitutes the essential comic element of *Changing the Past*) that "life" is being imagined by someone else (Hunsicker) who has been given the chance to re-author his own "life" within the larger framework of a novel by Thomas Berger, who, as author, has the power within the artifice of his narrative performance to freely generate the lives of his characters as he will.

The story is much the same in the other alternative pasts Hunsicker generates and experiences: a sudden change in circumstances or an accident provides an opportunity for the incipient novelist, comedian, or radio talk-show host to initiate a career that unwinds slowly and ends suddenly either when Kellogg has become culturally irrelevant and is "expunged" by Hunsicker, or when a second twist of fate cuts short the trajectory of his history. In the each of these instances, timing is of the essence, and the narrative pacing of these alternative histories serves to underscore the accidental nature of "origins" and the sense that "history" is a fugue of pasts as a rich businessman (a few hours in the life of the promiscuous slumlord "Jack Kellogg" is enough to convince Hunsicker that he does not wish to live long in this narrative); in each role he assumes the narrative focuses upon how, as a vocational identity, he "began." Hunsicker spends a good deal of time thus establishing "himself," but once his identity as novelist, comedian, or host is founded, the narrative speeds up and the years pass by quickly (recall the effect of floating calendar pages being torn off with increasing rapidity by some ghostly hand in films that signify in this visual trick the fleeting passage of time). The more Kellogg becomes himself, the more familiar he becomes to his author (Hunsicker), so that the details and the narrative compression that one experiences in the founding stories can be elided. To summarize Berger's technique in pacing the presentation of these stories: in each we observe a rapid, circumstantial beginning, the slow unwinding of the "career," and a sudden denouement once Hunsicker sees the handwriting on the wall—this invented character, too, will die essentially unchanged. As this summary suggests, all of Hunsicker's projected pasts are cast in the form of identity-narratives, and the "pacing" of these stories causes the reader to reflect upon how both the past, and the identity that "experiences" a past by repeating it in the trajectory of the future, are composed.

Each of Hunsicker's imagined pasts is, actually, the beginning of a novel in miniature, leading one to wonder if *Changing the Past* is not an album of the inceptions of novels that Thomas Berger might have written if he could change his authorial past—that is, change the canon of his work by writing different novels. The double-focus on "beginnings" in each narrative (the beginning of a novel; the founding of a new identity for Hunsicker/Kellogg) suggests that Berger is conflating the origins of a narrative and the origins of an identity as equally "unfounded," or unpredictably accidental. One of the reasons for investigating one's past, as is the case in autobiography, or for attempting to establish a causal relation between present circumstances and past events, as is the case in the detective novel, is to determine where the "I" or the "mystery" in each instance began. Yet, as Edward Said argues, the "aboriginal human need to point to or locate a beginning"[7] is confounded in the textual space of the novel by the authorial need to generate a wholly fictive "beginning whose intention is to make order out of chaos" (Said, 113), and the contradictory desire to create authorial distance from those beginnings: "The necessary creation of authority for a beginning is also reflected in the act of achieving discontinuity and transfer" that forges a connection between the beginning and a "new direction not so much with a wholly unique venture but with the established authority of a parallel venture" (Said, 33). In *Changing the Past*, the paradox of "beginnings" becomes the subject of the novel. With each new beginning, each new attempt to change the past (already paradoxical, because as one knows from *Gatsby*, to change the past is to repeat it), Hunsicker both originates a new "self" and succumbs to the parallel destiny that confirms the fact that he has never escaped from the old one. In other terms, as the alternative pasts he chooses unfold, his "beginnings" begin to look very much alike structurally, suggesting that, for Hunsicker, the beginning—the fictive origin of his identity—is ultimately a form of repetition. Given the opportunity to originate a new "self," Hunsicker replicates the identity he already has within the differing historical and personal contexts orchestrated for him by the little man. There is, in essence, no new beginning for Walter Hunsicker.

One of the chief comic effects of *Changing the Past* arises from the punch line to this rather cruel joke played by "the little man" (homunculus to Thomas Berger) upon his victim in this so-called experiment in free will: given that Hunsicker is who he is, what else could one expect? For no matter how much Hunsicker may attempt to create different identities for himself (and how different are they, really, from the multiple author/homunculus/protagonist portrayed in the novel?: the editor becomes a novelist; the comic writer casts Hunsicker as a comedian; the alternative-pasts master of ceremonies transforms his patsy into a talk-show host), he is always doubly constrained by his own limitations and by the circumstances of an intractable reality. Wherever he goes and whatever he becomes, Hunsicker cum Kellogg is made to confront the ugliness of life and of contemporary American culture: the poverty of the slums, which causes him to annihilate his identity as rich businessman; the banality and narcissism of show business, which compels him to expunge the miserable existence of a Jackie Kellogg who has made a living off of racism, sexism, and insult; the crassness and stupidity of the current "confessional" environment (with its Geraldo Riveras and Oprah Winfreys and Sally Jessy Raphaels) that nourishes the radio career of "Dr." John Kellogg; and the omnipresent violence of American society that obliges Hunsicker to "conclude another life" (276). One sees at work in *Changing the Past* Berger's humorous fatalism—his partial sense that people will simply have to put up with whatever practical jokes reality plays upon them in a world whose bottom line is mortality. The "choice," or more precisely, Berger's authorial choice, is to find ways to reveal, enjoy, and satirize the bizarre peculiarities of the human plight. Momentarily, it will be suggested in what ways Berger complicates these fatalities even as he authors them.

In *Changing the Past*, Berger engages in a comic form of what Said calls (not unironically) "molestation":

> Now, *molestation* is a word I shall use to describe the bother and responsibility of all these powers and efforts [to forge the beginning of a text]. By that I mean that no novelist has ever been unaware that his authority regardless of how complete, or the authority of a narrator is a sham. Molestation then is a consciousness of one's confinement to a fictive, scriptive realm, whether one is a character or a novelist. And molestation occurs when novelists and critics traditionally remind themselves of how the novel is always subject to a comparison with reality and thereby found to be illusion. Or again, molestation is

central to a character's experience of disillusionment during the course of a novel. To speak of authority in narrative prose fiction is also inevitably to speak of the molestations that accompany it. (Said, 84)

Said employs this odd and disturbing term in order to suggest how the inescapable fictionality of a novel is always in conflict with what has long been considered one of its primary functions, to imitate reality. But the process of establishing the authority and authenticity of the imitation initiated by "beginning" the fiction is always confounded, both by the "sham" of beginning itself (creating a false beginning since one is always, in reality, in the middle of language and narrative) and by the fact that "reality" is chaotic and unknowable until it is structured into a narrative. Thus, authors "molest" their characters by subjecting them to both their own authority and the "authority" of reality by confronting them (and the reader) with the untenability or illusory nature of their projections and insights—this, Said argues, arising from the "appetite that writers develop for modifying reality . . . as if from the beginning" (Said, 82).

Such a rich moment occurs in James's *The Ambassadors*, when Lambert Strether, gazing along a river, notices Chad rowing in a boat with Madame de Vionnet and suddenly realizes that he has been a fool in assuming Chad's "innocence." On this occasion, James's narrator, the reader, and eventually Strether himself are engaged in acts of "molestation" wherein the authority of one version of reality is checked, sundered, scrapped, and another new version authenticated and put in its place. But since this unfolding perception of what is going on is simply one in a succession that Strether experiences, the novel can be seen as a continual negotiation between molestation and authority, between versions of reality that can be momentarily accepted as the "real" and those that have been discarded as false. In this case, the process of "molestation" occurs at every level and as a series of multiple interactions between the author, narrator, reader, and protagonist—each checking the other at every moment for which authorized rendering of reality is presently installed.

Said insists that this movement between the polarities of authority and molestation constitutes the novel as such, and certainly in *Changing the Past* one is entertained by Berger's comic appraisal of this authorial process. The reader witnesses, as well, Berger's highly reflexive and sardonic self-positioning as a contemporary writer who had, by the time of the writing of this novel, spun off a series of alternative pasts, and who writes in a postmodern environment where, to employ Baudrillard's infamous phraseology, "reality" is composed of a play of simulations that are "no longer that of a territory, a referential being, or a substance. [They are] the generation by models of a real without origins or reality: a hyperreal."[8] In *Changing the Past*, Hunsicker is allowed to create and inhabit a series of Baudrillardian "simulated" identities that effectively constitute "a real without origins." Berger as author engages in this exercise both for the purposes of self-parody (for Hunsicker is an inept author; unlike "successful" simulations, his do not *dissimulate* enough) and in order to comment upon the plight of the author in high career, with a good portion of an authorial past behind him, writing in the age of the hyperreal. On the one hand, in this novel—as in all of his work—Berger implicitly protests against what might be termed the "fascism" of authority, the imposition of a single version of reality that is, by means of that imposition, constituted as the only true one. The idea of alternative pasts or different versions of history is appealing to him because he wants to suggest that one's present point of arrival is neither necessary (things could have come out differently) nor certain (one does not always know where one is in the present, and the reinterpretations of the past generate all conditional presents). But Berger is also wary of the definition of "the real" under Baudrillard's terms, which tell us why he depicts Hunsicker as a bumbling simulator. For it is precisely the constraints of "the real"—including the limitations of his own imagination and identity—that Hunsicker is compelled to confront as he engages in this experiment in "free will."

For Berger "the real" is neither singular nor wholly tractable; the past, or history, are both constructions of versions of the past, and repetitions of the past as it is made up from the perspective of a shifting present always in the process of being established. The past is infinitely repeatable for Berger, but in a far different sense than that articulated by Gatsby, who believes, paradoxically, that the "repetition" can be an original event. In contrast, Berger understands the past as the repository of possibilities or alternatives that only come into being by means of what can be imagined within the periphery of the present, that is, what can be construed *as repeatable*. This is Berger's authorial dialectic, and it is one that Hunsicker is subjected to as he attempts to negotiate an alternative past that is a true departure from the present and his identity as it exists in the present, but to which he always returns.

The ending of *Changing the Past* confirms and extends this conception of the past, and at the same time typically serves to confound those who want to carry away from a novel by Thomas Berger any easy conclusions. Hunsicker returns home to his wife, seemingly resolved to his singular destiny, settling for and accepting a domesticity that includes both the sustained love of his wife and his son's sexuality. More largely this might be viewed as an acceptance of mortality: since Hunsicker cannot change the past, neither can he change the future in which his son will most certainly die of AIDS and where the fact—if not the circumstances—of his own demise is assured. Yet the scene of domesticity is always depicted in unsettling terms in Berger's novels, and the "resolution" to *Changing the Past* is no less troublesome. Hunsicker and his wife, Martha, engage in a seemingly casual conversation about their past together, and how it might have been different if they had not met and married. In one moment, Hunsicker wishes to himself "that there were a means by which he could share his alternative lives with her at least as entertaining narrative, but it was also because he loved her that it could never be done: he could not alter her sense of him at this late date" (284). At the conclusion of the conversation, Martha opines that " 'I have no regrets. I did what I should have done, am what I should have been,' " and Hunsicker responds in the novel's closing lines, " 'So did I . . . so am I.' But something still remained to be said, and he said it. 'I couldn't even imagine another life' " (285).

In Said's terms, the novel's punch-line might be considered the ultimate "molestation" of a character by an author: so chastised is he by his doomed attempts to imagine alternative pasts that Hunsicker renounces the two roles in which he has been cast: author and character. He decides that he cannot relate "entertaining narratives" out of love for his wife, thus abdicating his author-ity and foregoing the possibility of communicating what he has learned from his encounters with alternative versions of himself; and he does so because, as a character in a novel, he is dead in the water: he cannot change, he cannot even imagine changing. Structurally, the novel ends at the right place, for Hunsicker the protagonist has ceased to exist as a "character" or identity in this novel. Here, he sheds the living relation to the past that Berger has portrayed throughout his work as the median of identity which conspires with "fate" in the dialectic that governs both the formation and development of his agents. That this relation is problematic for Berger—that it comes about through sleight-of-hand as well as re-search—is unquestionable, but in the end it is what narrative enables. Hunsicker ironically gives up on narrative at the last moment, and when he does, his fate is sealed.

That final line, " 'I couldn't even imagine another life,' " is both funny and chilling, both a moment of self-irony (indeed, he could not imagine one, even when given four chances) and an acquiescence to the death of the imagination. This last instance of molestation—the ultimate one, as is always the case when an author expunges the body or consciousness of a character—might be viewed as a protest on Berger's part: both against the imagined possibility of the end of imagining, and against his own author-ity in fashioning a Hunsicker who gives in so easily to the past. Yet, knowing Berger, Hunsicker might not be done yet. In the resuscitated futures one could imagine for him, the doorbell might ring, an unexpected guest might arrive, new neighbors might move in, his wife might confess that she has had a secret lover all these years, and Hunsicker will then be compelled to open up the closed book of the past, albeit with a different name in another novel by Thomas Berger.

Notes

1. F. Scott Fitzgerald, *The Great Gatsby* (New York: Scribners, 1925), 159.
2. See Hayden White, *Metahistory: The Historical Imagination in Nineteenth-Century Europe* (Baltimore: Johns Hopkins University Press, 1973).
3. For revealing assessments of Berger's deployment and parodying of received generic forms, see Brooks Landon, *Thomas Berger* (Boston: Twayne, 1989); David W. Madden, "Thomas Berger's Comic-Absurd Vision in *Who Is Teddy Villanova?*," *Armchair Detective* 14 (1981): 37–43; Alan Wilde, "Acts of Definition, or Who is Thomas Berger?," *Arizona Quarterly* 39 (1983): 312–50; Larry E. Grimes, "Stepsons of Sam: Re-Visions of the Hard-Boiled Detective Formula in Recent American Fiction," *Modern Fiction Studies* 29 (1983): 535–44; William Bloodworth, "Literary Extensions of the Formula Western," *Western American Literature* 14 (1980): 287–96; Jean P. Moore, "Thomas Berger's 'Joyful Worship': A Study of Form and Parody," *Studies in American Humor* 2 (1983): 72–82; and Max F. Schulz, "Thomas Berger: His World of Words, and Stereoscopes of Styles," *Studies in American Humor* 2 (1983): 87–100.
4. Here, I am indebted to Marc Chénetier's perception that Berger, Nabokov, Davenport, and others make " 'visits' to the cultural traditions of the past in order to recontextualize and renew those traditions" (my translation; Chènetier, *Au-delà du soupçon: La nouvelle fiction américaine de 1960 à nos jours* [Paris: Seuil, 1989], 282). The idea of "visiting" the literary past is quite apt for Berger, whose novels often depict the comic intrusions of visitors and neighbors.
5. Thomas Berger, *Changing the Past* (London: Weidenfeld and Nicolson, 1989), 3. Further citations noted parenthetically.
6. Wallace Stevens, *The Collected Poems of Wallace Stevens* (New York: Knopf, 1972), 165; hereafter cited in the text.
7. Edward W. Said, *Beginnings: Intention and Method* (Baltimore: Johns Hopkins University Press, 1975), 5; hereafter cited in the text.
8. Jean Baudrillard, *Simulations* (New York: Semiotext(e), 1983), 2.

INTERVIEW

◆

An Interview with Thomas Berger

David W. Madden

I met Thomas Berger in 1982 and began a correspondence with him that has continued for thirteen years. In 1989 I suggested we undertake an interview, and he agreed, though cautioning me that "I do interviews *only* in writing." On the surface such an arrangement is without the usual anecdotes—what Berger's house or study looked like, how he was dressed, what books lined the shelves—and naturally there were none of the "usual" surprises. However, surprises, for me at least, came frequently and always promptly in the mail. In response to some queries, he was positively expansive, and others he dispatched briefly, only to be pestered again with the question inelegantly rephrased. I have always found Mr. Berger to be an affable, witty, and pleasant correspondent, and this interview, although a long while in the making, was simply the most recent installment in what I hope is our continuing friendship.

DM: The naming of your characters has fascinated me for some time. If you don't mind, I'd like to ask about some of them. For instance in *Reinhart's Women*, Edy Mullhouse has a father named Edwin. Were you alluding here to Steven Millhauser's novel *Edwin Mullhouse*?

TB: Never, until receiving your letter, had I so much as heard of Steven Millhauser or a novel of his entitled *Edwin Mullhouse*! Extraordinary! Indeed, I had utterly forgotten that I gave Edy's father a name, cannot remember that I mentioned her having a father!

DM: I know you did graduate work on George Orwell; is Georgie Cornell in *Regiment of Women* an anagram of his name?

TB: As to Georgie Cornell's name, again I did not consciously select it with reference to anything other than my need to call the hero something. But of course I do not rule out unconscious influences. Perhaps even in the case of Edwin Mullhouse I had seen the name somewhere, years ago, and unconsciously stored it away.

This interview was conducted for this volume and is published with the permission of Thomas Berger and David W. Madden.

DM: I'm also curious about the name Earl Keese, why that particular spelling of his surname?

TB: I was thinking of spelling it "Keyes" but decided on "Keese," so that no one would pronounce it as "Kize," which seemed possible with the other. The irony is that John Belushi delivers it with an emphatic sibilant in the film, so that we hear "Keess." My use of the name, of course, derives from the Edward G. Robinson character in the movie version of *Double Indemnity*: Fred MacMurray uses it again and again as he dictates his confession, if you remember, into Robinson's machine—not, I believe a tape recorder; the era's too early for that; probably the so-called Dictagraph, which recorded onto wax tubes. I'm sure you know the film, one of the all-time greats. Forty years ago, before it was fashionable, my cousin, who's slightly older than I, could recite passages of dialogue from the movies we both saw at least once a week. I can still remember lines from *Gunga Din*, starring Victor McLaglen, Cary Grant, and Doug Fairbanks, Jr., made in about '38, not as they came from the actors, but as my cousin delivered them, mimicking the actors. I don't know the James M. Cain novel of *Double Indemnity*, but I suspect the Robinson character's name is spelled Keyes. I think his desk, in the film, has one of those name boards on it, but I cannot see, in my mind's eye, what's printed on it.

DM: Could you comment in general, then, on your practice of naming characters?

TB: Indeed I am always concerned to find the right names for my imaginary people. Dickens has served as my inspiration in such an effort, though to be sure his names would be somewhat overblown in our era: e.g., Poll Sweedlepipe in *Martin Chuzzlewit*. In the twentieth century my favorite is the guy named Klipspringer, in *The Great Gatsby*, who comes to the otherwise deserted mansion after Gatsby's death to look for some tennis shoes he left behind as a houseguest.

DM: Are the names, then, serendipitous or do they actually precede the character to the point that that figure's personality grows out of or around the name?

TB: I think I usually get a character's name at the time he first appears, just as one newly meets a human being. But I do keep a list of names that come to me at other times, and occasionally refer to it when I meet a character who needs naming. On this list, which dates back to the beginning of my career, I find, at random, Ruth Goodge, Dolly McElroy, Mitch Pratt, Lucas Oakum, and Jerry Esposito. I've already used Hunsicker, Teddy Villanova (which I heard on TV), Gus Kruse (a walk-on character in *Vital Parts*), and the name "Babe" for a woman.

DM: I'm curious about the character of Tony Gamble in *Changing the Past*; is he modeled after Frank Sinatra?

TB: Tony Gamble differs from Sinatra as often as he resembles him, but Tony does suggest what might result if all the prominent figures in Sinatra's milieu were compressed into one. The spitting of the half-chewed sandwich into the hands of a long-suffering lackey I stole from a reportorial account of a backstage visit with Jerry Lewis. You were quite right in your review when you said *Changing the Past* is not funny. It wasn't supposed to be. But I have a hard time evading reviewers who insist that whatever I write is a "comic novel."

DM: I'm pleased that my caution that *Changing the Past* is not a comic novel per se met with your approval. However, I still remain curious about your long-standing reluctance to see your works described as comic. Could you explain why you don't see them as such or why you reject that description?

TB: On the subject of whether my work is comic or not, I can only say that my intention is to tell a straightforward story for my own entertainment. Surely there are funny passages, but my purpose is not to inspire laughter except incidentally. What I dislike about being called a "comic novelist" is that reviewers who don't like my books find it too convenient to condemn them for not being funny enough.

DM: Your answer to the above provokes this—when writing do you do so with any sense of audience in mind? Nabokov once said, for instance, that he wrote first for himself, next for his wife, Vera, who typed his manuscripts, and last for a few informed, sympathetic readers.

TB: My sole serious motive for writing is to entertain myself. I rarely think consciously of the audience, and when I do, it's usually to assume that they will probably not get my point. Thus I am always astonished when I read the rare critical piece (like those of yours) that displays an authentic sympathy for my work.

DM: Given your abiding fascination and precision with language, how do you arrive at a voice for your characters—does it precede them or issue from their personae?

TB: As to the characters' peculiar voices: each creates his own as he proceeds, with the possible exception of Jack Crabb. His came to me already fully developed, I don't know how. I simply heard it when I sat down at the typewriter. A couple of people have mentioned my debt to Mark Twain, and no doubt I owe one, but I was not consciously echoing him, and the only book of his I had read within fifteen years of writing *Little Big Man* was *Roughing It*. I *was* consciously influenced by the dialogue of the character called Kit Carson, in Saroyan's play *The Time of Your Life*. One of the colorful personages who frequent the bar therein, this aged coot tells tall tales about the Old West. It would be more precise to say that in his case, as I remember, he promises to tell such stories but either never gets around to them or is brushed off by the other characters when he makes the attempt.

DM: I've been struck by how prolific you've been, especially in the 1980s. After you finish a novel, are you set to move on to another or do you pause and let the well fill up?

TB: While I'm writing one novel I generally have another idea waiting in the wings. When I was younger, it was almost invariably the case that the next one I began after finishing the latest did not work out: that is, the idea might have been okay, but somehow I couldn't live up to it. I think my imagination needed more time between books. But for a while now, I haven't had that trouble but have moved rather easily from one novel to the next. Perhaps that's because I am older and don't have as much time left!

DM: I remember in the interview you did with Richard Schickel when *Neighbors* was published you mentioned that "Harry and Ramona may be better people finally than Keese, despite their outrages, for the reason that they are fundamentally more generous than he." In considering Chuck Burgoyne's relationship with the Graveses in *The Houseguest*, do you consider him a fundamentally better sort than they?

TB: Harry and Ramona are endearing people even though, as my friend Zulfikar Ghose uniquely saw on his first reading, they are Angels of Death. But Chuck Burgoyne is a vile fellow. The Graveses are simply worthless. Lydia is the only decent person in that book.

DM: Do you consider Lydia's position at the end of the novel as similar to, better, or worse than Earl's at the end of *Neighbors*? One can read the ending to the latter in very different ways: for going against his essential nature, Earl winds up killing himself, or at the moment when he is released from his former self, he shuffles off the mortal coil.

TB: At the end of *The Houseguest* she is in quite a different situation from Earl Keese's in *Neighbors*. Earl is done, whereas she's really just beginning adult life. Earl by the way is already dying when his story begins: here and there I mention his high blood pressure, as I recall, but more seriously, he is morally moribund. Harry and Ramona in one sense give him the coup de grace, but, in another, provide him a final twenty-four hours of vivid existence. By the way, I regard *Neighbors* as being, with *Little Big Man*, my best book. It's about Death but is a happy story, all in all.

DM: I agree that Lydia is the central character in *The Houseguest* and that she is clearly superior to the Graveses, Chuck, and the Finches. However, the conclusion seems rather enigmatic to me, for she aspires now to assume the role of houseguest, a role that's been revealed to be rather dubious. How do you see her, especially at the novel's close?

TB: I think that at the conclusion of *The Houseguest*, Lydia is prepared to become a tyrant, though perhaps a more honorable one than Chuck. At least her intentions are better than his, for he is nothing more than a scoundrel. The subject of that novel is power, whereas that of *Neighbors* is dying.

Though in neither case did I arrive at that understanding until the final word was written.

DM: My students are often very concerned about Chuck's rape of Lydia. It seems one of the novel's many unresolved enigmas—Lydia claims he has, Chuck argues he was invited, but our narrator offers no opinion. Do you want to have a say about this?

TB: I suppose you have to say that Chuck rapes Lydia insofar as he doesn't have her consent, but he takes her by deceit and not by force. She really is asleep at the outset. As soon as she is conscious, she throws him out of bed. The situation is really unambiguous. Chuck's saying she invited him is, I believe, the standard self-serving excuse of a certain kind of rapist. I don't want to be pious on this subject: I despise cockteasing, but detest rape. Not that Lydia does any of the former, in my memory.

DM: Whom would you describe as the protagonist or hero of *The Feud*?

TB: The hero of *The Feud* or anyway the central character, though perhaps he's more of a *raisonneur*, is Jack—though I confess to you that I forgot his name completely and had to turn to the book now to get it! By the way, he was omitted entirely from the movie.

DM: Do you have any plans for future additions to the Reinhart saga?

TB: I'd like to write one more Reinhart, about R. as an old man.

DM: At the conclusion of *Who Is Teddy Villanova?*, Russel Wren comments that "Peggy was not . . . serving her novitiate in venery." Could you interpret his remark? The answer seems obvious, but my students, and some very good ones, have interpreted that line in wildly different ways.

TB: All that Russel Wren means when he makes his final comment on Peggy Tumulty is that she is far from being the frigid virgin he has taken her for throughout the narrative.

DM: The unprinted subtitle to *Neighbors* is "A Tale of Harassment." While that certainly refers to the involvements of the characters, doesn't it have other implications, especially for the reader who finds him- or herself trying to find some stable ground in the shifting allegiances and motives of the characters?

TB: I take it you mean *Neighbors* is harassing not only to its characters, but also to its readers. That may be so: my grocer made such a complaint. The effect was not intentional on the author's part: what I so like about *Neighbors* is that in effect it wrote itself. At no point in its composition did I use any ratiocination. I was eager each day to get to the typewriter and see what happened next.

DM: In a class discussion of Harry and Ramona—their mysterious origins, outlandish pranks, threatening gestures, and general unruliness—one of my students said they reminded him of Germanic tribes, the "barbarians" who would lay siege to a castle, win it, only then to destroy it by fire or some other means, but not inhabit it. He argued that they shunned such places because they believed that to live in them would be to inherit the spirits and values of its predecessors, and they wanted none of that but to cleanse the place of earlier influences. He then wondered whether, since you were of German-American origins, you weren't availing yourself of this bit of cultural lore in creating Harry and Ramona, with their laying siege to Earl's life and castle and burning down the house they briefly claim. Do you have any response to this theory?

TB: Your student's idea that in the case of Harry and Ramona I might have had Teutonic barbarians in mind is intriguing, but I had no such conscious intention. However, who knows whether it might not be valid as to my unconscious inclinations. In preparation for the writing of my first novel, *Crazy in Berlin*, I steeped myself in German lore, going as far back as Tacitus' work on the savage tribes met by the Romans, and no doubt some of this stayed with me.

DM: Ramona seems to me an especially complex and fascinating character. Initially she appears as an importunate temptress, but later, especially in her dealings with young Greavy after the fire, she is a figure of deep intuitive resources and one who possesses a strong, almost moral, force over others. How do you see her?

TB: Yes, Ramona is an extraordinarily wise figure, underneath it all, and so is Harry. Being heterosexual, my bias is in favor of the female, though both of them have godlike attributes. Just about my favorite scene is when Ramona disposes of the younger Greavy, who has been such a terror to Keese. One almost feels sorry for the lout when she's done with him. She also says something great at some point to the effect that "they'll nail you to the wall if your sequences are off."

DM: When writing do you see your work as participating in some critical debate—as a deconstructionist, poststructuralist, or whatever fiction?

TB: As a graduate student at Columbia, forty years ago, I had some interest in critical theory. I have had none whatever in the years since and have successfully kept myself totally ignorant of the -isms you mention.

DM: Another novelist has mentioned to me that he felt any writer has a finite number of deeply held ideas to which he or she returns frequently. Without being hopelessly reductive, can you share some of those you are consciously aware of?

TB: I am not aware of having any deeply held ideas to which I return frequently in my fiction, though no doubt critics could find some: that's their job, not mine.

DM: In various critical analyses of your work, writers have noted influences of existential thought. Have you been influenced by the existentialists, and if so, could you comment on that influence? Also along the same lines, I have noticed lately that your works (*Being Invisible*, *The Houseguest*, and *Changing the Past*) have been referred to as modern "morality" tales. Do you agree, especially given your aversion to Shaw and to instructing anyone about anything?

TB: I have no conscious philosophical intent in my novels. Nor do I preach morality, though I am interested almost exclusively in moral situations.

DM: But surely there are at least echoes of existentialism in your works. I see it over and over again, particularly in *Being Invisible*, but by no means in this one novel. Is this an intellectual influence, and do you see it figuring in this novel?

TB: I always thought that the Indian parts of *Little Big Man* are existential, and got a chance to say so in an interview published in a Parisian newspaper at the time the French translation was published! What I did not say, however, was that I always despised Sartre and had not read much of Jaspers and none of Heidegger. Martin Buber would be my influence, if there was one.

DM: Do you, then, agree with John Carlos Rowe's contention that *Neighbors* and subsequent novels amount to a rejection of existential humanism?

TB: Perhaps. In any event, I am fascinated by Rowe's essay.

DM: Could you explain? Are you ambivalent, uncertain, or still deciding? I would assume that the influence of Nietzsche is profound enough that you have some strong opinions about existentialism one way or another.

TB: My only own philosophy is an amalgam of Nietzsche and Simone Weil, who may superficially be seen as impossibly divergent but come together in a stern *amor fati*: one must "not merely bear what is necessary, still less conceal it . . . but *love it*" (Nietzsche). "I saw it [the love of fate] as a duty we cannot fail in without dishonoring ourselves" (Weil). But my conscious purpose in writing novels is not to promote my beliefs or even to suggest or reflect upon them: it is rather, as I have continued to insist, only to amuse myself. Therefore I can say "perhaps" to almost any reasonable interpretation.

DM: What role does setting or landscape have in your works? I ask because it seems to me that setting in so many of your novels—*Regiment of Women*, *Sneaky People*, *Neighbors*, *The Feud*, *The Houseguest*, to name just a few—is of major importance. These aren't simply convenient locations for activities; in my view they are as strong a narrative force as the characters themselves. How do you see the role of setting in your fictions?

TB: The setting of a novel is indeed often important to me, but usually I'm not aware of that until I get well into the narrative. Just as the characters begin as formless blobs and sketch themselves in by what they say, the physical situation gradually reveals itself, just as it does in life when one moves into a new house, a new town, a new country. I never have even a mental floor plan until I am far into the narrative. When Keese goes downstairs for the first time, what he sees was news to me: I hadn't known of the shower there, for example. Outside, I hadn't been aware of the swampy area next to the house until Harry's car sank into it. And so on.

DM: I know that you have a high regard for Vladimir Nabokov, and in rereading *Little Big Man* I was struck by the character Snell who writes the insane and self-serving introduction and epilogue. Were characters like Nabokov's John Ray, Jr., Ph.D., in *Lolita* and Charles Kinbote in *Pale Fire* any inspiration—conscious or otherwise—for Snell? Brooks Landon, in his introduction to the most recent edition of the novel, mentions Nabokov.

TB: Indeed I was, and am, an admirer of Nabokov. Perhaps I was influenced by John Ray, Jr.'s foreword to *Lolita* when writing the one signed by Ralph Fielding Snell, but if so, I was not thinking consciously of it. I needed another voice than Jack Crabb's to make some acknowledgment of recorded history, in which despite Crabb's claims to have participated in and survived the Last Stand (and to have known most of the celebrated figures of the Old West), there is no reference whatever to this person. Snell serves to make such a point, but he is otherwise a pompous ass.

DM: Could you expand on a remark in a letter to Zulfikar Ghose in which you write, "My recent [Dec. 1977] books mean little if taken literally: the meaning disappears if the text is unravelled."

TB: What I meant in my 1977 comment to Ghose was that if *Who Is Teddy Villanova?* and even *Arthur Rex* were synopsized, abstracted, or paraphrased, they would be meaningless: the text is the meaning and the meaning is the text. To some degree that's true of all of my books, which is why throughout my career, I have paid little attention to editors, who are by nature without interest in words.

DM: I'm also curious about another remark in which you say, "plot is something I have never given ten seconds' thought to throughout my career. Such plots as I use have developed organically, as it were, from the style." There is a similar technique I find in many of your novels, a movement between the actions of various characters and suspensions in time and focus. Does this shifting and pausing have any thematic connection? (For instance, the nature of "reality" which in your works is *never* linear but fractured and truncated. By the way, this also reminds me very much of the practice of many eighteenth-century novelists who delight in the episodic, often simply for its own sake, such as Defoe, Fielding, Smollett.)

TB: I never consciously make fictional plots because to do so would be to stifle that which is natural and organic and replace it with dead artifice. When a work of mine goes well, the Muse steps in and writes it for me, and being a lazy fellow with limited talent, I welcome this process. I never know what's coming next, nor which characters, which is why writing fiction has always been so exciting for me. Yes, Smollett is one of my favorites, all of whose principal novels I read at the outset of my career. I think you are shrewd in finding his scent here and there in my forest.

DM: Why in the early seventies were you more enthusiastic about drama than fiction and do you still write plays? Are there any plans for the plays to be collected and published; I've never seen them in print.

TB: A play of mine called *The Burglars* was published in *New Letters* a few years ago (along with an interview full of typos, one of which criminally misrepresents me as making a libelous pun to the effect that too many "crooks" spoiled the pot of the *Neighbors* movie!). And one act of *Other People* appeared in a paperback book-magazine, published by the Literary Guild under the title, *Works in Progress*, 1972. *Other People* was performed for the first two weeks of the season of 1970 at the Berkshire Theatre Festival in western Massachusetts. Despite the prestige of that event, the producers were unable to raise the money for a Broadway production, and that was the end of my career as a playwright, though I wrote two other plays in quick succession during the same era. I enjoyed my brief experience in the theater, but I am fundamentally a writer of fiction, in which I'm not dependent on anyone else to realize a work. Writing a play, unless it's intended to be kept in the closet (which surely must have been the case with some of the plays written in the nineteenth century by people like Shelley), is only the first phase: it's not a complete work until it's performed.

DM: I'm also curious about your use of various structures or subgenres of the novel—detective story, utopian novel, knightly romance, futuristic fiction, the Oresteian saga. I know you have said that these spring from your appreciation of these forms, but is there another provocation—whom you are reading at the moment, an opportunity for a stylistic challenge, or perhaps a thematic exploration?

TB: As to why I've tried my hand at various genres of fiction, when I admire and enjoy something I am generally inclined to try my hand at it: e.g., after years of pursuing my interest in food exclusively by eating it, it occurred to me that I should learn to cook, and I did so. I always loved the way sports cars look, and arrived at a point at which I wanted to own and drive one. Being about forty at the time, I thought it too late to think about a career in competition driving (though I may have been wrong about that: whenever Paul Newman began, he is still racing, and he's my age), but I had a lot of pleasure on public roads with an E-Type Jaguar and other high-performance machinery, especially when I lived in then speed-limitless England. I have always enjoyed tales of crime, Westerns (though curiously enough, not in print but rather on film: the only Western novel I think I ever read was Zane Grey's *Riders of the Purple Sage* as a boy and didn't care for it), the Arthurian legends, and so on. I have never cared for space operas or horror stories and avoid both if I can: you will notice that I have written no novels with any reference to any venue but Earth and none that features haunted houses, the residents of ancient Indian burial grounds, or malignant wraiths. (Though I admit to having produced a piece of short fiction in 1988 for *Playboy* entitled "Planet of the Losers," in which some inept visitors from space land in an American field, and an attempt at a ghost story, many years ago, which went unpublished, so I can't be too self-righteous. But I don't quite know why I wrote those things, because I despise the genres.)

DM: You dedicated *Changing the Past* to Ralph Ellison, and for some time I've been curious about your selection of the surname "Reinhart." Is there any connection with Ellison's Rinehart (different spelling I realize)? Both characters are chameleons in a sense, ever-changing figures who wander through their worlds. Where Ellison's is threatening, even an incarnation of evil, yours is far more benign, even benighted. Would you care to comment?

TB: Though Ralph Ellison was a friend to my work early in my career and though I was and am a great admirer of *Invisible Man*, I did not (consciously, anyway) lift the name Reinhart from his character Rinehart. I chose the name because, as I say somewhere in *Crazy*, the meaning of the German original is Pureheart. Also, about one of every ten persons in the town where I grew up had that name in one or another spelling: e.g., the chap to whom I dedicated *The Feud*, one Mick Mooney, had a mother maiden-named Reinhart.

DM: A detail in *Sneaky People* occasions, this next question—Laverne's make-shift version of Roman Catholicism and penance. I may have asked you once if you were Catholic (and I believe you said no), but a number of Catholics appear in your books. Can you explain this; have you studied or been influenced by Catholicism?

TB: No, I haven't ever been a Catholic, but I was raised among Catholics and several of the girls and women with whom I have been close were of that persuasion. Most of the rest of my associations, with only a few exceptions, have been with Jews, and I'm not Jewish, either. I am usually interested in the other and not the same.

DM: I'm curious what provoked you to return in *Nowhere* to the character of Russel Wren.

TB: Russel Wren simply seemed the appropriate fellow to send to *Nowhere*. I first thought of a Utopian novel of which Reinhart was the hero, but that seemed too far-fetched.

DM: In deciding on the utopian genre for *Nowhere*, were you writing with any particular examples or models in mind? Were you responding, obviously in the twentieth century, to the work of specific writers from other eras?

TB: I had read many of the familiar treatments of the theme, More, Butler, Bellamy, and the others, including a (at least to me) lesser-known example by my fellow Ohioan William Dean Howells, but I don't remember thinking of any of them when writing my own. This is as appropriate a place as can be found to confess that *Nowhere* satisfies me least of any of my novels. Mind you, I should not have published it at all had I considered it unworthy of me—more than once I have discarded huge fragments of works—in progress and on one occasion the manuscript of a complete book of more than four hundred pages—but in this case I think I was a bit too impatient to complete the project and so fulfill a legal obligation to a publishing firm at which a great friend to my work had been replaced by an enemy, who nevertheless, presumably so as to do me as much damage as possible, would not release me from the contract. Without such a distraction I might have been more patient and remembered at the outset I had hoped Russel Wren would enter into a romance with a desirable young woman in San Sebastian and thus provide some relief from the prevailing didacticism. I should also say that *Nowhere* as it stands displays some of the things I do best, though again I leave it up to others to say just what they might be.

DM: One critic of your work has argued that a reader can deduce *you* from evidence in the fictions. How do you feel about such a proposition?

TB: Since receiving a photocopy of the essay to which you refer, sent me five or six years ago by someone who unaccountably admired it, I have made almost annual efforts to penetrate the ungodly jargon in which it is couched, but have failed to the degree that I cannot so much as recognize the *Muttersprache* from which it is derived—except to rule out English. As I therefore have been unable to identify the answer this practitioner gives to the question he asks of himself (surely the ultimate authority), "Who Is Thomas Berger?" it may well be that I lack the credentials that would empower me to dismiss him out of hand when, for all I know, the mystery may well have been solved, only to be concealed anew, this time under a compost pile of critical gibberish. . . . But given his example, why should I be restrained by ignorance?

Borrowing from Pound and then Proust (*Contre Sainte-Beuve*), I might say my Penelope is Flaubert, with whom I agree that the "writer's life is centered in his work, and that the remainder exists only 'to provide an illusion to describe.' " This statement might be taken by our commentator to justify his effort, which would be okay by me could I recognize anything of myself in the trivialities accessible to translation: for example, the "fear of Otherness" that he ascribes to the puppet he scissors from the whole cloth, stuffs with his own delusions, and calls "Berger."

DM: More specifically, I'm interested in this man's conclusion that evidence in your novels suggests homophobia on your part. Would you care to address this contention?

TB: Obviously I cannot comment on the sexual preoccupations of our critic, but I can aver, with the authority of experience, that American young men of the working and lower-middle classes (from which I take my own origin), in military and civilian life, consistently manifested, during the eras in which the earlier Reinhart books were set, what might seem to the sheltered spirit an obsession with heterosexual virility. Now, this might be seen as fustian (concealing a latent attraction to sexual inversion), fascist (lording it over those who, like the rest of us, had no alternative to being what we are), or farcical (and often unfunnily cruel)—or as having no significance whatever—but that's the way it was. The most popular form of jocular spoken abuse in every Army outfit with which I ever served, from Denver to Berlin, heard incessantly, was "queer" or one of its variants. That this is still the case half a century later, at least with the civilian equivalents of my wartime comrades, was confirmed for me by the banter exchanged by the score of carpenters, plumbers, electricians, et al., who renovated my house last fall. Indeed, it was sometimes even true of the homosexual man (and his visiting friends) with whom my wife and I shared a home during the period in which I wrote one of the novels desperately ransacked by our scholar for evidence that I hysterically fear homosexuals. Perhaps the hysteria, if such there be, is not mine. It might be stretching a point (despite my admiration for Balzac, Gissing, Norris, and Dreiser) to call me a realist, but I do strive for sociological authenticity.

Now, in a passage in *Vital Parts*, Reinhart in his own fashion makes much the same point as I do above, and our *Besserwisser* even quotes it on one of his endless pages—only, as usual, to provide an interpretation that is at once fatuous and laden.

DM: Elsewhere in that article, in discussing your style, the writer comments, "whatever else Berger's fiction achieves, it is rarely delicate inflections. Indeed, as an instrument of discrimination and nuance, Berger's style often seems remarkably blunt, even awkward." Would you care to comment on this assessment?

TB: It is axiomatic that one cannot speak of one's own delicacy with a straight face, and it should be apparent to anybody who is guided by reason that I would wear a smirk when I predicted to the *New York Times Book Review* that the "tin-eared will fail to hear the delicate inflections" of the language of *The Feud*. To which our ponderously disingenuous commentator responds, "At the risk of joining the ranks of the tin-eared, I have to say . . . ," etc., and proceeds to display a pair of the very metallic auricular organs of which I spoke, legitimizing the jest.

Yet I would myself be less than candid were I to say, that late in the game, I was surprised to see the trap close on his foot: by then I had long since understood that this disquisition had very little to do with either my work or me, both of which are simply (or elaborately) used as pretexts for an extended exercise in self-regard.

DM: I'm curious about something you just mentioned about writers you admire, and you include Norris. What do you like about him? Today his standing among academics is not especially high, though I have always admired and taught *McTeague*.

TB: *McTeague* is of course Norris's masterpiece, to which, by the way, I pay tribute in *Little Big Man*: at one point when McTeague is boarding a train at some remote railway station, an Indian comes up to him and hands him a "filthy, crumpled letter . . . to the effect that the buck Big Jim was a good Indian and deserving of charity; the signature was illegible." McTeague returns the letter without a vocal response, and neither does the Indian speak. The latter "did not move from his position, and fully five minutes afterward, when the slow-moving freight was miles away, the dentist looked back and saw him still standing motionless between the rails, a forlorn and solitary point of red, lost in the immensity of the surrounding white blur of the desert." The book would be great if only for that brief passage. In any event, Old Lodge Skins presents such a letter to the wagon train at the beginning of *Little Big Man*, a moment stolen from Norris. But *McTeague* is not his only triumph. Anyone living in the Bay Area should know the excellent portrait of San Francisco as given in *Vandover and the Brute*, space for which on one's shelf should be made by discarding Kerouac's drivel. And every Californian should know *The Octopus*, and any American *The Pit*, a rare example in serious fiction of dealing with finance, in this case the commodities market in Chicago: scarcely an attractive subject on the face of it, but Norris is an artist of the Balzacian breed. He was also, as this alas all too short list displays, remarkably versatile. His death was a great loss to American literature. Californians, so often the object of Eastern cultural scorn, can show in Norris a writer who can hold his own in any company. He is by the way somewhat less melodramatic than Dickens and less sentimental, but the great ones like Norris and Dickens sometimes employ such effects for their own good reasons, which in both cases are good enough for me.

DM: I'm also curious about your remarks about Goethe. What significance does *Wilhelm Meister* have for you?

TB: My particular memories of *Wilhelm Meister* are very vague indeed after forty-three years: I have never returned to it since reading Thomas Carlyle's translation, except for looking up from time to time, the New Melusina episode in the *Wanderjahre* in which incidentally is to be found one of my favorite passages in literature, the tale of the so-called New Melusina, in which a chap marries a beautiful girl who is secretly one of the tiny people but can magically transform herself at times into a person of normal size. When she in effect runs out of steam, however, she becomes minuscule, a state in which her husband first discovers her when, taking a nighttime journey in a stagecoach, he sees a little shaft of light issuing from a valise she has packed, applies his eye to it, and sees within a tiny drawing room containing a even smaller wife, sitting before a blazing fireplace! The memory of this scene has so delighted me throughout the forty years since I first read Goethe's novel that I conclude, but only now, that I should do an updated version thereof.

From the *Lehrjahre*, the mysterious circus child Mignon also comes to mind, and of course the marvelous lyrics, famous in German literature but like so much of Goethe altogether ineloquent in English and therefore to be sought out in the original: "Kennst du das Land wo die Zitronen blühn" (Do you know the land where the lemon trees bloom); "Wer nie sein Brot mit Tränen aß" (Who has never eaten his bread with tears); "Nur wer die Sehnsucht kennt" (Only those who know what longing is), and others. By the way, the melody to which that third one has been put is, or was, well known. As to my general feeling about the novel, it was and is much like yours, that here is something unique. Goethe always contains multitudes, and one is enriched by every exposure to him, but he is perhaps the most mysterious of the Olympians, at least to those outside German language and culture. He is by the way, like Nietzsche and so many of the greatest German cultural figures, nothing at all like what non-Germans believe Germans to be.

DM: Could you explain how you see the theme of time in *Killing Time*?

TB: My memory of the novel is confused with that of the real-life case which it follows quite closely—or rather I should say it follows the accounts I read of the murders—and, as I recall, the human killer, the predecessor of the fictional creation, had a theory of time to which I helped myself and perhaps subsequently elaborated upon. To answer your question responsibly, I should have to reread both my version and the source material, and while the latter task would merely be tiresome by now, the former would be unbearable. I never return to the scene of any of my own crimes.

DM: Yes, but the theme of time is a persistent concern of yours, and in *Meeting Evil* references to time abound. How conscious is your treatment of this theme and could you comment on your treatment of the theme in this novel.

TB: My treatment of time is rarely conscious—I cannot remember any example of it except for a sentence in *Crazy in Berlin*, where (if memory serves) a twenty-one-year-old Reinhart speculates briefly on where *his* time has gone. But it is true that in life I am obsessed with time, and all the more so when I reflect that as each year ends I have one less.

DM: If you could stand back for a moment and take a somewhat Olympian view, how would you describe the development of your career as a writer? What changes, developments, emphases do you detect over time?

TB: Over the decades my style has become leaner than it was at the outset. Not leaner and meaner, however, for with age my authorial voice has grown sweeter—while as a person I have become less generous with the years. As to what other changes have taken place, I could not say without resorting to the kind of fakery I deplore. I write not as I wish but as I must.

DM: Since I've got you taking the long view, can you comment on who or what provoked you to write fiction?

TB: As a child I always loved to read and exercise my imagination. I have a vague memory of wanting to grow up to be a foreign correspondent, but that had to do almost entirely with wearing a trenchcoat, and I think that before I got too old I understood the difference between journalism and fiction and came to prefer the latter as being more likely to serve the truth: I mean of course, using Pascal's distinction, the truth of the heart and not that of the reason, which is to say the serious truth as opposed to that of expediency and vulgarity. I regard myself as a teller of tales that are intended primarily to enchant or at least entertain myself. Only by living in the imagination can I successfully pretend I am a human being.

DM: I'm also struck by a rather consistent technique in your novels—plots develop quietly around a small mystery (which the reader may not initially see as mysterious) that is solved in a surprise or twist revelation later. For instance, Naomi Sandifer's surreptitious career as writer of erotica, Bobby Beeler's affair with Harvey Yelton, the question of Peggy Tumulty's virginity, Amelia's exact relationship with Jack Crabb, etc.

TB: Yes, and those things are as mysterious to me as they are to my characters. Almost all the principal personae in a novel of mine—with the exception of *Arthur Rex*—have appeared by accident. I generally, though not always, have my hero at the start. I climb into his skin as if it were a suit of clothes, and from there on, what occurs is revealed to me, particular by particular, by what is said. But you protest, *"What is said? Aren't you doing the saying?"* Perhaps that is true (for there is no Muse of fiction), but when things are going well, my imagination performs so independently of my self that I can seldom get a word in edgewise. When things go badly it is because my imagination refuses to proceed on its own and I am forced consciously to manipulate matters: the result lacks spirit, life, art, and, to me, sense. I have written and subsequently discarded perhaps a thousand such pages.

DM: It seems to me the sense of mystery extends even further. In almost every novel, the protagonist is someone not only on the outs with the world about him but someone who feels that he's alone in this condition, that others know how things work and where everything is headed (young Ralph Sandifer and Tony Beeler, Jack Crabb, Russel Wren [in each book], Walter Hunsicker, Earl Keese, et al.). Could you comment on this?

TB: I see, with the greatest discomfort, that you have violated the cardinal rule of the critic and arrived at a truth to which the author of the work under examination could honestly assent. This is so rare a phenomenon that

I need a moment in which to compose myself. . . . To resume, in saying that my typical "protagonist is someone not only on the outs with the world about him but someone who feels that he's alone in this condition, that others know how things work and where everything is headed," you have not only hit the nail on the head with respect to Reinhart, Jack Crabb, Earl Keese, Russel Wren, and all the others, but you have identified my own secret as well. In that sense, and that sense only, I can borrow Goethe's statement to the effect that each of his works is a fragment of a great confession.

DM: Ken Phipps in the short story "Gibberish" would appear to be an exception to this rule. He begins in confusion and isolation, is unexpectedly catapulted into a position of esteem, apparent honor and comradeship, only to be undone by the very powers that have launched him just a few hours before. How do you see Phipps and his relationship to other of your protagonists?

TB: Ken Phipps is an example of what happens when my typical protagonist does finally acquire "esteem, apparent honor and comradeship": he displays what Zeus sees as hubris and is soon struck down by a divine emissary.

DM: In one interview you comment that "I write each novel in a trance that is peculiar to that book alone." Could you expand on that statement; for instance, is there anything in particular that can provoke or stimulate that trance? Does music, another artistic medium, in short anything act as a stimulus?

TB: I get into the trance only after writing for a while. Indeed, the only way I know that I am serious about a piece of work is when I reach the point that it begins to write itself. This might take a chapter or two. *Neighbors* was an exception. From the first sentence on, it was like automatic writing: I never consciously thought about it at all, but would rush to the typewriter each morning, eager to see what would happen next. Yet I remember a review that called the novel "contrived." This is yet another example of why I take very few reviews seriously—including many that praise my work!

DM: At another point you remark, "real life is unbearable to me unless I can escape from it into fiction." Do you still feel this way (perhaps even more intensely so) fifteen years later?

TB: Indeed I do.

DM: You reveal that you often abandon projects because of their unsuitability. Do you throw whole manuscripts away or store them, like *Nowhere*, to sometime resuscitate them months or years later?

TB: Usually I destroy them altogether.

DM: In speaking of dedication to your art you answer, "devotion to one's work is greatly sustaining, but one must be prepared to become a monster." Could you comment further, especially in what sense(s) one must become a monster?

TB: I think it's monstrous to live most intensely in make-believe. It's probably only one step from the madhouse, two from blowing out one's brains. Except for a handful of sublime moments, my most vivid memories concern that which never happened except in the imagination. But I confess this neither as apology or excuse.

DM: There you also mention that *Neighbors* is your tribute to Kafka; more specifically, in what sense did you mean that (in the novel's unpredictability and constantly fluid shifts in motive and action)?

TB: What has always struck me most forcefully in Kafka is the hero's being not only totally without power but also having not even a vague idea of what's happening to him, yet trying with all his strength to maintain his standards nevertheless: just because the effort is hopeless, utterly doomed, is not an acceptable reason for quitting, even if he knew to quit, which he doesn't, but that doesn't matter, because he wouldn't!

DM: Are you familiar with Samuel Beckett's fiction, and if so, would you comment on your estimation of his art?

TB: Yes, I have read Beckett's major novels, and have seen several of his principal plays, and except for a split-second or two in *Godot*, have been bored to the point of suffocation and could identify nothing of merit anywhere in those of his works to which I have been exposed. In view of the world's regard for him, I can only believe the fault is mine. I also find Whitman unbearable but am willing to concede nevertheless that he is a great poet. I confess that my trouble with Beckett is that he—I should really say not he (since I am in sympathy with what I know of the man)—but rather the authorial voice one hears in his works: to me it has always seemed, simply, demented. Make of that what you will; I think I remember that you admire him greatly.

DM: I'm curious how versed you are in various myths of the trickster figure? There is, of course, Hermes in Greek mythology, but worldwide the trickster is a common figure.

TB: I don't think I'm well versed at all in that area. Aside from the abridged *Golden Bough*, I've read very little in anthropology, except that which concerns American Indians, and not much in mythology beyond the Greek, Roman, and Norse. I have however been interested in the rogue as he appears in European literature.

DM: In all the reading you did about Native Americans, how much concerned itself with Indian mythology? More specifically, are you familiar with trickster cycles in these mythologies? Are you familiar with Paul Radin's classic study of the trickster in Winnebago myths?

TB: Not much, as I remember from almost three decades ago. I don't know Radin's work. My source for Cheyenne ways was principally the work of Grinnell.

DM: If you are familiar with any of these, were you consciously working with them in writing any of these novels? I vaguely remember in Thomas Edwards's review of *Neighbors* his mentioning some Norse or Scandinavian myth; I always thought this was far-fetched, though the figure of Loki is a prominent one in Norse mythology.

TB: I had no such thing in mind when writing the book. Having said which, I remember being fascinated with the milieu of Loki, Thor, Wotan/Odin as a child, which I read about in books written for children, and then reencountering it as a young man in the Wagnerian operas.

DM: At one point in another interview, while discussing *Arthur Rex*, you mention that Merlin's prophecy ("Saturn shall rain malignity upon the earth and destroy all humankind as with a crooked scythe") "was right on the money and that everything we do nowadays is posthumous." Could you expand on the latter statement, especially with regard to the idea that all today is done posthumously?

TB: I'm afraid that any attempt of mine to expatiate on such a wisecrack would vitiate whatever point it has. But I have asked it from time to time in my passage through life: what if this is really death?

DM: With the various uncollected short stories and plays you've written, are there any plans to collect these, shortly or in good time, for book publication? Do you have any desire to do this or see it done?

TB: I have published fewer than a dozen stories (and the two that were not published have been destroyed: they were rejected with good reason). I think I should probably write several more before putting a collection together. As to the plays, I suspect they will be unpublished as all but one have gone unperformed. Scholars and teachers, who work for fixed wages, are sometimes not aware of how the public career of a professional free-lance writer is affected by commercial considerations. Collections of plays, even those that have won prizes and filled theaters, rarely sell well, and thus not many such are published.

DM: I've noticed a trend recently for reviewers to denounce what they regard as your misanthropy. Would you care to respond to this evaluation?

TB: As to my recent reviewers: for some reason several of them have been sour, in what would seem an obeisance to trashy and simpleminded trends that will inevitably be out of fashion within a decade—yet at their worst theirs are superior to many of the reviews my earliest novels received, including *Little Big Man*.

DM: A couple critics have quoted Splendor Mainwaring from *Reinhart in*

Love when he says, "The truth of life is that things are exactly as they appear, and symbols are the bunk." Do you agree with Splendor's acceptance that appearances and essences are so easily joined?

TB: I probably agree more with Splendor than I disagree. I think the interpretations of symbols has some validity, and it is usually an amusing exercise, but by sticking to appearances alone you'll be right at least more than half the time: better odds than most available to mortals.

DM: A number of critics have also cited Melville as either an influence or a writer with whom to compare you, and you have occasionally mentioned him in interviews. Would you like to expand on your estimation of him?

TB: I worship Melville and am lighted by his refulgence, of course, as I am by that of Shakespeare, Goethe, Dante, and the other greatest masters, but it is difficult to say whether his work has influenced me in a particular way. If it has so done, then the immediately influential works would be some of the tales and shorter novels, "Bartleby," "Benito Cereno," and *Billy Budd*, with their moral complexity and *Israel Potter*, with its amalgam of history and fiction. Frederick Turner, in an early essay, shrewdly discerned the connection between the last-named and *Little Big Man*.

DM: Do you agree with one critic's assertion that Reinhart in *Reinhart in Love* believes that "social life offers a satisfying pattern for working out human destiny." Do you see social life in those terms?

TB: Though I suffer from a distaste for organized religion (while nevertheless finding it preferable to collectivist political movements), I am not an atheist. I do not therefore see social life as being sufficient to determine destiny. If Reinhart does, and he may, then so much the worse for him. But in the last of *Oedipus Rex* we are told that a human life cannot properly be assessed until it is over. When last seen, Reinhart was only in his fifties. Perhaps he has time to widen his horizons.

DM: On the surface Joe Detweiler and Richie in *Meeting Evil* seem to have a great deal in common; how do you see these two; do you see significant similarities or differences between them?

TB: To me, Joe Detweiler and Richie have little in common, their respective moralities being utterly opposed. Detweiler is benevolent in intent, whereas Richie is altogether malignant. Detweiler as I remember is the only character in *Killing Time* who has any values, and his are demented—at any rate, it was my intention so to present him. Richie on the other hand is pestilential, without a redeeming feature. The matter of *Meeting Evil* is concerned almost exclusively with how long it will take John Felton, a decent man of mediocre gifts and few attainments, to recognize, first, that Richie must be destroyed and, second, that the job must be done by him, John, with no help from anyone else. I have no sympathy for Richie as he is presented in this book, and in life I keep a double, twelve-gauge insurance policy against an invasion by him or his growing tribe. On a Detweiler, however, I should probably trustingly turn my back—and perhaps get zapped when his mood changed without warning. But until then he would be rather likable.

DM: There is a Thomas Berger who has written a British children's book, *Stan Bolivan and the Dragon*; this is not you, I assume.

TB: No, the British children's book author T. Berger is not I. There is also a Canadian Thomas Berger who is an anthropologist. Brooks Landon once sent me a Canadian sci-fi comic book in which the writer of the text said he was influenced by TB. Landon assumed I was the one referred to, and therefore so did I—and was so intrigued I wrote to ask the guy how he had been so influenced. I never received an answer. Only later on did I hear elsewhere of the anthropologist Berger, obviously the one referred to, being himself a Canadian. Very embarrassing. And the worst of it is I do not care at all for science fiction!

DM: Do you agree with the critic who says, "Even Berger's most frivolous games are signals to indicate that this wonderfully articulate novelist *does not trust language*"? This is certainly true of Detweiler, but is it of you?

TB: Yes.

DM: Is your lack of trust with others and their uses of language, with its cavalier use in the world and our quotidian experiences, or with your own uses as a writer whose primary and cherished medium is language?

TB: Language is untrustworthy by its very nature. The names for an apple (*apple, Apfel, mela, manzana,* etc.) are not the fruit itself, and the difference must always be remembered, even when eating one's own words.

DM: Still another critic states that you are a writer of "stringent moral parables." We've discussed your concern with moral issues, but do you see yourself as a writer of parables?

TB: I think I could reasonably be called such.

DM: Would you characterize yourself in that way; how strongly do you feel about that label?

TB: I am happy to be called a moralist, which by the way does not conflict at all with my stated intention of writing only to amuse myself. What amuses me are tales of moral significance: my own are always personal inventions, even when I use history or established legend, but hardly ever self-regarding.

DM: Could you give me a chronology of composition for the plays. *Other People* was begun in 1969, and, I take it, worked on for some time. What about the other two; I assume the early 1970s, and then *The Burglars* sometime around 1986 or 1987? When did the last appear in *New Letters*?

TB: *Other People* was written in 1969 and revised, during rehearsals and in between performances and then once again during the months after the Stockbridge run, in 1970. *Rex, Rita, and Roger* was written in 1970, and *The Siamese Twins* in 1971, as I remember. Throughout some of 1971 I also worked on certain plays that were never completed. One of these concerned a restaurant that began as a beanery in Act I and, through the succeeding acts and generations of characters, rose to be a temple of gastronomy frequented by epicures. Another was to be about a famous showman, but while writing the early scenes I realized that what it needed was music. I have no such talent myself and was not quite sure how to get hold of the right kind of composer, so put it aside. So somebody else (who really knew what he was doing) later brought Barnum to Broadway. *The Burglars* was written, probably, in 1987 and was published in *New Letters*, Vol. 55, No. 1, Fall 1988.

DM: Written some ten years or so before novels like *Neighbors*, *The Houseguest*, and *Meeting Evil*, your plays seem clearly prophetic of the turn your fiction would later take. As you look at them now, were the plays in the 1970s warm-up exercises for later novels; did you feel freer to let your imagination run wild in ways that it might not in fiction?

TB: Perhaps the plays were forerunners of the novels to come, now that you mention it, but to me they were primarily an opportunity to write entirely in dialogue, then my favorite of the modes of narrative expression. No doubt I could, following the examples of Thomas Love Peacock, Ivy Compton-Burnett, and one of my favorite novelists, Henry Green, have written some mostly- or all-dialogue fiction, but I wanted to set up a proper stage in my imagination, with exits and entrances in rooms of three walls and a curtain to drop from a proscenium arch. Which is to say I doted on the stylizations and mechanics of playmaking.

DM: Brooks Landon concludes his book on you by discussing the influence of Nietzsche, and we've touched on him in this interview. Could you comment on what his works have meant to you?

TB: I have not joined Landon in looking for Nietzsche's influence on my novels, though that doesn't mean it is not there: it means only that the matter is the critic's business and not mine. In life, my life, on which I am the sole authority, I can say that Nietzsche has given me a sense of what intellectual courage, probity, honor, and nobility are. If I can seldom, if ever, attain to any of those virtues, I can at least aspire to them, defying my instinctive urge to be cowardly and lazy, and to resist a natural tendency to let existence be a "thoughtless accident."

DM: Name a writer of the second half of the twentieth century whom you admire without qualification.

TB: Barbara Pym, whose masterpiece is *Quartet in Autumn*.

DM: You have commented frequently on what writing and language mean to you; could you please comment on what fiction, or the novel in particular, means to you?

TB: As Henry James said of himself, I am an "inveterate proser," and therefore it is fiction that has been the means by which I can see myself as a wizard, ebulliently making things from the void.

PLAY

♦

Trysting with Thalia

THOMAS BERGER

On a whim of much the same kind as those that have inspired my novels, but with the significant difference that this one called for the dramatic and not the fictional form, I began *Other People* in 1969 as I was simultaneously writing *Vital Parts*. My procedure in so doing was to work on the novel for a while (most of my books have been written in daily sessions of from one to two hours; three- or four-hour stints are possible but improbable), then set it aside, put a new sheet of paper in the machine, and write one page of dramatic dialogue as fast as I could type. After three months I had in this fashion completed a play, which I then showed to my agent, an ardent theatergoer, and asked him whether reproducing it in the professionally mimeographed scripts that producers demanded, an extra expense, would be justified. His verdict having been cautiously affirmative, we ordered a supply.

I sent a copy to my friend Howard Sackler, whose extraordinary *Great White Hope*, of a few years earlier, was only the second play in history to have won all three major American prizes for drama; and another to Arthur Penn, who was then preparing his film based on *Little Big Man*. The generous response of both men exceeded the demands of friendship. Howard urged me to let him take the play to the Mark Taper Forum in Los Angeles, with which he had an association, and Arthur, then a leading force in the Berkshire Theatre Festival, offered to sponsor it as the first production of the 1970 season at the Stockbridge, Massachusetts, site.

Meanwhile my agent, Don Congdon, had offered *Other People* to an array of Broadway producers and quickly found an excellent prospect, one of the then big names on the Great White Way. When I met with this man, he told me his enthusiasm for the play was such that he intended to bring it to the stage with every advantage, including a director whose name was a familiar word in at least every show-business household. But one condition had to be met: certain parts of my negotiations with him must be concealed from the playwrights' craft association, the Dramatists Guild, of which, as already a member of the related Authors Guild, I would be automatically enrolled as soon as *Other People* reached the boards. By now I

This essay appears in print for the first time and is published with the permission of Thomas Berger.

have forgotten just what he wanted me to hide, but this was too negative a beginning to lead to any positive resolution, and I had no further dealings with the gent. Instead I accepted Penn's invitation to come to the Berkshires, preferring it over Sackler's suggestion because Stockbridge was closer to New York City, where I lived in those days.

Other People was performed at the festival during the first two weeks of July 1970. As Arthur was still immersed in the editing of the *Little Big Man* movie, he assigned his close associate Gene Lasko, a theater veteran, to direct the play. Lasko was of invaluable help to a dramatist whose latest acquaintance with the stage had been as actor in public high school productions in his little Ohio hometown, thirty years before. While the original text had been written at blinding speed, few of the virgin lines remained intact once rehearsals began, and though I usually reject the advice of book editors (on the ground that I have written more novels than they), I was so eager to accept not only the suggestions of the director, but also those of the actors, that Lasko felt at one point he had to warn me against being too acquiescent: this was unprecedented behavior for a playwright and might spoil people rotten.

The producer of the play for the Berkshire Festival was another distinguished practitioner, Lyn Austin, whose Broadway productions, often in partnership with Oliver Smith, had claimed their place in the cultural history of the time. Therefore I took Lyn seriously when she assured me that *Other People* was the most exciting play she had seen in years, if not ever; that it would be a smash in New York in the following season, earning a fortune for all concerned; and that furthermore I would be misguided to continue writing novels: I should immediately bring that phase of my career to an end and henceforth write only for the theater. Unlike the many others who have given me extravagant advice on what I should do with such talent as I possess, Lyn was no fake or fanatic, and therefore I spent much of the ensuing year acting on her suggestion. I let *Regiment of Women* simmer while I cooked up two other plays and also continued to revise *Other People*, before, during, and after the Stockbridge run.

But by the early autumn of 1970, Lyn's efforts to bring my first play to Broadway having been unsuccessful, she dropped the project altogether. Nor was she keen on my other plays. So eventually I returned to novels, none the worse for the detour, for working with the gifted people at Stockbridge was the most delightful and rewarding experience involving others that I have ever known as a writer. A novelist's professional joys are usually and necessarily those of solitude. Fiction in its making is a very personal matter, at least with me, and the response of others to my product, even when laudatory, lack the reality of the satisfactions, and sometimes the thrills—and in my case often the astonishment—of doing work that is acceptable to the private conscience. But plays—at least those not confined to the closet—are communal enterprises. Perhaps this is why theater people kiss one another a lot and are attracted to utopian political causes. If all the world were really a stage, it would be a nicer place, harder-working, kinder, sweeter, with momentary tiffs and temporary tantrums replacing wars.

A dedicated actor at work is an awe-inspiring spectacle: in that state he or she is beyond the range of love or money, food or drink, or the need for rest, will rehearse continuously and perform forever unless forced to desist. I never knew just what it is that actors do until I collaborated with the company who did *Other People*: they take a play from its author and then from its director and make it their own. Marian Seldes, the brilliant Tony-winner who played my Gretchen, at one point created a bit of business with a potted geranium, an eloquent stroke that obviated an entire page of dia-logue; and Emmett Walsh (who has since gone on to a prominent career as character actor in the movies), playing Hal, improvised a walk to downstage center, where his anguished stare at the audience intensified the lines I had given him so far beyond their force as written as to make the scene a new and wondrous event. Richard Mulligan had more than enough energy after a bravura portrayal of General Custer in the *Little Big Man* film to represent the character first called Stewart Poole with great *brio* (I forget why we changed the name to Peele). He has since won an Emmy in a long-running television comedy series, but not before playing, in another movie, a madman who *thinks* he is General Custer! I should also note that Jane Czack, then a teenager in her first role as an actress, not too many years later became Sylvester Stallone's first wife.

This is the first time the entire text of *Other People* has appeared in print, but Act I was included in *Works in Progress* (No. 6, 1972), an occasional paperback anthology published by the Literary Guild.

David Madden has asked me to account for my brief excursion into playwriting in the early 1970s (unique in my career except for an even briefer term in the late 80s, when I wrote a short comedy entitled *The Burglars*, which was published in the quarterly *New Letters*), but I cannot do so. At the time I wrote *Other People* I had not seen the performance of a play in many years, except for Sackler's and a couple of comedies by other friends and acquaintances, to all of which I got free tickets and by none of which I was influenced in any way. Nor had I read much in the drama since Bernard Shaw, and what I had read did not speak to me. Among my old masters would be Aristophanes (especially the *Thesmophormiazusae*), Molière (espe-cially *L'Avare*), and Shakespeare, though perhaps not so much for his come-dies as for the comic passages in the tragedies, the gallows humor of Iago, Hamlet, et al. But their influence would necessarily be remote on someone writing in the vernacular of the late twentieth century.

My best guess as to why I embarked on a short but passionate tryst with Thalia is that fiction has no Muse of its own, and I was suddenly, and unbearably, lonely.

Editor's Note to Other People

♦

Early in planning this volume I wrote to Thomas Berger, hoping to secure an as-yet unpublished story, a discarded chapter from a novel, or some other squib that had not yet appeared in print. He graciously but unambiguously told me that he had saved nothing and could therefore make no contribution. A couple years later I asked again, and again he declined, wittily noting that he did "not maintain a file of literary gems unsullied by printers' fingers." In the final stages of preparing the collection, I inquired a third and last time, specifically mentioning his unpublished plays; to my shock and delight he sent me *Other People* as well as photocopies of his other three plays. Each of these works bears his unique stamp, and they form intriguing counterpoints to various of his novels. One hopes that for the sake of scholars and readers alike all four plays will be gathered and published in a single volume one day soon.

OTHER PEOPLE
A Comedy in Two Acts

Thomas Berger

Note:

OTHER PEOPLE was performed at the Berkshire Theatre Festival, 1–11 July 1970, produced by Lyn Austin and directed by Gene Lasko.

Stewart Peele	Richard Milligan
Gretchen	Marian Selds
Valerie	Jane Czack
Dwight	Riley Mills
Harold Winter	M. Emmett Walsh
Marjorie	Carolyn Coates
Rebecca	Catharyn Tivy
Author	Simm Landres

Characters

STEWART PEELE, an attorney at law
GRETCHEN, his wife
VALERIE, their seventeen-year-old daughter
DWIGHT, their twelve-year-old son
HAROLD WINTER, an accountant
MARJORIE, his wife
REBECCA, their eleven-year-old daughter
AUTHOR, a man of parts
A large woolly dog

This play appears in print for the first time and is published with the permission of Thomas Berger.

ACT I

SCENE: A loft on the top floor of a deserted building near the waterfront. The entrance is in the center rear, behind a bookcase hinged to serve as a door. There are plywood partitions, left and right, with doors leading to the bedrooms and kitchen. Down left is a desk; behind it, a ladder to the skylight. A sofa stands to the left of stage center. Down right are a table and chairs. There is a window on the extreme right.

The bookcase swings back now, and STEWART PEELE enters, carrying two valises and a gun case. He is followed by GRETCHEN, also burdened with luggage. Behind her appears VALERIE, who carries a portable phonograph and a cosmetic case. Finally, in comes DWIGHT, with a pillowcase full of possessions.

PEELE

Quite a climb, but it would have been playing into their hands to take the freight elevator.

DWIGHT

(With false animation)
How so, Dad?

PEELE

They would have known at which floor we deboarded.

DWIGHT

The indicator was broken.

PEELE

Then they could have made a calculation based on elapsed time.

DWIGHT

Do you believe we are pursued that closely?

PEELE

That must always be our assumption, son.

GRETCHEN

(To DWIGHT)
The whole thing seems rather extravagant to me, but I'd do anything to sustain your father's faith in himself.

PEELE

(Annoyed)
I heard that.

GRETCHEN

I wasn't trying to keep it from you. I'm not embarrassed by my opinions.

PEELE

I suppose you will insist you did not see that sallow man lurking at the corner.

GRETCHEN

He was making a cat's cradle from a rubber band.

PEELE

I don't know about that. He had a face like a lizard. He kept us under constant surveillance. Our lair may be known.

GRETCHEN

The game is up. We may as well go back to our comfortable house.

PEELE

Not so fast. We took measures to delude him. That is why we entered the building next door, climbed two flights, then crawled across that plank between the windows, over the airshaft, and—

GRETCHEN

Don't remind me. I tore my stockings.

PEELE

Clothes are meaningless here.

VALERIE

That's neat.
    (SHE begins to unbutton her blouse)

GRETCHEN

What are you doing?

VALERIE

He said we didn't need clothes.

GRETCHEN

Your father spoke metaphorically.
    (To audience)
She's an idiot.

VALERIE

I heard that!

    (A MAN steps from the wings. He is dressed as a California Highway
    Patrolman: helmet, goggles, glossy boots)

POLICEMAN

    (Raising his goggles)
You are not supposed to respond to those asides.

GRETCHEN

Who are *you*?

POLICEMAN

(Archly)
I wrote this vehicle.

PEELE

I never saw you before in my life.

AUTHOR

I wore a different disguise at rehearsals.

PEELE

Oh.

DWIGHT

You were the guy who filled the soda machine, "Dr. Pepper" embroidered on your back and "Richie" over your breast pocket.

POLICEMAN

There is no soda machine in this theater.

DWIGHT

I'm the sort of person who will lie if the spirit moves me.

POLICEMAN

You're a fascinating little fellow. How'd you get into the business?

DWIGHT

It's a charming story. How much time do we have?

GRETCHEN

Jesus Christ!

PEELE

(To POLICEMAN)
We're trying to give a performance, and you are obstructing us. Do we hang over your shoulder when you're seated at the typewriter?

DWIGHT

(To PEELE)
You're bitter because it's my career he wants to discuss, not yours.

VALERIE

I'm forgotten in these vulgar squabbles.
(Does a forlorn bump and grind at the POLICEMAN)

POLICEMAN

(To PEELE)
I wonder if you're miscast? I wrote the part for a much more versatile actor.

PEELE

(Stung)

Listen, you hack, I'm doing you a favor. I don't need show business. I could be kept by my choice of rich old ladies.

POLICEMAN

(Impressed)

I'm sorry. I didn't know that.

(HE exits in shame)

GRETCHEN

(Toward departing POLICEMAN)

Our public servants are so uncouth!

DWIGHT

(To his FATHER)

You hurt his feelings. He'll get you for that. I happen to know how madly all of you need the work.

PEELE

(Frightened)

I'll butter him up during the intermission.

VALERIE

I'll give him a piece of ass.

PEELE

We find ourselves in an extreme situation.

GRETCHEN

I always detested children even when I was myself a child. Why should I change now?

(SHE laughs shrilly)

I have always loved old ladies.

PEELE

Let's get serious. In preparing this hideaway—the work of months—I tried to think of every eventuality.

(Points to bookcase)

Note that this part of the wall turns on a hidden swivel. There is no door as such. Locked into place, it gives the illusion of being solid. No one would suspect there is an enormous living space behind it, containing four human beings.

GRETCHEN

The stairway suddenly comes to an end for no apparent reason, confronting one with a blank wall? Whom would that fool?

PEELE

That will never be questioned, Gretch. Toiling up a height not only taxes the body. It numbs the mind.

DWIGHT

Why is the bookcase on the *inside*, hiding the secret door from *us*?

PEELE

A shrewd question, son. It's there for the psychological effect. We must forget the outside world and hope it returns the favor.

GRETCHEN

You are convinced we are being hounded by these diabolically clever enemies, with their fiendish cunning?

PEELE

Must I go through all of that again? You saw the mutilated newspaper this morning, the container of homogenized milk, cleverly pierced so that when I tipped it toward my coffee, my lap was inundated. And could that stray dog have got in by himself?

GRETCHEN

There are animals who can open doors with their noses.

PEELE

He made straight for my BarcaLounger and lifted his leg. These are not chance occurrences, Gretch.

VALERIE

I sure wish I had a dog. Somebody I could communicate with, without having to listen to.

PEELE

Life did not get this vile all by itself.
  (Holds up gun case)
They may get me eventually, but when I go I'll take along a few of them.
  (Frowns)
I hope my gun permit hasn't run out. I don't care about my driver's license. I'll never use it again. Before abandoning the car I obliterated engine and body numbers and took off the plates.

DWIGHT

Hundreds of cars are abandoned on city streets and highways every year. They have no value. Dealers won't buy them, and the owners certainly won't pay to have them hauled to the dump. Therefore they are left at some curb. At last the Sanitation Department removes them, but it often takes months.

GRETCHEN

Why are you so pedantic?

DWIGHT

It helps pass the time in this stupid place.

PEELE

There'll be plenty to do, Dwight. We must not fall into complacency merely because we're safe and sound here. That would be playing into their hands.

DWIGHT

Whose hands?

PEELE

That's not our first concern, son. Rather, when and how. Their identities can be verified by searching the bodies.

VALERIE

I sure wish I could expose myself. I never know what to contribute to a conversation.

PEELE

(To DWIGHT)

I'm appointing you chief of security, Dwight. I know you're reliable. We're ten stories above the street, and that—
    (Pointing to bookcase door)
—is the only entrance, and it is absolutely impregnable. Still and all, be on the lookout for foul play. They are cunning devils. Remember that TV repairman last spring? Two hundred forty-three dollars and fifty cents later, the baseball players still appeared as hydrocephalic dwarfs, but now their complexions were purple, and a dirty jockstrap was hanging from the rooftop antenna.

    (DWIGHT takes a tape measure from the pillowcase he is carrying, and begins to measure the distance between arbitrary points)

PEELE

I have laid in enough canned goods to keep us for years, as well as a deep-freeze chock full of frozen provender. Waste disposal has not been overlooked. Nonorganic rubbish goes in here.
    (Indicates waste chute in wall)
And is channeled to a lower floor.

GRETCHEN

I doubt that the tenant down there will approve.

PEELE

This building is empty, Gretch. Empty, isolated, and forgotten. I have chosen it with care. As to edible wastes, you will find your all-electric kitchen equipped with the familiar Dispose-All.

GRETCHEN

The manufacturers warn against peach pits, pork chop bones, and percolator caps.

DWIGHT

(Has reached VALERIE and is measuring her behind)

Wow, what a spread.

VALERIE

I have what is known as a lush, fecund body, made for the act of love. Men dream of being imprisoned between my pulsating loins, breathing stertorously, heaving, gasping, slavering, turned into savage animals, pounding into my firm flesh. My sharp talons lacerate their shoulder blades as they rise to the insane paroxysm.

(Pause)

They dream of that, but when they approach me in reality, they propose deviate acts.

PEELE

(Impatiently)

That's part of growing up, Valerie. We've all been through that phase.

DWIGHT

I haven't.

PEELE

Then you have something to look forward to, son.

GRETCHEN

I have had a lifelong constipation problem. On the other hand, childbearing was simple for me. I just don't like what they become when they grow up, else I'd have had a dozen kids. Babies and old ladies. I say to hell with everybody in between.

PEELE

Let's get squared away. I'll take this stuff to the master bedroom, Gretch, and I'd be obliged to you if you would unpack the clothes. Plain gas-pipe racks and open shelves. Rough but serviceable. Slabs of foam rubber on plywood platforms—all the bed we'll need. Wait till you see your rooms, kids! It's a fun place as well as a fortress.

(HE takes suitcases and exits)

GRETCHEN

This might humiliate me before my friends if I had any friends. I am not a gregarious woman. Yet I have known moments of quiet happiness.

(SHE smiles brilliantly at the audience and exits)

VALERIE

Once when I was nine years old I saw a horrible old wino in a park who had twisted his pocket around and was peeing out of it. Ever since I have suffered from a sense of wonder. I'm the clown of my gang. I do impressions and funny walks.

(Does funny walk)

DWIGHT

Val, I want to ask you something.

VALERIE

Speak.

DWIGHT

Do you think Dad is clinically insane, or is this a temporary nervous condition?

VALERIE

These things are relative.

DWIGHT

We left an eight-room house in the suburbs to hide out in a deserted building on which a "condemned" sign is clearly posted.

VALERIE

People are all different. My idea of pleasure may not be yours, and vice versa. We each have our little peculiarities. I have a friend who likes the smell of sweat.

DWIGHT

Male or female?

VALERIE

Her own.

DWIGHT

Call me reckless, but I don't find that odd. But whatever the nature of Dad's problem, we are being forced to share it. Who is after us? And if they are, what do they want?

VALERIE

Hordes of men would like to ravish me.

DWIGHT

If that were true, no power on earth could force you into hiding.

VALERIE

Oh, yeah? I suppose you get a lot?

DWIGHT

I'm discreet about my erotic life. The intrigue interests me more than the flesh, per se.

VALERIE

My childhood was quite different from yours. Everybody said I looked like an angel and then proceeded to ignore me. Flattery is one way of disregarding other people.

(A MAN in a green shirt and matching trousers and a black bow tie comes in through the main entrance. This role, along with those of the OTHER INTRUDERS who appear from time to time, is played by an actor playing the AUTHOR)

MAN

I'm here to read the meters. Gas-and-electric company. You people just moved in, right? Peele, right?

DWIGHT

(To VALERIE)
There's a fortress for you.
(To MAN)
How'd you get in?

MAN

I pushed the wall.

VALERIE

We're hiding out here.

MAN

(Looking around)
Very nice place, too.
(To DWIGHT)
Hey, sonny, how about a Good Humor? The guy's out front. Here's a buck.

DWIGHT

Gee, mister, that's real neat. Oh boy.
(Grimaces at audience, but takes money and goes upstage)

MAN

He's not going outside.

VALERIE

He's not allowed to.

MAN

(Unbuckling his belt)
I don't like a kid watching me.
(Shrugs and opens his fly)

VALERIE

What are you doing?

MAN

(Dropping his trousers)

Get your clothes off, doll. I haven't got much time today.

VALERIE

I'll scream if you expose your shame.

MAN

(Pulling up his pants)

This is the kind of nightmare you always imagine you will find yourself in someday. It's clear I have been the victim of a malicious joke. How can you ever forgive me, Miss?

VALERIE

I think of myself as a tolerant person.

MAN

We meter readers get into every place of living all over the city. You'd be surprised at the range of types we see—

VALERIE

(Interrupting)

I don't want to hear your philosophy. I just want to know why you thought you could march in here and get some cooze.

MAN

I'll say one thing, with all respect. You certainly talk like a whore.

VALERIE

No, I don't. Prostitutes always call it "going out."

MAN

(Reflecting)

That's true. I'm wrong again.

VALERIE

Do I look like a hooker?

MAN

Very much. Also, there's a pimp outside.

VALERIE

Are you serious?

MAN

I'm not the kind to force my attentions on respectable ladies. I put women on a pedestal.

DWIGHT

(Coming downstage)

Time's up. You only get a quickie for a buck.

MAN

I think I've been had. I should stick to my job. Where's the meters?

VALERIE

How should we know? We're not supposed to be here.

(Pause)

Is there really a pimp outside?

(PEELE enters. HE stares at the MAN)

VALERIE

Daddy, this is—

MAN

(Grinning)

Hi there.

VALERIE

He came to read the meters.

PEELE

(With false hospitality)

Welcome to our little hideaway.

MAN

(Apprehensively)

It's a kind of paradise.

PEELE

We like to think so. But let me show you around the place. It might surprise you to know that we have a sauna.

MAN

You're kidding, aren't you?

PEELE

Not at all. We've also got a ten-lane bowling alley. Come on, I'll show it to you.

MAN

Another time, maybe. I really have to read the meters.

PEELE

(Forcefully)

I insist.

(HE gives the MAN a far from friendly push.

MAN looks fearfully at VALERIE and DWIGHT, but THEY remain noncommittal. PEELE pushes him out)

DWIGHT

There's no sauna here, and there's certainly no ten-lane bowling alley. Dad is acting very weird.

VALERIE

Far be it from me to sneer at the fantasies of others.

(An anguished cry, diminishing as if from a falling MAN, is heard from offstage. PEELE enters shortly afterward

VALERIE is horrified)
What have you done to that man?

PEELE

(Gets his shotgun)
Any more of them?
(Searches room)
How'd he get in? That was a close one. Like a fool I left the gun in here. That could easily have been my last mistake. You see how cunning they are.

VALERIE

What did you do to that man who came about the meters?

PEELE

I pushed him out the window in Dwight's room.

DWIGHT

That's fabulous, Dad!

VALERIE

(Hysterically)
You're no father of mine. You're an insane killer.

PEELE

When you've had time to reflect, Val, I'll expect an apology. These are trying times. He was of course a spy. If not himself the assassin, then he was casing us for the gunman to follow. Mercy would be wasted on a terrorist like that.

DWIGHT

You wrung a confession from him?

PEELE

No, sir. This one was a real professional. He was in the act of displaying his company identification when I defenestrated him. The forgery was of a very high quality.

VALERIE

Sadist!

DWIGHT

"Defenestration" means pushing out the window, Val. It's from the Latin.

VALERIE

Even so, I am far from being mollified. I was just getting to know and love all his little ways. We had a growing affinity, which is always the case with people who at first sight dislike each other. Now I will never know what would have transpired. That's my tragedy.

PEELE

That is your inconvenience, Valerie. The tragedy is his. To sell himself to a vicious cause, to hound poor devils like us—he deserves no sympathy.
(Piously)
Yet he was a man for all that. We must never forget the essential dignity of the human condition.

DWIGHT

Hear, hear.

(GRETCHEN enters)

GRETCHEN

Did I just hear a peal of merry laughter?

DWIGHT

That was a scream of terror. Dad just threw a stranger out of the window.

GRETCHEN

What a rash thing to do. I would have welcomed someone to talk to. I'm getting stir-crazy.

PEELE

We've only been here half an hour. Gretchen, I wish you would take this seriously. This is no game. They're out for blood.

GRETCHEN

Stew, have you considered taking up archery, the wood-turning lathe, or volunteer work? I know you pooh-pooh that sort of thing, but you shouldn't reject out of hand the concept of creative leisure.

PEELE

(Impatiently)
Oh for Christ's sake.
(To DWIGHT)
I'm going to check on the body.

(Brandishes gun)
I don't mind saying I'm proud of myself. I've had no training in violence.
A busted eardrum kept me out of the service. I went in for tennis at school,
but never the contact sports.
(Exits)

DWIGHT

Gone to gloat over his victim. That killing did Dad a world of good.

GRETCHEN

Dwight, such jests are in the worst of taste. Imagine your father killing a
stranger! He couldn't even kill a friend.

VALERIE

He was the man who came to read the meters. I now see it as fortunate.
Our love never had a chance to pall. There are many ways of looking at the
same experience. Winning or losing are not the only alternatives.

GRETCHEN

I'm glad to see you settling down, Val. The young often waste themselves
on youth, as the saying goes.

DWIGHT

The man thought Val was a whore, whereas Dad thought *he* was an enemy
agent and therefore defenestrated him.

VALERIE

(Smirks)
I tell myself he's not the only fish in the sea.

GRETCHEN

Who?

VALERIE

Daddy's recent victim.

GRETCHEN

Don't let him hear you use such language, Val. It would break his heart.
Things are not always what they are, but rather what they seem.

DWIGHT

(Shaking his head)
Sometimes I feel like a motherless child.
(Exits.

PEELE returns)

PEELE

By leaning way out the window, I could see the body at the bottom of the airshaft. It fell against the wall and is sitting there now like a Mexican at siesta, though of course without the tilted sombrero.

GRETCHEN

Tijuana is not really Mexico.

VALERIE

To hear that brings back all the horror. Is life so cheap a thing?

PEELE

That depends on where you price it. However, I'd hate to think that fleeing corruption, I have become myself corrupt. Perhaps he *was* a meter reader. Maybe I went off half-cocked.
(Shaking off this idea and becoming furious)
Those painters we hired last year: a leg of my pajamas was sticking out of the closet door—they ran their rollers right across it. Last week a drunken waiter ladled oxtail soup into the crown of my hat, lying on the table nearby. And you've hardly forgotten the time that gas-station attendant lighted a stogie while filling the tank of our Honda Civic, blowing it to smithereens. All he himself lost was a cheap cheroot. What gets me is that none of these gentry ever apologizes.
(Peers at GRETCHEN)
And you think this happens by accident?

GRETCHEN

Is that why we came here? To escape minor discomforts?

PEELE

Placed in sequence, Gretchen, they constitute a massive effort to make existence unbearable. It took me a while to see the design in it. At first I took them as unconnected phenomena. Stepping outside in the morning, I would find half-filled beer cans in the hedge, still cold, and deep-fried chicken parts often untouched by human teeth. On the train I was forced to inspect the seat before lowering my rump onto it. The upholstery might be smeared with library paste or littered with cross sections of kielbasa. And tell me this: why, at whichever bus stop, on any corner in the world, do I step off the curb and invariably feel the squishing of dog shit underneath my soles?

GRETCHEN

(Wisely)
Stew, you're hiding something. You were expelled from your club for some disgusting practice, and you have slunk away, unable to bear the humiliation of exposure.

PEELE

(Obliviously)

Have you ever called the weather bureau? You are answered by a recording. What the fuck is a 40 percent probability of precipitation? Who are these anonymous voices? What are they concealing? And strange, sinister things come in the mail—

GRETCHEN

Dildoes, for a ten-day trial period. Candid photos of nude old men.

PEELE

Rejections for credit cards for which I have never applied. Entry blanks for contests in which the prizes are bedpans, resort wardrobes, and an all-expenses-paid weekend at the re-creation of the Donner Pass catastrophe.

GRETCHEN

I don't remember that one.

PEELE

Trapped by snow in the High Sierras, members of the party fed on one another. In the simulation they eat dummies made of marzipan. Believe me, it's a filthy mockery of the human condition.

(Pause)

At public urinals men in adjacent stalls peer contemptuously from the corner of the eye. Pure competitiveness! "I can piss longer than you." That sort of thing.

GRETCHEN

And can they?

PEELE

I hold my own, but what a way to live!

GRETCHEN

Do these enemies have a name?

PEELE

Of course! Other people.

GRETCHEN

Let me push that around a bit with the toe of my mind.

(VALERIE has gone to the window and is looking out)

PEELE

(Seeing her)

Get away from the window!

VALERIE

I don't see any pimp down there.

PEELE

Gretch, there's a roll of monk's cloth behind the desk. I want you to cover that window. The skylight will provide sufficient illumination during the day. After dark we must be careful about showing lights or making silhouettes that will draw their fire. Ventilation will come from the windows onto blind airshafts, like the one through which I airmailed that Mexican. Now, if you'll excuse me, I haven't taken a leak since getting out of bed this morning.

(Exits.

GRETCHEN covers window with monk's cloth throughout following dialogue)

GRETCHEN

I often wonder what became of the sleek, olive-skinned youth who made me an indecent proposal on the beach at Puerto Vallarta. My reply was an inscrutable smile. I also tendered him a crumpled peso.

VALERIE

I didn't know we had a bathroom.

GRETCHEN

Your father had a lot of work done here. I wonder if it occurred to him that the carpenters and plumbers would know someone would move in.

VALERIE

He probably knocked them all off.

GRETCHEN

Workmen have no curiosity. I know a rich woman who had an elaborate tomb built for her pet armadillo when it died after eating a tainted quince. Not one of the stonemasons asked a single question.

VALERIE

Well, you brought up the problem.

GRETCHEN

Only to resolve it, Valerie.

VALERIE

You hate me.

GRETCHEN

That's a preposterous accusation. My teeth have been in poor shape ever since you were born. You took away all my calcium. But have I complained? Not me.

VALERIE

I don't remember that.

GRETCHEN

With your allowance you bought candy and offered it to strange men in cars if they would take you for a ride and molest you.

VALERIE

(Smiling)
Oh, yeah.
(Frowning)
You've always been jealous of me.

GRETCHEN

I've pitied you, Val. Nature has given you rather modest endowments. You must accept that and not squander your days in the venting of spleen. You can still make something of yourself. Take a course in speed-writing. There are all sorts of opportunities these days for plain girls who apply themselves.

VALERIE

Did you ever see one of those video tapes of a girl balling a Shetland pony?

GRETCHEN

Horses are the most stupid animals on the face of the earth. Know what's smart? Rats. Crows. Most of the creatures classified as vermin.

VALERIE

I wear my heart on my sleeve.

GRETCHEN

Truck drivers are wont to shout filthy words at me. I seem to provoke that sort of thing. But I sense I am getting beyond your depth.

VALERIE

I'm glad we had this little talk, Mother. It has convinced me that I was one of the babies who are always being given to the wrong parents by the stoned personnel in maternity wards.

GRETCHEN

(Throws up her hands)
All right, be a foundling if you want. I have never stood in your way.

(DWIGHT enters)

DWIGHT

May I have a word with you?

GRETCHEN

Certainly. I'm just leaving.

DWIGHT

I mean, with you. And—

(Points to VALERIE)
—in confidence.

VALERIE

I'll make myself scarce. I'll go to my room and pick my nose.
(Exits)

GRETCHEN

She's basically a sweet girl.

DWIGHT

Easy for you to say. She was never your sister.

GRETCHEN

However, I have more sisters than you.

DWIGHT

That's a funny thing to be competitive about.

GRETCHEN

Much of life is spent in rivalry, Dwight. It would be a disservice to conceal that from you.

DWIGHT

Speak for yourself, Mom. I either win fast or I quit.

GRETCHEN

My, aren't we spiteful? You'll be bitterly sorry when I'm dead. Now what did you want to talk to me about?

DWIGHT

What's Dad up to?

GRETCHEN

Suffice it to say that your father is trying to give you something to believe in. A viable mystique.

DWIGHT

By moving us into a loft in a condemned building?

GRETCHEN

(Desperately seizes and fondles him)
I've got a neat idea, dear! Why don't I make up a picnic lunch with all your favorite foods—Velveeta, pimento loaf, Wonder bread, and Devil Dogs—and find a quiet corner somewhere and pretend it's a park? Afterward you can show me how to catch a forward pass in your first-baseman's mitt.

DWIGHT

(Suspiciously)

Mother, what are *you* up to?

GRETCHEN

(Pushing him away)

Well, I tried to be nice. It's not my idea of pleasure to see you revolving a huge white pasty mouthful of bread and cheese.

DWIGHT

Val is probably in there playing with herself.

GRETCHEN

Is self-sufficiency a crime? Dwight, you are growing up without values. Why don't you run away from home?

DWIGHT

That would be hard to do, considering that our whole family has run away from home. If I went anywhere, it would be back.

GRETCHEN

Be patient and enjoy yourself. That's not much to ask.

(The bookcase-door opens and a GROUP enters: HAROLD WINTER, his wife MARJORIE, and their daughter REBECCA)

WINTER

(Dropping suitcases)

Excuse me, do we have the right place? Would you be Mrs. Stewart Peele?

GRETCHEN

(Dramatically)

God knows I try to be, against all odds.

DWIGHT

(To audience)

More desperate hooligans. Watch Dad fix their wagons.

WINTER

(To MARGE)

This is it.

MARGE

(Looking around, sourly)

Uh-huh.

GRETCHEN

(Shouts in panic)

Stewart!

(PEELE rushes in, carrying shotgun at the ready, but drops the muzzle when HE sees WINTER)

PEELE

(Jovially)

Hi, Hal. Jesus, am I glad to see you made it. Were you followed?
(Pumps WINTER's hand)

WINTER

I don't think so. I took every precaution. Meet my family.
(Introduces MARGE and BECKY, and PEELE in turn presents GRETCHEN and DWIGHT)

PEELE

And I also have a daughter.
(Calls VALERIE)
Where's the rest of your luggage?

WINTER

Outside. I wanted to check first if I had the right place.

PEELE

I think you'll find it cozy in its own way.

WINTER

Sure there's room?

PEELE

(Expansively)

This is a vast establishment. We have the whole floor. There's a bedroom for you and Mrs. Winter, and your daughter can double up with mine.
(Calls VALERIE again, and SHE enters)

VALERIE

Hi, everybody! My name's Val, and I'm known for my sense of humor.
(Performs clownish walk)

BECKY

Hi, Val. You probably compensate for your basic shyness by being silly, but I know I'm going to like you.

VALERIE

I have always wanted a younger sister with whom to share my fancies and simper girlishly.

BECKY

(Grimaces)

Do you really live here?

VALERIE

Don't ask me why.

(DWIGHT has been roaming around the WINTERS, inspecting them carefully. Now HE pries open the suitcase that WINTER dropped, and searches it)

GRETCHEN

(To audience)
Just as I begin to acquire a certain peace of mind it is shattered by a new event. Who *are* these people?
(To the WINTERS)
Welcome, welcome.

MARGE

(Sees DWIGHT going through suitcase and kicks him in the rump)
Mrs. Peele—

GRETCHEN

Please—Gretchen.

MARGE

I didn't expect to find anybody else here.

WINTER

(Quickly)
It was my little surprise. But let's get settled first and then we'll compare notes.

PEELE

I'll go get the rest of your things.

WINTER

(Hurrying after him)
Please, I insist.
(THEY exit)

GRETCHEN

(Going to sofa)
Come sit down, Mrs. Winter.

MARGE

Marge.

(THEY sit down on the sofa. DWIGHT is fascinated by MARGE and hangs around)

                              GRETCHEN
You children go about your own business. Show Becky to your room, Val.
Dwight—

     (SHE points the way out)

                              DWIGHT
     (To MARGE)
In my opinion, zero coupon bonds are overrated.

     (MARGE grimaces and looks away)

                              GRETCHEN
     (Pointing)
Out.

     (DWIGHT slinks out)

                              MARGE
Unusual sort of boy, your son.

                              GRETCHEN
Yes, isn't he?

                              MARGE
I meant no offense.

                              GRETCHEN
None taken.

                              MARGE
Seems mature for his age.

                              GRETCHEN
Do you understand the situation here?

                              MARGE
I haven't the foggiest.

                              GRETCHEN
Are you English, by chance?

                              MARGE
If I were, it wouldn't be by chance.

                              GRETCHEN
It was just an impulse. I hope you weren't offended.

                              MARGE
Not at all.

(SHE makes a severe smile)

GRETCHEN

I was dragged away from an eight-room house in Oakdale. I swear to you that until now our life has been routine, commonplace, predictable—or at any rate as much as anyone else's. Meals more or less on time, commuting schedules, that eerie quiet that strikes you when everybody leaves in the morning, bracketed between the rushing sound of passing cars, the *plink* of an acorn fallen from furry squirrel-paws . . .

MARGE

Are you sure that is what you want to say?

GRETCHEN

Marge, would you please tell me what you're doing here?

MARGE

Hal is the most materialistic person I have ever known. He's proud of trading in his car every year and throwing his socks away when they get holes. We have the only refrigerator with a built-in gadget for freezing a bottle of Aquavit in a block of ice, and our Volvo wagon has one of the only 306 cellular phones.

GRETCHEN

Ivy Village is a wonderful community.

MARGE

I was born and raised there, and therefore usually disparage it.

GRETCHEN

I don't care why you're here. I'm going to like you.

MARGE

Let me finish.

GRETCHEN

I don't want to know, really. Please don't tell me.
  (Puts hands over her ears)

MARGE

In view of his instincts I think it was a manly act for Hal to come here and hide out for the rest of his life. I can remember when he wouldn't leave the house for fear it would be burgled or burned down in his absence. Whereas this morning his final gesture on stepping over the threshold was to ignite the morning newspaper and fling it into the foyer. Then he locked the door. By now the house is surely a blackened ruin.

GRETCHEN

I know we're going to be best of friends under trying conditions. There is only one bathroom here for seven human beings. Then there's the matter of meals. People tend to quarrel more about eating than anything else, I have found. Once we shared a resort house with another family, and haven't spoken to them since. Eggs, especially, are troublemakers, owing to the many styles in which they can be prepared.

MARGE

On the other hand, they're the easiest dish to prepare to individual order, as opposed to steak or chicken.

GRETCHEN

I imagine ours will be powdered. Because of our peculiar circumstances, fresh foods will not be at hand.

MARGE

Have you thought of schooling for the children?

GRETCHEN

No I haven't.

MARGE

Now, don't panic. I'm pursuing a train of thought. We'll set up classes and teach them ourselves. Isn't that what the pioneers did?

GRETCHEN

It just hit me that this is not a joke.
(SHE begins to sob.

PEELE and WINTER enter, the LATTER carrying all the luggage)

PEELE

(Raising the shotgun and addressing GRETCHEN)
Did another one get in? Have you been attacked?
(Swings gun around wildly)
Take cover, Hal!
(HE makes a search of the room)

GRETCHEN

(Explaining to MARGE)
Stew allegedly threw a person out the window.

MARGE

(To PEELE)
Don't you know better than to play with guns?

WINTER

Now, Marge.
(To PEELE)
Don't mind her. The important thing is she'll come through when the chips are down. Last year when my appendix burst—

MARGE

I called the doctor.

WINTER

Still, it was damn quick thinking. Don't sell yourself short, Marge. You're up there with the biggies, for my money.

MARGE

(To GRETCHEN)
Hal has this idea that any problem can be glossed over with a simpleminded compliment.

GRETCHEN

(Smiling at WINTER)
And he's not far wrong.

MARGE

This is no joke. One of them got in just before you showed up.

WINTER

Are you serious?

PEELE

I dropped him like a bad habit. Come on, I'll show you the cadaver.
(THEY start to exit)
Don't forget the luggage, Hal.

(HAL picks up the bags and THEY exit)

GRETCHEN

I suppose I should go too. I can't just sit here wondering.
(Rises)

MARGE

Perhaps this individual was trying to commit suicide, and Mr. Peele grabbed at him hoping to save him—and that's what you saw.

GRETCHEN

I did not witness the incident, but you emanate good sense, Marge. I hope you can put up with my flightiness. But I can't rest till I see what happened to that body.
(Exits)

MARGE

(To audience)
She's the kind of person you can put up with without really liking. Vanity without pride.

(BECKY enters)

BECKY

Valerie's all right, but she's sex mad.

MARGE

She's probably just shy, doesn't know how to make friends easily.

BECKY

Her ambition is to pose for pornographic pictures, but she doesn't know how to get started in that field.

MARGE

You can't expect to start at the top, I'll tell you that. You might wait years for that one big break.

BECKY

That Dwight is always showing off. I just hate him.

MARGE

All boys are like that. Later on they run out of steam and turn into men like your father and Mr. Peele. If I were you, I'd pretend to be impressed. We need all the friends we can get. You'd be weird, too, if you had a mother like his.

BECKY

You never take anything seriously. If I were to die tomorrow, this would be all of life that I had had. Don't you realize that?

MARGE

I just don't see it as an excuse to be self-indulgent, Becky. You might have become one of the great ballerinas of our time if you had kept up your dancing lessons.

BECKY

But I might have broken my leg or got a horrible disease, and all that work would have been wasted.

MARGE

I've said it before, and I'll say it again: you are a shallow child.

BECKY

I don't like the people who run things.

(GRETCHEN returns)

GRETCHEN

Excuse me for that little scene before. There's nobody down there. If there ever was one, it's gone now. Stew is furious, incidentally—his heart was set on having a corpse to show off. Dwight made a very sick joke about defenestrating Mr. Winter. That boy has a diseased imagination.

BECKY

He has some comic books that aren't on the approved list, full of monsters and degenerates and the worship of force. Yanks smashing little yellow-faced Japs with rifle butts and plunging gory bayonets into their bellies and kicking out their buckteeth—

MARGE

You may leave us now, Becky. I know you love to bore adults, but you have used up your ration.

(BECKY exits obediently)

GRETCHEN

She has beautiful manners. My kids act like apes, I'm sorry to say, but I have always been reluctant to stifle their creative impulses.

(A silence)

MARGE

My husband's an accountant. He works for a firm, but he also does income-tax work on his own for friends and relatives and keeps the books for the many organizations of which he is a member. He is also a notary public, puts that little seal on things.

GRETCHEN

I suppose he is an old friend of Stew's. Stew has never shared his friends with me, though I know he has a good many. Sometimes they call and leave messages, as if I were the maid. For example, he never mentioned you lovely people.

MARGE

Oh, he and Hal just met recently, on the train. Hit it off immediately. The windows were filthy, as usual, the seat was ripped, the conductor surly.

GRETCHEN

Stew has this feeling the world's out to get him. And maybe it is.

MARGE

Hal came home one night and said, "I've got the answer." I was breading a veal cutlet at the time.

GRETCHEN

Wiener schnitzel à la Holstein?

MARGE

No, a simple tomato sauce. Hal doesn't like me to tart anything up.

GRETCHEN

You're certain you're not English?

MARGE

Not bloody likely.

GRETCHEN

Have you ever tried that bread they fly over fresh every day from Paris?

MARGE

I find it rubbery, don't you?

GRETCHEN

(To audience)

I can't say a word to this woman without her using it against me somehow.

MARGE

I heard that.

GRETCHEN

You mistake my meaning, Marge. I am grateful for your reactions. I *am* a foolish, giddy person. Imagine entertaining the idea that Stew threw a man out the window. He's always been a terrible coward—not physically but morally. He apologizes when another person collides with him on the sidewalk, even though he, Stew, has clearly the right of way. He even thanks the people who sell him things.

MARGE

That's a sinister trait.

GRETCHEN

So Hal came home and said he had the answer.

MARGE

I asked the "answer to what?" As you might expect.

GRETCHEN

And he replied with a cryptic statement.

MARGE

No, he was crystal-clear. "To everybody else," he said. "To the entire spectacle. We must flee. This was made obvious to me," he said, "by a madman and/or genius."

GRETCHEN

Do people actually say "and/or" in speech?

MARGE

Hal does.

GRETCHEN

Could he have been referring to Stew?

MARGE

The next morning we packed our suitcases.

GRETCHEN

That was this morning.

MARGE

Perhaps it was.

(The WOMEN embrace, and while THEY do so PEELE and WINTER come in. PEELE is agitated)

WINTER

(Seeing the WOMEN)
Will you look at that. Why can't men get away with that sort of thing?

PEELE

(Impatiently)
It begins in childhood. Girls can dance together while boys cannot. Forget about it, Hal. I can't get that missing stiff out of my mind. That means there's more of them. He didn't just get up and walk away.

(Goes to his desk, WINTER following)

GRETCHEN

(Pulling away from MARGE)
Stew can be so unfair! I've seen him throw comradely arms around male pals of his.

MARGE

It wasn't your husband who said it, but mine, and you are too shy to point that out. If we are going to live together, we'll have to get beyond that kind of delicacy. For example, if you see my child do something that deserves punishment, I want you to hit her.

GRETCHEN

But I don't strike my own children.

MARGE

I will.

PEELE

They're vicious, Hal. Don't try diplomacy on them. They'll laugh in your face.

(HE makes an ugly laugh in WINTER's face, and WINTER recoils. HE pushes his gun into WINTER's belly)
Both barrels in the gut—that's their language.

(WINTER looks ill.

PEELE takes gun away and claps him on the shoulder)
Don't lose your nerve, old buddy! That's what they want. We'll stand shoulder to shoulder against the tide of scum.

(HE seizes a small megaphone from the shelf and puts it to his mouth) I want to say right here that Hal Winter is sharing expenses fifty-fifty. We are all of us on an absolutely even basis here. Nobody is boss.

WINTER

(Doubtfully)
But we don't want anarchism, do we? That doesn't mean that anybody can do what he wants at all times?

MARGE

What about the ass-kisser who wants only to do what other people like? I always think of that type when anybody talks about freedom.

WINTER

Is that an oblique thrust at me?

GRETCHEN

Oh, let's not wrangle about incidentals. Does the idea of lunch appeal to anyone? Why don't you just go ahead to the kitchen, Marge? I'd only get in your way.

(The bookcase-door opens slowly, and the torn and bruised figure of the METER READER appears)

Yes? May we help you?

MAN

(With difficulty)
I was here earlier.

PEELE

(Raising shotgun)
You sniveling jackal!
(To WINTER)
Keep him talking.
(Circles MAN and, keeping him covered, slams door)

GRETCHEN

Are you the person who was supposedly defenestrated?

MAN

I believe so. I'm a bit foggy.
(Falls to his knees)

GRETCHEN

And so am I. How did you survive?

MAN

I don't know. All I remember is a rush of wind in my face followed by several collisions.

PEELE

You people thought I would be passive, did you? Push me far enough, and I revert to utter savagery.

(VALERIE and BECKY enter, see the MAN, and scream in unison)

MAN

(To the GIRLS)
Oh, knock it off. If you want to help, get some bandages.
(To VALERIE)
I know you. You're that hooker. You sure play a rough game.

PEELE

(Pointing gun at MAN and addressing the COMPANY)
Take a good look at him. That's your enemy. But he's not triumphant now.
(To MAN)
I'll give you a better break than you would give me. You may make a short statement, explaining
(HE begins to shout)
why you won't let me alone!
(Cocks gun and puts it to MAN's head)

MAN

I suppose it's useless to beg for mercy?

PEELE

Try me.

MAN

I'm the sole support of my aged mother.

PEELE

(Scornfully)
I'd have more respect for you if you went out shrieking defiance.

MAN

My wife's in an iron lung.
(HE starts to walk away on his knees)

PEELE

You will die with a cheap jest on your lips.
(Shoots him)

MAN

(Mortally wounded, HE hands PEELE a postcard)
To insure uninterrupted service, take the meter readings yourself, enter them on this card, and mail it promptly to the company.

(Dies.
DWIGHT runs in)

WINTER

You've got some dad!
(DWIGHT searches body)

DWIGHT

(Taking a card from the wallet)
Look, here's a card that says: "I suffer from an exotic disease. If I am found unconscious please do not think I am drunk, but call my next of kin at 473-6200."

PEELE

There's cunning for you. I recognize the number. It happens to be Alcoholics Anonymous.

GRETCHEN

(To MARGE)
Stew licked his own problem.

PEELE

(Looking around)
Now do you believe me? This man was a terrorist. The sick humor is typical. Nothing is sacred to these people.

WINTER

(To MARGE)
What did I tell you about my old buddy Stew?

MARGE

That you hardly knew him.

GRETCHEN

Where *do* we get our electricity, Stew?

PEELE

(Impatiently)
You wouldn't understand if I told you. An extremely complex hookup, underground, to somebody else's line. We can't have mailmen traipsing in here with bills. Forget the outside world, Gretch. We have disaffiliated, with all that that implies.

WINTER

(To PEELE)
I wonder if I know you well enough to ask a favor.

PEELE

(Expansively)
Anything.

WINTER

Would you let me hold the gun while it's still warm?

PEELE

(Covering him)
Anything but that.

WINTER

No offense?

PEELE

None taken.

VALERIE

(Looking at body)
I guess he was too old for me anyway.

CURTAIN

ACT II

VALERIE and the AUTHOR, who is dressed as a doctor, come
out in front of the closed curtain.

AUTHOR

(Holding end of the stethoscope that is around his neck)
I don't like the sound of that cough. Open your blouse.

VALERIE

(Suspicious)
You were the only one who was coughing.

AUTHOR

(Puts stethoscope to her behind and listens briefly)
Uh-huh.

VALERIE

What's "uh-huh" mean?
(Tries to elude the stethoscope)

AUTHOR

I'm afraid it's not good news.

VALERIE

(Worried)
I've always been in perfect health.

AUTHOR

Get those clothes off. I must begin operations immediately.

VALERIE

What are you going to take out?

AUTHOR

My instrument. You'll see: in no time at all you'll be saying, "Oh, doctor, I feel so-o-o-o good."
(Does bump and grind)

VALERIE

(Does bump and grind of her own)
Am I getting it?

AUTHOR

I wish *I* was!
(Rolls eyes and does Groucho walk)

(PEELE comes out of curtain)

PEELE

(To AUTHOR)
Why are you out here, doing old burlesque routines? The second act is beginning.

AUTHOR

I'd do anything to be loved.

PEELE

Why don't you try disappearing?

AUTHOR

(To VALERIE)
Next time we'll do "Floogle Street."
(HE and VALERIE bump-and-grind their exits)

PEELE

(Watches them, shaking his head. When they have gone through the curtain, he says:)
The time of this next and final act is the morning of the day after the one that preceded.

(The curtain opens as he speaks. DWIGHT is onstage)

DWIGHT

Morning, Dad. How they hanging?

PEELE

(Jovially)

To the left, as always! Son, what are you up to these days?

DWIGHT

You act as if you haven't seen me for weeks.

PEELE

Little pretenses are refreshing, I find. After a good night's sleep I'm bright-eyed and bushy-tailed. I'm going to find Hal and give him his orders for the day.

(Exits.

DWIGHT sits down on couch. GRETCHEN and MARGE enter through different doorways)

GRETCHEN

Good morning, Marge.

MARGE

Uh, good morning, uh . . .

GRETCHEN

Gretchen.

MARGE

Gretchen, where's Hal?

GRETCHEN

He was up an hour ago. He's in the kitchen, doing French toast.

MARGE

(Makes a face)

That's a specialty of his. I find it awfully dry.

GRETCHEN

Weak tea is about all I can face in the morning.

MARGE

A sizzling kipper is lovely.

GRETCHEN

Come on, Marge, admit you're English.

MARGE

Why should I?

(WINTER enters)

WINTER

Everybody up? Where are the girls? Two more minutes.

(Exits)

GRETCHEN

(To DWIGHT, without looking at him)
Dwight, go get your sister and her little friend.

DWIGHT

Not on your life.

MARGE

Do as you're told, Dwight, or I'll whip your smart ass.

DWIGHT

Yes, ma'am.
  (HE exits)

GRETCHEN

(Smiling at MARGE)
You're so good at these things, Marge. I suppose I should be jealous, but I admire you too much. I have no feeling whatever about your sleeping with Stew.

MARGE

Neither have I.

GRETCHEN

I thought I would be embarrassed.

MARGE

I wish I were.
  (SHE shrugs cynically.

  PEELE and WINTER enter, PEELE first, proudly carrying the platter of French toast, WINTER following anxiously. DWIGHT furtively comes along behind)

PEELE

Get 'em while they're hot!

  (VALERIE and BECKY enter and EVERYBODY sits down at the table)

VALERIE

I hope it's waffles!

BECKY

No, pancakes!

DWIGHT

Spanish omelet!

WINTER

I hope you like French toast.

VALERIE

Not me.

DWIGHT

Ugh!

BECKY

I'll just have a glass of milk.

(Then THEY eat voraciously)

WINTER

I hope you like this, folks. The secret's the sour cream.

PEELE

We have no sour cream.

WINTER

I brought along a container.

PEELE

Any more secret supplies of anything must be be reported to me immediately. Is any of the sour cream left?

WINTER

Most of it. Look, I'm sorry, Stew. I didn't realize you would be so upset.

PEELE

(Rises)
This whole thing will have to come out in the open.
(Exits)

MARGE

Careful, Hal. He's probably gone to get the shotgun.

WINTER

(Laughing nervously)
Come on, Marge.

DWIGHT

He'll defenestrate you first.

(WINTER stops eating and waits apprehensively. PEELE returns with container of sour cream)

PEELE

Here, Hal. Smash it into my face.

WINTER

I couldn't do that.

PEELE

No, but you could sneak it in here behind my back. You've challenged my authority, so go ahead and add gross humiliation to it, if you've got the guts.

GRETCHEN

(To MARGE)
Do you understand any of this?

MARGE

(Eating placidly)
I'm ignoring it.

PEELE

Are you going to do as I ask, Hal?

(DWIGHT throws down his fork in disgust, seizes container, and grinds it into his FATHER's face)

PEELE

(With a faceful of sour cream)
I'd be ashamed of myself, if I were you, Hal. Letting a boy do a man's work.

WINTER

I get your point.

PEELE

Then it served its purpose. I'll go wash up and we will never mention this incident again.

(Exits)

WINTER

Say what you want, old Stew understands power. I would follow his flag anywhere.

GRETCHEN

Yet I would not call you effeminate.

WINTER

You're learning something, Gretch.

MARGE

(To CHILDREN)
All right, let's wind this up. Time for school.

(The GIRLS rise obediently and carry out the dishes. DWIGHT keeps eating)

GRETCHEN

(Whining)
Now, Dwight . . .

(MARGE reaches under the table, brings out a huge club, and strikes DWIGHT over the head. HE rises dizzily)

DWIGHT
(To MARGE)
Then you're not indifferent to me?

MARGE
(Affectionately)
I always wanted a son like you.
(Kisses him)

DWIGHT
The whip and the carrot. There's nothing new under the sun.
(Takes dish and staggers out)

GRETCHEN
You're making a man of him.

MARGE
How long have you had this feeling of ineffectuality?

GRETCHEN
All my life, really. When I was only five years—

MARGE
No childhood reminiscences, please.

WINTER
They've forgotten I'm here.

MARGE
No, I haven't.
(Strikes him with club)

WINTER
(Takes club from her and addresses audience)
Funny, in spite of the size of that bludgeon, you can hardly feel it. It's balsa wood, I guess. That sort of effect fascinates me. I love movie fight scenes with breakaway chairs and fragmenting bottles made of some harmless plastic.

GRETCHEN
I fear a repetition of an earlier series, now that this club has proved non-damaging. First I am appalled at a violent act, then it turns out to be harmless or at least not permanent in its effect—like the defenestration of that man—and then I relax, and then he really is killed and I am not disturbed at all.

MARGE

I suggest you just sit tight. The ancient Greeks had a superstition about calling a man's life happy until it had ended.

GRETCHEN

I never finished college.

WINTER

One thing I have never been able to endure, and that is listening to women talk among themselves.
(Exits)

MARGE

Nevertheless, I can't do all the teaching myself. You'll have to lend a hand.

GRETCHEN

I might manage a little class in interpretive dancing, but certainly not geography or social studies, and I still have nightmares about mathematics.

MARGE

Go fetch the students.

GRETCHEN

Yes, ma'am.
(Exits)

MARGE

I can't stand that woman—even though I am sympathetic to her.

(PEELE and WINTER enter)

Do you guys want to help with the school?

PEELE

(Peers at her)
Don't try it, Marge.

MARGE

Try what?

PEELE

That's woman's work. Don't try to pull me down. You haven't got the balls for it.

MARGE

Neither has Hal.

WINTER

Come on, Marge.

(To PEELE)

She's a great little kidder.

(MARGE and PEELE are staring at each other)

PEELE

All right, get going, chop-chop.

(THEY continue to exchange stares. Suddenly a rock, with a note tied to it, comes through the window.

(PEELE spreads his arms)
Everybody back.
(HE gingerly approaches the rock, then stops and gives a peremptory order to MARGE)
Get a bucket of water.

(MARGE does not move)

WINTER

I'll get it, Stew.

PEELE

Take cover, Hal. This may go off at any moment.

(WINTER falls to floor behind couch

PEELE addresses MARGE)
Goddammit, that's a direct order!

(MARGE shrugs and moves indifferently away. PEELE takes a cushion from the couch and, holding it in front of his chest, hurls himself onto the rock. Carefully HE withdraws, picks up the rock, loosens the string, and takes off the note.

HE reads it aloud)
"This building is condemned, you horse's ass." Aha! Come here, Hal, and see what you make of this.

(WINTER rises and joins PEELE)

WINTER

(Takes note and reads it)
"This building is condemned, you horse's—"
(Breaks off hastily)
That seems to be what it says, all right.

PEELE

What's your interpretation?

                              WINTER

I'd hate to say.

                              PEELE

You don't recognize the handwriting?

                              WINTER

    (Guiltily, though HE is innocent)
Can't say I do, Stew.

                              PEELE

You're quite sure about that?

                              WINTER

I've never seen it before.

                              PEELE

    (Nodding ironically)
Uh-huh.

    (MARGE is watching them)

Let me tell you something, Hal. You're skating on very thin ice.

                              WINTER

Aw, Stew. You can't believe I had a hand in this.

                              PEELE

After all, what do I know about you? A chance acquaintance on the train.
Now that I think about it, that meeting was suspicious in itself. How did
it happen that you were sitting in the seat into which I flung my attaché
case? I admit I was at first taken in by your howl of pain, your pretense
that your nose was broken. Then your sniveling apology followed, and I was
hooked. So here I am, cheek-by-jowl with an enemy agent.

                              MARGE

    You don't have to take that sort of thing, Hal.

                              WINTER

    (Laughing fearfully)
Come on, Stew.

                              MARGE

I call it sickening.

    (DWIGHT, VALERIE, and BECKY enter)

                              PEELE

Come over here, Dwight.

(DWIGHT comes, and PEELE gives him the note)

Take a look at this.

DWIGHT

(Reads it to himself)
They've got you there, Dad.

PEELE

(Saving face)
It's probably a hoax. I think you're late for school, son.

(The CHILDREN sit down at the table)

MARGE

Good morning, children. Today we're going to talk about what we did on our vacations. Dwight?

DWIGHT

I went to scout camp. In the woods I saw a big black bear, a little red chipmunk, and a middle-sized degenerate, and also a lot of aluminum beer cans that will never rust throughout eternity.

VALERIE

He's lying. We stayed home all summer and he gave an obscene puppet show.

BECKY

This is a lousy story.

MARGE

We'll have the critiques later. Have you got an ending for it, Dwight?

DWIGHT

The scoutmaster was arrested for crimes of a carnal nature.

MARGE

You need to do more work on your point of view, though your pace and detail are quite good.
(Looks at her watch)
I see it's rest time, already.

(The CHILDREN lower their heads onto their folded arms and go to sleep.

PEELE is at his desk, still studying the note. WINTER sits on the floor at his feet)

WINTER

(Looking up apprehensively)
I will say this, Stew. I did see some such notice downstairs when we came in.

PEELE

Oh you did?

WINTER

A notice of condemnation.

PEELE

Uh-huh.

WINTER

It said about the same thing as that note, without the abusive epithet.

PEELE

I suppose you will say that it did not occur to you that I might have nailed that up, myself, to throw pursuers off the trail.

WINTER

In fact, that's exactly what did occur to me, Stew. I thought it was very clever.

PEELE

(Staring at him)
Oh, you did, did you?

WINTER

But perhaps someone else did not figure that out.

PEELE

You're working up to something pretty slimy, aren't you, Hal? Looking for a scapegoat? You've got only women and children to choose from.

WINTER

(With an air of discovery)
I couldn't have thrown in that note! I was with you all the time.

PEELE

(Slaps the desk)
Hal, I want you to level with me. Did you or did you not have anything to do with this note?

WINTER

I swear.

PEELE

(Produces a little pistol from the desk drawer)
See this, Hal. A lethal weapon.
(Gives pistol to WINTER)
Now you are armed, and I am not. Do you understand?

WINTER

No.

(Tries to give it back)

PEELE

(Pushes the pistol away)

No, no, not on your life. I want to get this settled. You're either with me or against me. If the latter, I hope you have the guts to shoot. I fear treachery, not death.

WINTER

This is a nightmare.

PEELE

(Clamps WINTER's hand around the weapon and puts WINTER's finger against the trigger, then pulls it into his own belly and supports it)

Pull the trigger, you deceitful hyena!

(THEY struggle.

MARGE snaps her fingers, and the CHILDREN awaken)

MARGE

Your turn, Valerie.

VALERIE

My summer was a blur of longing.

MARGE

That's enough narrative for the moment. Quick now, do this one in your heads: Farmer Brown has two chickens, five ducks, and a drinking problem. He is politically reactionary, wears the same underwear all winter, and underpays his moronic hired hand. What crop has he planted on the back forty?

BECKY

Soybeans.

MARGE

Correct.

VALERIE

That was rigged. I don't like this school. It caters to the individual.

DWIGHT

Doesn't sound like Brown has much of a farm.

MARGE

A very good observation, Dwight, leading us right into the economic question. You see, Mr. Brown doesn't have to farm to make a living. He does very well at his mail-order business. Novelties from all over the world. Cuckoo clocks from the Black Forest, bumper stickers which deride the truths we live by, and a cunning little model of an outdoor toilet which, when you open the door, discloses a small boy who whirls around and pees on you.

DWIGHT

That happened a lot at scout camp.

MARGE

It has a reservoir you fill with tap water.

(PEELE and WINTER come onstage again, still struggling. PEELE at length gives up his effort to get WINTER to shoot him, and puts the pistol against WINTER's forehead)

PEELE

You've had your chance. Now say your prayers, buster.

WINTER

Now I lay me down to sleep—

PEELE

Sorry I can't wait for the punch line.
(HE pulls the trigger. Nothing happens. HE lowers the pistol)
Misfire. Okay, I never go against fate.
(Shakes WINTER's hand)
As far as I'm concerned, that's the end of it. I'll never mention it again.
(HE returns to his desk.

WINTER collapses)

MARGE

Who can tell me the current population of Lahore, Pakistan?

BECKY

1,296,477.

MARGE

Correct. Which of the following are real animals, and which are mythical? A. The unicorn. B. The hobbyhorse. C. The postcoitum tristis. D. The duckbilled platypus.

BECKY

E. None of these.

MARGE

(Triumphantly)
Wrong!

DWIGHT

When are we going to get to history? I'm big on that.

MARGE

Any minute now. Do you have a favorite period?

DWIGHT

Yes, the reign of Lady Jane Grey, who was queen of England for nine days in 1553, after which she was imprisoned. The arts flourished in this period, and peace was maintained by a subtle balance of power. The importunate peasantry was mollified by certain superficial reforms, and a new type of leader appeared on the scene, dressed in simple homespun but with an embroidered codpiece. The barriers of intolerance fell. It was not unusual to see horse dung in banquet halls. Dirks, poniards, and bodkins were manipulated in public. There was a popular game called the beast with two backs.

MARGE

An excellent report, Dwight. I'm giving you an A-plus.

VALERIE

I know something about ancient Sparta. In ancient Sparta naked boys competed in athletics with naked girls. This was one of the causes leading to the Pubic Wars.

BECKY

I know how Balto the noble sled dog got the serum to Nome though suffering from the mange.

MARGE

We have just a moment before the bell. Here's your homework for tomorrow: write an epic poem in dactylic hexameter. For biology, trap an animal of any species and give him a cute name. Draw a picture of some member of your family in a humiliating situation. School's out, school's out, teacher's eating sauerkraut! Do they still say that?
 (Exits with the GIRLS.

DWIGHT finds pistol on the couch, where PEELE tossed it)

DWIGHT

Oh, *there's* my pistol.
 (HE points it at WINTER and soaks him with a stream of water, then exits)

WINTER

(Incredulous)
That was a *water* pistol?

PEELE

Filled with a virulent acid, it could be deadly. Never disparage a toy, Hal.

WINTER

(Dumbfounded)
You terrorized me with a water pistol?

PEELE

Would you rather I used the shotgun? Be sensible, Hal. I had to establish your loyalty conclusively. These are perilous times.

WINTER

I don't question your motives. It's my performance that disgusts me.

PEELE

(Expansively)
There are two kinds of people, those who do good and those who do well. You belong to the former, old buddy.

WINTER

I just hope I can earn your trust.

PEELE

One thing is certain. We mustn't allow ourselves to be panicked by a little piece of paper.
(Claps WINTER on the shoulder)
Get hold of yourself, Hal.

WINTER

I'm trying to.

(THEY exit.

The AUTHOR appears, dressed as a cowboy in ten-gallon hat, sheep-skin chaps, and spurred boots. HE is ineffectually trying to spin a limp rope)

AUTHOR

I never met a man I liked.
(Tries to spin rope)
I'm getting it now. There. . . . No. The hell with it.
(Throws rope down)
Much of my life has been wasted in an effort to charm other people. . . . No, that's not true. I want to make them feel guilty, which is quite another thing. Sometimes I walk along the street with a false limp. . . . Actually, I can spin a rope reasonably well when nobody's looking.

(As HE says this, the end of the rope erects itself, like the snake of an Indian charmer. AUTHOR draws his six-shooter and fires at the rope, which collapses)

I go armed at all times. Everyone is distracted these days. I fire off a round or two to get the attention of department-store clerks, post-office employees, and the like.

(Pause)

I myself played the role of the man who was murdered in the first act of this melodrama, but in rehearsals we used a series of actors in the part and actually killed one at each performance. Not only was this expensive, but it lacked dramatic verisimilitude.

(PEELE sticks his head through a doorway)

PEELE
Will you stop interrupting this play?

AUTHOR
If you know so much about personality, why do you represent someone other than yourself?

(PEELE retreats)

(To audience)

They have to say whatever I write. That's what they can't stand. I hope you have been refreshed by this little relief from make-believe.

(Bows and exits.

PEELE, WINTER and DWIGHT enter and sit down on couch, DWIGHT in the middle)

PEELE
Dwight, you're shaping up very well. Were we a primitive tribe, you would already have taken your first head and shrunken it.

WINTER
(Putting an arm around DWIGHT)

Think of me as your Uncle Hal.

DWIGHT
Know something, Uncle Hal? Your breath is enough to knock me over.

PEELE
Perhaps you could suggest a good mouthwash, son. You shouldn't just leave a man with information of that kind.

DWIGHT
I don't like the way any older person smells.

WINTER

I can remember feeling that way myself, squashed between the grownups in church. I would almost suffocate.

PEELE

Getting serious, Dwight—
(Gives him the note)
What's your judgment on this note?

DWIGHT

It's the work of person or persons unknown.
(Studies note further)
Notice the way the writing slants to the right. That would strongly suggest that the penman was left-handed and deliberately trying to give the impression he was right-handed.

PEELE

(Eagerly)
Yes, yes. Go on.

DWIGHT

Probably a German.

PEELE

How so?

DWIGHT

Observe how careful he is to avoid the use of an umlaut—which would give him away.

PEELE

(To HAL)
What did I tell you, Hal? I knew Dwight would have a contribution.

DWIGHT

Finally—
(Takes pen from his pocket)
It is suspiciously easy to imitate this script.
(Writes on paper and gives it to PEELE)
Even a little kid can do it.

PEELE

(Looking at note)
Right as rain, Dwight! You're on to something.

DWIGHT

(Rises)
My pleasure, Dad.

(Shakes WINTER's left hand)

Auf wiedersehn, mein Herr.

(Exits)

PEELE

(Stares suspiciously at WINTER)

He's a bright boy.

WINTER

Now wait a minute, Stew.

PEELE

He and I are very close.

(Ominously)

Let's play a little game of free association. I'll mention a word and you tell me the first thing that comes into your mind.

(Pause)

Knockwurst.

WINTER

(Helplessly)

Sauerkraut.

PEELE

(Laughing)

Threw a scare into you, didn't I?

(Shakes his hand)

Don't worry, Hal. I don't go back on my word. I said I trusted you, and I do. I know you'd lay down your life for me.

WINTER

(Relieved)

It won't be for lack of trying. I'll say that, Stew.

PEELE

But that still leaves this second phenomenon unexplained. First that bogus meter reader walks right in, and now the murky figure of a left-handed German may or may not be in the picture. Tell me this: do you trust the women?

WINTER

Implicitly.

PEELE

(Nods)

Mmm.

(An AMERICAN INDIAN walks in, wearing a war bonnet and fringed leggings)

Marge, for example, has made many remarks that I would call snide.

INDIAN

I was a simple, healthy barbarian until the white devils came across the Big Water with their thundersticks and syphilis. Many moons ago—

PEELE

(Furiously)
Oh, shut your fucking mouth!

INDIAN

Isn't this the Mohican Convention?

PEELE

No, it isn't.

INDIAN

When was the last time you saw kids playing Cowboys and Wops?
(Exits.

WINTER snickers, in spite of himself)

PEELE

You think he got the better of me?
(Looks for shotgun)

WINTER

I wouldn't say that.

PEELE

(Finds shotgun and runs to doorway)
I'll fix that insolent redskin! If anybody else shows up, shoot to kill.

WINTER

I'm not armed.

PEELE

Then play for time.

(Exits.

WINTER wanders about, brooding. A FLAMBOYANT PERSON appears, dressed in colorful leisure-wear. WINTER sees him at last. THEY stare at each other for a while. Then)

FLAMBOYANT PERSON

Hi, handsome.

WINTER

Hi. How did you get in?

FLAMBOYANT

I saw the light.
 (Pause)
A penny for your thoughts.

WINTER

I used to compete, but it wore me out. I just didn't have the stomach for it. I think I missed something the way I was brought up. My parents were sex maniacs. I grew up in a house in which orgies were a regular Saturday night feature, people going at it hammer and tongs on the beds, sofas, even the floor. My whole boyhood was lived in a kind of blue movie. I suppose that's why I respond so readily to Stew's tyranny. I need something to believe in.

FLAMBOYANT

Be kind to me.

WINTER

I don't care for that sort of thing.
 (Hastily)
I don't mean to criticize you of course.

FLAMBOYANT PERSON

I come to town for some amusement. All week I'm a game warden upstate. This is my way of relaxing. I get out of my wool shirt and heavy boots. . . . Let's go down to the wharves and look at the oilslick on the water.

WINTER

You've got the wrong fellow, believe me.

FLAMBOYANT

Why are you so glum?
 (Chucks WINTER under the chin)

WINTER

I'm warning you!

FLAMBOYANT

Aren't you fierce! Let's go up to the woods and slaughter some deer.

WINTER

I oppose killing except in self-defense.

FLAMBOYANT

Please, no maudlin sentimentality! Nature itself is red in tooth and claw.

Besides, the deer herd is overstrength. It should be weeded out for the sake of the remaining animals. Have you ever eaten venison?

                    WINTER
Never.

                    FLAMBOYANT
     (Seductively)
It has *such* a gamey taste . . .

                    WINTER
Look, I've tried to be nice—

                    FLAMBOYANT
Why?

                    WINTER
     (Gets control of himself)
No, I refuse to be provoked.

                    FLAMBOYANT
I pity you. You don't know how to enjoy yourself.
     (Exits)

                    WINTER
I'm a target for weirdos of all kinds, because I look sympathetic. Actually, I'm not. I seethe with malice. One of these days I'll get fed up and then look out!
     (Puts his face in his hands.

     GRETCHEN and MARGE enter)

                    GRETCHEN
Sometimes I feel like I'm playing house.

                    MARGE
You are.

                    WINTER
     (Looks up indignantly)
How do you like that for nerve!

                    MARGE
What?

                    WINTER
You missed him. Some importunate game warden. It was all I could do to keep from killing him, I'll tell you. Fresh bastard!

GRETCHEN

(Smugly)

No matter how wild your fantasies, someone has already performed them in reality. Remember that, and you will never be frightened again.

WINTER

Me? He was the one in danger. It was all I could do—

MARGE

Remember that guy who used to follow you around at the beach?

WINTER

(Rigidly)

I should have known better than to try to talk to a couple of women.

(PEELE enters)

PEELE

He vanished in thin air.

WINTER

The game warden?

PEELE

The Indian.

WINTER

I wonder if we might be imagining these intruders.

MARGE

There's the curious case of Our Lady of Fatima.

PEELE

I suppose you didn't see anything fishy?

(Stares hostilely at MARGE)

MARGE

I haven't seen anything normal since I entered this place.

WINTER

He claimed to be a game warden, a state employee!

PEELE

I didn't encounter him. I assumed it was hyperbole. Forgive me, old comrade. It must have been a frightening experience, alone and unarmed as you were. From now on stick close to me.

MARGE

That's what the game warden wanted him to do.

PEELE

Marge, you and I are moving toward a showdown. I'm damned sick of your wisecracks. It's not enough that I have to defend this place singlehandedly against vengeful Indians—

GRETCHEN

I had a toy birchbark canoe when I was a little girl. Souvenir of Niagara Falls, but I do believe it was made in the Orient.

(PEELE glares at her, and seems about to say something when the door opens and in comes a JAPANESE, dressed in the uniform of the American Society for the Protection of Cruelty to Animals)

JAPANESE

(Bowing, smiling)

I'm from the ASPCA. We have received a complaint that someone here is mistreating a dog. Incidentally, were you aware that perverts flock to zoos at mating season, where they congregate in an informal group known as the Cock Watchers?

PEELE

We keep no dog here. You are welcome to inspect the premises.

JAPANESE

I think it's only fair to warn you that I easily go berserk at the sight of a brutalized animal—though I am normally a mild-mannered individual.

(Exits)

GRETCHEN

Who can that Asiatic person be?

PEELE

I can't be sure.

WINTER

You were about the man from the gas and electric company.

PEELE

That was a different matter. Animal people are not so easy to deal with. They have no sentimentality when it comes to human beings.

(JAPANESE returns, leading a large woolly dog)

JAPANESE

I apologize, folks. He looks like a healthy little fellow, well fed and with a glossy coat, wet nose. You're clean as a whistle so far as I'm concerned. The complaint was probably put in by one of the many cranks in this city.

PEELE

No offense taken.

WINTER

(Indignantly)
What's this?

JAPANESE

I must confiscate him, though. He is not properly licensed.

WINTER

Who do you think you are?

JAPANESE

Who is anybody, under the aspect of eternity? We are all expendable, my dear chap. I'm interested only in the problem of pain.

WINTER

That makes you some kind of hero? I think you're a prick. How do you like that?

PEELE

Take it easy, Hal.

WINTER

I don't intend to let this bastard walk in here and push us around. This is our home.

JAPANESE

Can't we conduct ourselves like gentlemen?

GRETCHEN

Stew, where did that dog come from?

PEELE

I have no idea.

WINTER

What difference does that make? You're not going to let him walk out of here?

PEELE

I am handicapped by my suspicion that he is probably legitimate, Hal. I frankly can't see any motive for a Japanese to pretend he is an ASPCA officer—and notice that he carries a revolver on his belt. Were he here to do us violence he would have made use of his weapon by now. And, most important of all, he did find a dog. I'm in an embarrassing position. That's the kind of monkey I am. I have to feel I'm morally right. He's got the goods on me, I regret to say.

JAPANESE

You're wrong there, sir. I never go into motives. You look like an honorable

individual to me, but it's none of my business if you're not. My concern stops with fur, feathers, or fins.
(Goes to door, then stops)
Goodbye, all. I'm double-parked outside with a van full of yapping curs.
(Looks at dog)
Be assured we'll put him to sleep in a humane way.

WINTER
(Approaches him threateningly)
Just a minute, fella. I don't know how that dog got in here, but you'll take him away over my dead body.

JAPANESE
(Regretfully)
Oh, dear me. I did hope there would be no violence.

WINTER
A man has to take a stand somewhere.
(HE advances on the JAPANESE)

JAPANESE
In the end, I suppose most of us die for clichés.
(HE draws a pistol and shoots WINTER)

WINTER
They always say you never hear the shot that kills you. Another lie.
(Falls and dies)

PEELE
Christ, he did it. He really did it!

JAPANESE
Of course, I did.

PEELE
I mean Hal. You are nothing to me.

JAPANESE
Well, you saw the whole thing. It was self-defense. I really have to run now. Bye-bye.
(Bows and exits with dog)

GRETCHEN
Who ever would have known a Japanese ASPCA man would be armed?

MARGE
(Shrugs)
You can't repel a mad dog with a wet towel.

(The CHILDREN enter)

DWIGHT

Gee, Dad! You bagged Uncle Hal!

PEELE

(Incredulous)

He did it for me.

(VALERIE sniffs in distaste and walks away)

BECKY

(Stepping over body)

Please don't think me heartless, but I am still in a state of disbelief. Later no doubt I will mourn.

MARGE

Ego. The important thing to her is her own reactions. Why should we care whether she mourns or not?

GRETCHEN

(Piously)

He was her father, Marge. My own ran away with a cheap little manicurist. A girl notices these things.

MARGE

Well, she's not special. Everybody's the child of someone.

PEELE

(Kneeling next to body)

Hal, Hal, old chum. Forgive me.

(Pokes body)

Come on, pal, get up and make us some lunch, huh?

(Pokes body)

Come on, Hal, don't clown around like this. It's bad taste, old son.

(DWIGHT pushes PEELE away and searches the body)

GRETCHEN

Dwight, what a rotten thing to do!

DWIGHT

(Going through the wallet)

I just thought he might have some ice-hockey tickets he couldn't use.

PEELE

What do you think, Marge? He'll pull through, won't he?

MARGE

If he does, he better not eat soup. It'll leak out through that hole in his belly.

VALERIE

(Repelled)

I ignore things like blood and vomit and bodily wastes. They just don't fit into my worldview.

(Exits)

DWIGHT

(Holds up some photos)

Hey, naked pictures!

MARGE

Give them here, Dwight.

(Takes snapshots)

He took these last year on one of our ski weekends.

(Shows picture to GRETCHEN)

Here's me and Gwen Hanschman, only an hour before she broke her wrist.

GRETCHEN

You're not in the nude.

MARGE

No, we're just about to take the lift.

(Hands her another picture)

Hot cocoa in the lodge. That's Bill Rego, Nancy Welch, Mr. and Mrs. Harvey Viking, and—

GRETCHEN

Those names mean nothing to me. Hey, who's this swarthy little character in the knitted cap?

MARGE

He's a chimpanzee. Belongs to Dr. Peter Pomerantz, the leading gynecologist. He can ski like a whiz. But it *is* shocking to see that hairy little figure shoot by you on the trail.

BECKY

If my daddy is dead, who will handle the charcoal grill? I like everything well done. I won't eat meat that has the slightest bit of red showing. I am allergic to everything red—tomatoes, pimentos, and lobsters. Blotches appear on my face and my skin feels all creepy. But pink is okay, like shrimps.

PEELE

(Looking down at body)

Speak to me, Hal. Tell me it isn't so.

(HE staggers to couch, and sits down, his head in his hands)

GRETCHEN

Hal was wonderful in bed.

MARGE

(Astonished)

He was?

GRETCHEN

He never touched me all night.

MARGE

Stew's acting rather spooky, isn't he?

GRETCHEN

I don't think we should disturb him.

DWIGHT

(Goes to couch, sits down alongside PEELE, and pats him on the shoulder)

Buck up, Dad. Marge will probably get married again.

PEELE

I'm not much of a model for you.

DWIGHT

Nonsense! *You* survived. It was Uncle Hal who got killed.

MARGE

(Joins PEELE on sofa)

Stew, you're not losing your nerve? Don't blame yourself for Hal's death. You're responsible for his one great moment.

PEELE

That's generous of you, Marge, but don't waste your sympathy on me. I don't deserve it. Leave, Marge, save yourself. Go home, for the love of God.

MARGE

Hal burned our house down.

PEELE

What a massive spirit he had!

MARGE

Be that as it may, you can't get rid of me now.

(SHE leans possessively against him.

BECKY comes and sits on PEELE's lap. GRETCHEN tries to find a place for herself on the sofa, fails, and sits on floor.

VALERIE enters)

VALERIE

I was all alone back there. I'd rather be in here with the corpse.

(SHE joins the GROUP at the sofa.

PEELE is engulfed for a moment, and then HE shakes EVERYBODY off and rises)

                              PEELE

I've been too soft up to now. Somehow I haven't been able to shake off the sentimental conviction that a certain basic decency remains in the human heart no matter how depraved. I was wrong. Our enemies are conscienceless scum.

                              DWIGHT

Man is a wolf to man.

                              PEELE

The old free-and-easy style must be put aside. No more dolce vita. This is war, no quarter given and none asked.
    (Shouts)
Half rations for everybody, drinking water will be dispensed by the spoonful, the curfew will be observed, and God help that sentry who sleeps at his post. There will be a continuous identification check on all personnel.
    (Points to BECKY)
You there. Come here.

    (BECKY marches toward PEELE, as HE counts cadence)

Hut two, hut two, hut two. Halt, hut two! Who goes there?

                              BECKY

Rebecca Margaret Wint—
    (SHE looks at body and breaks off)
Rebecca Margaret *Peele* age eleven.

                              PEELE

You may pass.

    (GRETCHEN marches up)

                              GRETCHEN

Gretchen Elizabeth—

                              PEELE

Cut the comedy, Gretch.
    (Turns to DWIGHT)
Let's police up this area, son. The Hal we knew and loved is no more. The mighty spirit has fled and what remains is a stiff, pure and simple.
    (HE drags the body to the refuse chute and with very little help from DWIGHT, slides it from sight)

MARGE

(Yawning)

Well, I suppose I should rustle up some lunch.

PEELE

(Brushing off his hands)

Marge, you rustle up some lunch. Girls, go check all the windows. If you come across either the Indian or the game warden, report to me immediately. Don't try to apprehend them yourself. They're rough customers. Dwight, maintain your roving reconnaissance. You are called upon to be a man before your time. I know I can count on you.

Gretch, try not to get in anybody's way and above all, no hysteria.

(Examines bookcase-door)

This is too easy to breach.

(Exits through bedroom door)

GRETCHEN

I must say you are taking this very well, Marge. Your home is burned to the ground, your husband is slain, and you have to work as a short-order cook. But do you complain? Not you.

MARGE

I am that rarest of human beings, the happy person. I suppose you think me cold.

GRETCHEN

Not at all!

MARGE

Just because I see people as interchangeable.

GRETCHEN

That makes sense.

MARGE

I lead a charmed life. I have attended dinner parties at which every guest but me got hepatitis from the clam dip. I have never received an obscene phone call.

GRETCHEN

Dwight makes a lot of those.

MARGE

Or a poison-pen letter.

GRETCHEN

I have.

MARGE

Whatever happens, I'll survive. I'm only sorry I can't pass on my magic to you, but you are a born loser.

GRETCHEN

But I'm serene enough in my own little way. I feel no pressure. There is a kind of security in knowing you will always come out on the short end of the stick.

MARGE

I'll make some peanut-butter sandwiches.

(THEY exit)

BECKY

Let's go look for the Indian.

VALERIE

And the game warden. Maybe we can straighten him out.

(THEY exit.

DWIGHT lurks about, and when PEELE enters, carrying dynamite sticks and wire, DWIGHT takes cover and watches him go out the bookcase-door)

DWIGHT

(To audience)
There goes the only character in the play who doesn't mean well.
(HE exits.

PEELE reappears)

PEELE

I've still got a few tricks up my sleeve. I can't wait till the next one tries that door.

(A WORKMAN opens door PEELE has just closed, and enters)

WORKMAN

Hey, bud! Better get out of here pronto. We're gonna demolish this building.

PEELE

I posted that notice downstairs. It's a fake.

WORKMAN

What difference does that make to us? It's how we earn our living.

PEELE

You can't tear down a building because of a hoax.

WORKMAN

Why not?

PEELE

It's against the law!

WORKMAN

So is unnecessary blowing of your auto horn, but does anybody pay attention to that?

PEELE

Are you insane?

WORKMAN

Naw, I'm a *professional*. We got our crane and big iron ball ready to swing. Look, sometimes that goddam crane will topple over and crush a crowd of sidewalk superintendents. Is that *my* fault? I work hard, fella. Can you say the same? Last week we got the wrong place altogether and razed a building still under construction. That caused a real stink with the steelworkers.

(Takes off his helmet and points to his skull)

See that? I took a rivet in the head. Did you pay my medical expenses?

PEELE

I'm sorry about that, but—

WORKMAN

I ain't asking no favors. Just get your ass out of here. This building is coming down in ten minutes.

(Starts to leave, then stops)

Just remember there are other people in the world, for God's sake.

(Exits)

PEELE

I booby-trapped the landing out there, and he walks right in!

(Thinks for a moment, and then calls out)

Marge! Marge!

(MARGE and GRETCHEN enter. MARGE hands PEELE a sandwich)

Marge, I want you and your daughter to leave.

MARGE

We've been through all that.

PEELE

No quips now, please, Marge. I'm touched by your loyalty, but the situation has changed.

(Takes keys from pocket)

These are the keys to our house. I'm no Hal Winter. I didn't have the guts to put it to the torch when we left, so unless it's been vandalized overnight—and it may well have been—it's still standing in Oakdale, 272 Hessian Avenue—take a left at Lafayette and another at Cornwallis, go past the giant ice-cream cone—

MARGE

Stew, I can't get over the feeling that you are a thrill-seeker.

PEELE

No, Marge, no sympathy, please.

(Points)

Leave.

(MARGE shakes her head and exits)

GRETCHEN

Stew, have you discovered the truth about that dog?

PEELE

(Absentmindedly bites into sandwich, chews, and grimaces)

Jesus, peanut butter!

(Sees GRETCHEN)

Listen, Gretch, you too can leave if you'd like. Tell the kids. Only make it fast.

(Looks at his watch)

Eight minutes.

(MARGE, BECKY, VALERIE, and DWIGHT enter. MARGE and BECKY carry suitcases)

GRETCHEN

(Brightly)

That was quick.

BECKY

We never unpacked.

DWIGHT

Hey, Dad, see the crane out there?

PEELE

(Hastily)

Goodbye, Marge.

MARGE

(Affectionately)

You know, Stew, underneath it all I've always kind of liked you. If you reconsider, you can always come home.

PEELE

Goodbye, Marge, and God bless you.

BECKY

Goodbye, Mrs. Peele. Goodbye, Valerie.

VALERIE

Take care, Betty.

BECKY

Becky. Good-bye, Dwight. Good-bye, Mr. Peele. Perhaps one day you will beat your gun into a plowshare.

(SHE and MARGE exit)

GRETCHEN

I wonder why Marge left so soon. I must have offended her in some way.

PEELE

Oh, my God! I forgot I booby-trapped the landing.
  (Rushes to door, opens it, and looks outside)
Well, once again it didn't work.
  (HE exits left)

DWIGHT

He's disappointed.

GRETCHEN

It just goes to show you how wise I've always been to make no friends. They might be blown up. Then where would I be?

VALERIE

Betty spilled my cologne. Still, I don't like to think of her being blown up.

(PEELE returns with a can of gasoline and sprinkles it about)

DWIGHT

What's your rationale for that, Dad?

PEELE

I'm putting this place to the torch.

DWIGHT

  (To audience)
I think it would be prudent of me to seek new alliances.
  (Exits)

VALERIE

I sure would like to find that Indian. Maybe he could use a piece of white meat.

(Exits)

GRETCHEN

Stew, you must talk to that girl.

(PEELE has finished dousing the place with gasoline. HE tries to light it with a lighter that won't work. DWIGHT enters, seizes the shotgun, and covers PEELE)

DWIGHT

I'm doing this for my own good. Ruthlessness is no longer entertaining when it's inefficient.

PEELE

So my own son turns out to be other people.

DWIGHT

It's an existential situation.

(HE opens the bookcase-door, and the AUTHOR enters, wearing dinner jacket)

AUTHOR

(To DWIGHT

A beautiful job. You'll get the reward you deserve.

(To PEELE)

I'm putting you under arrest.

PEELE

You and what army?

(Runs out the door, and an explosion is heard)

DWIGHT

It finally worked.

GRETCHEN

I hope Stew learned his lesson.

AUTHOR

(Looking around the room and rubbing his hands)

It looks as though I've disposed of most of the cast and can now bring in Fortinbras, just back from smiting the sledded Polacks on the ice.

DWIGHT

What are you going to do about us? They're ready to knock down the building, and Dad gave our house away. Not to mention we've lost our meal ticket.

GRETCHEN

Dwight, have you no pride?

(To AUTHOR)

Forgive this young person, sir. And could you direct me to the nearest facility for distressed gentlewomen?

AUTHOR

Didn't your late husband carry any insurance?

GRETCHEN

What an ingenious man you are! And where do you make *your* abode?

AUTHOR

This was *my* loft before the building was condemned.

DWIGHT

It was cunning of you to fob it off on Peele.

(GRETCHEN smiles and takes one of the AUTHOR's arms and DWIGHT takes the other)

AUTHOR

I guess I asked for this.
(To DWIGHT)
Bring the shotgun. We'll need it to defend whatever home we find.
(To the audience)
I'm wearing my tuxedo because I thought somebody might like to invite me to a party after the show. We'll hang around for a while just inside the stage door.
(THEY exit.

VALERIE wanders in)

VALERIE

I wonder where everybody went. I can't even find my dog. As usual, nobody tells me anything. I feel like I am standing at the curb long after the parade's gone by. Strangers will wonder, who is that girl with the sad, sweet smile? You can never know how you figure in the fantasies of other people.

CURTAIN

Index

♦